# MISPLACING OGDEN, UTAH

# MISPLACING
# OGDEN, UTAH

RACE, CLASS, IMMIGRATION,
*and* THE CONSTRUCTION *of*
URBAN REPUTATIONS

●

## PEPPER GLASS

Copyright © 2020 by The University of Utah Press. All rights reserved.
First paperback printing 2023.

 The Defiance House Man colophon is a registered trademark of The University of Utah Press. It is based on a four-foot-tall Ancient Puebloan pictograph (late PIII) near Glen Canyon, Utah.

LIBRARY OF CONGRESS CATALOGING-IN-PUBLICATION DATA
Names: Glass, Pepper, author.
Title: Misplacing Ogden, Utah : race, class, immigration, and the
   construction of urban reputations / Pepper Glass.
Description: Salt Lake City : The University of Utah Press, [2020] |
   Includes bibliographical references and index. |
Identifiers: LCCN 2019042812 (print) | LCCN 2019042813 (ebook) | ISBN
   9781607817598 (hardcover) | ISBN 9781647691547 (paperback) | ISBN 9781607817529 (ebook)
Subjects: LCSH: Ogden (Utah)--History. | Ogden (Utah)--Social conditions.
Classification: LCC F834.O3 G53 2020  (print) | LCC F834.O3  (ebook) | DDC
   979.2/28--dc23
LC record available at https://lccn.loc.gov/2019042812
LC ebook record available at https://lccn.loc.gov/2019042813

This work incorporates material originally published as "Dividing and Defending Ogden: The Intersection of Race Making and Space Making in a Diverse Community." *Ethnic and Racial Studies* 40, no.14 (2017): 2520–38. Available from the publisher's website, www.tandfonline.com. Used here with permission.

Errata and further information on this and other titles available online at UofUpress.com

Printed and bound in the United States of America.

# CONTENTS

List of Tables   **vi**
Preface   **vii**

1. Introduction   **1**

**PART ONE: INSIDERS AND OUTSIDERS**   **23**
   2. Promoters and Challengers of Urban Reputations   **25**
   3. A City Defined by Difference   **34**

**PART TWO: BOUNDARY WORK**   **43**
   4. Defending a Working-Class Place   **45**
   5. A Hesitant Community   **62**
   6. Immigrant Perceptions of Place   **76**

**PART THREE: THE CONTEXTS OF URBAN REPUTATIONS**   **93**
   7. Historical Echoes   **95**
   8. The Moral Frontiers of Outsiders   **107**

**PART FOUR: TRANSFORMATION**   **117**
   9. Boundary Maintenance and Boundary Blurring   **119**
   10. Interventions   **135**

   11. Conclusion   **148**

Epilogue   **159**
Appendix   **167**
Notes   **173**
Bibliography   **191**
Index   **213**

# TABLES

Table 1.1. Perceptions of Ogden as Reflections of Residence and Status   **18**

Table 3.1. Percentage of Ogden Employment by Industry, 2017 Five-year Estimates, with Margins of Error)   **36**

Table 3.2. Percentage of Household Income, 2017 (Five-year Estimates, with Margins of Error)   **37**

Table 3.3. Race by Percentage of the Population, 2010   **40**

Table 6.1. Race of Ogden Residents, 1960–2010   **79**

Table 7.1. Race of Weber County Residents, 1870–2000   **98**

Table A.1. Ogden Reported and United States Estimated Violent Crime Rate per 100,000 Residents, 1985–2014   **169**

Table A.2. Ogden and Salt Lake City Reported Violent Crime Rate per 100,000 Residents, 1985–2014   **170**

Table A.3. Ogden Reported and United States Estimated Property Crime Rate per 100,000 Residents, 1985–2014   **171**

Table A.4. Ogden and Salt Lake City Reported Property Crime Rate per 100,000 Residents, 1985–2014   **172**

# PREFACE

When I moved to Utah, I quickly realized that the city of Ogden was the "East Saint Louis" of the region. Growing up in a suburb just outside of Saint Louis, Missouri, I never visited East Saint Louis—a city just across the Mississippi River in Illinois. I saw that place as a destitute and forbidden hellscape, only viewing it from highways as I quickly rocketed past, imagining what horrors could await me there.

This was like many childhood fears, except that everyone I knew believed in this boogeyman. East Saint Louis was a well-known symbol of disrepute, disorder, and danger. Warnings about this place from my family and friends were, on their surface, about people's safety and well-being. Yet, our concern never extended to the inhabitants of East Saint Louis, although they were exponentially more likely to be victimized by the crime and other problems found there. Underlying such talk about the city was a moral lesson about two communities, one welcoming and the other menacing. As people who fell on the "good" side of this moral line, we felt the need to either avoid or overcome the threat from those on the other side of this line.

Although I passionately embraced ideals of equal opportunity and social justice in the abstract, in practice the terrifying image of East Saint Louis—deeply implanted from a young age as a commonsense understanding—created in me profound fear and avoidance. Thus, I was taken aback when, in my early twenties, a coworker told me that he regularly journeyed into the bowels of this ominous place. In fact, *he actually lived there!* Not only had I spent the first two decades of my life completely isolated from this community, I believed that my separation from the people living there—a population that was almost completely black—was not only sensible but also important to my safety.

Ogden inspired a similar fear in the hearts of many Utah residents, leading them to shun this city and the people who lived there. The word "misplace" means either losing something ("misplacing your keys") or an erroneous feeling or attitude ("misplaced sympathy"). Both of these definitions fit the case of Ogden. The city found itself in the wrong place or even lost. Greatly differing from the rest of the region, Ogden seemed like it was *misplaced*—like it should be somewhere else. Because of this difference, Ogden's residents suffered from the loss of resources, status, and strong feelings of connection and unity, among other things. This loss happened because people felt what I argue is a *misplaced* vilification and fright, fearing Ogden far beyond any threat that it or its residents posed. Not coincidentally, the city that inspired such terror was, like East Saint Louis, home to a large number of lower-income residents and people of color.

Social scientists have extensively exposed and analyzed many ideas that uphold systems of inequality. This book is a modest attempt to unearth and chip away at one more of these—the bad reputations of urban areas. The project was many years in the making, and it relied on the support of many people. Here I want to celebrate their efforts.

First and foremost, those who worked as part-time research assistants on the project, Jose Chacón, Viviana Felix, and Emily Jordison, were invaluable to the research. They spent long and tedious hours recruiting people, interviewing them, transcribing interviews, translating some of them, and other crucial tasks. Also invaluable were others who collected, usually transcribed, and occasionally translated interviews with residents: Leon Araujo, Adrienne Atkinson, Hans Bergen, Mikayla Bowers, Christa Boyd, Amber Corbridge, Heather Couturier, Chaley Diarte, Melanie Cuevas, Heather Edwards, Andrew Hyder, Timothy Isom, Thomas John, Eric Martindale, Mirian Maya, Diego Esquivel Meza, Calan Moore, Scott Odenwalder, Stephanie Quinn, Brent Shearer, Jonathan Warren, Jay Paul Werner, and Alexis Wiley.

Many others at Weber State University supported me in this research. My colleagues in the Department of Sociology and Anthropology—Brooke Arkush, Rosemary Conover, Joanna Gautney, Huiying Hill, Ron Holt, Belinda McElheny, R. C. Morris, Marjukka Ollilainen, Rob Reynolds, Mark Stevenson, Carla Trentelman, and David Yoder—offered a constant flow of support, assistance, suggestions, sources, and conversations. I would especially like to thank Rob for help with research on religion, and Carla for being there for my constant complaints and consternation while giving condolences and corrections. The university, with the help of the Hemmingway family, provided funding for the study, allowing me to hire and train assistants, among other financial support. I thank the various Research, Scholarship, and Professional

Growth committee members for believing in the project and approving its funding. I also thank Frank Harrold, dean of the university's College of Social and Behavioral Sciences at the time, for his help and support with the project over the years. Luis Lopez's assistance was crucial for connecting me with Ogden's immigrant community. Sarah Singh and Melissa Johnson at Special Collections of the Weber State University Stewart Library provided assistance with the historical research. Lonna Rivera at the Stewart Library also helped by finding census data.

I also received much support from the wider Ogden community. Charlie Trentelman provided much help, especially by giving me historical sources from the local newspaper. Presentations to Ogden's city leaders and public also helped me develop and disseminate this research. Thank you to Viviana Felix (again) and Ogden City's Diversity Commission—Adrienne Andrews, Kathie Darby, Azenett Garza, Taylor Knuth, Priscilla Martinez, Ami Noshiravan, Marcy Rizzi, Enrique Romo, Betty Sawyer, Jeremy Shinoda, and Jayson Stokes—for inviting me to present this research to them as well as their interest, encouragement, and support. Thanks also to Megan Fitzpatrick and Weber County Libraries for hosting a public presentation of this research.

The following people also gave guidance, suggestions, support, and other help: Leticia Alvarez, Julian Chan, Annie Fukushima, Sarita Gaytán, Esperanza Granados, Omar Guevara, Gary Johnson, Brenda Kovalewski, Aaron Londe, Jonathon Marshall, Richard Price, and Mariel Sevilla. Also, I would like to thank those who were central to my training in sociology—Bob Emerson, David Snow, and Carol Warren.

I would also like to thank the people at the University of Utah Press, especially Thomas Krause and John Alley, for their expertise and support. Thanks to Ashly Bennett, for providing the meticulous copyediting, and Bill Nelson, for creating the fantastic maps of Ogden. Three anonymous reviewers also provided insightful and valuable comments that greatly improved the manuscript.

Finally, I would like to thank my family, my parents, and my sister Sarah, for their love and support throughout the years. And Brenda—you have helped me more than you will ever know.

# 1
# INTRODUCTION

A reputation can at times seem impossible to reign in; one event, whether tragic or celebratory, or one popular media depiction has the potential to affect more opinions of a place than its official promoters ever could alone. And an ongoing series of events and depictions, all centering upon impressions of vice, rebellion, and depravity, can create an overall impression that is difficult to dislodge.

—*Alicia Barber*

To those from outside Utah and companies considering doing business in Ogden, Utah: Ogden is dangerous. Sure, public officials would like everyone to think Ogden is some liberal, conservation-minded, outdoor sports and activities mecca, but in actuality, it's not.

—*Ogdenisdangerous.com*

The reputations of places—how we collectively understand areas as sedate or unruly, safe or dangerous, reputable or disreputable, good or bad—are a central force by which we organize our lives. These spatial meanings are powerful. We use them as tools to decide where to live, work, and visit, as we carefully negotiate streets and neighborhoods based on them. We flock to reputable areas, and they receive resources of enhanced growth, investment, and development, entertainment and tourist dollars, and increased quality of life for their residents.[1] At the same time, we shun and stigmatize areas with bad reputations, maintaining their existing disadvantage and blight or hurling them into decline and decay. A few disreputable neighborhoods can taint the image of an entire city.[2]

Urban reputations act as symbolic shorthand for determining the quality of places, but also the quality of the people, practices, and ideas associated with them.[3] Divisions between good and bad areas reverberate widely, reflecting social divisions and inequality while also reinforcing them. They are connected to identities. Those who live in reputable places tend to see themselves as good, while seeing those who live in disreputable places as suspect and threatening, lacking in abilities, ambition, intelligence, and self-control.[4] People use place-based terms such as "ghetto," "hood," or "trailer trash" to describe those who they see as unsophisticated and unsuccessful. Urban reputations shape who we perceive as upstanding or deficient, affecting who we choose to share our lives with on a day-to-day basis—who we hire for jobs, befriend, or make our romantic partners. This influences who has access to opportunities and benefits and who is shut out from them.

The praises or warnings of family, friends, and acquaintances, as well as information and images from the news and other media, mold our ideas about place.[5] We accept this popular consensus as a reflection of the reality found there, whether it is attached to our firsthand experience or not. People frequently have very strong feelings about places that they have never visited. Transforming these views can take decades. People's feelings about many places do not shift much over their lifetimes. They also can change in an instant, such as following a tragedy or other dramatic event.

Despite the sweeping influence of urban reputations, as well as their central place in so many people's lives, the mechanisms underlying perceptions of place—how they develop, continue, and change—remain underexplored to the point of being obscured from our view. We even see these symbols as a passive reflection of disparities in resources and other structural influences. In answer, this book analyzes urban reputations as the active cultural products that they are. I take a social constructionist view,[6] asserting that perceptions of place are not just based on evaluations of the features found there. Instead, they are the result of a process of collective meaning-making. We invoke urban reputations in order to preserve or increase our status as members of groups. Those who benefit from being on the "good" side of this boundary—higher-status people who live outside of disreputable places—do symbolic work to adopt and promote these physical divisions. Such boundaries help to maintain their standing. In contrast, the residents of disreputable places seek to elevate their status by mending these rifts, merging with more respectable people and places.

To help uncover the construction of urban reputations—revealing and explaining the meaning-making, social division and unification, as well as the contexts involved in their creation, maintenance, and outcomes, I draw from the extended example of Ogden, Utah.

## INTRODUCING OGDEN

A city of around eighty-five thousand people, Ogden is in Northern Utah, about thirty-five miles north of Salt Lake City. This places it in the western region of the United States, about a day's drive from Denver to the east, Phoenix to the south, and San Francisco to the west. Fur trappers founded the town in 1846, and it is named after trapper Peter Skene Ogden. The course of the city began to change dramatically the next year, after followers of the prophet Joseph Smith (who are generally referred to as "Mormons") entered the region.[7] Leo Tolstoy reportedly called Mormonism "the American religion,"[8] and Utah remains the center of it. Members of the Mormon Church see the area as the special home of those who have heard and accepted the religion's truths. Change came to Ogden again in 1869, when the city became a major railroad junction, linking the eastern United States with western cities. Promontory Summit—where rail lines from East and West met in 1869, joined by the famous Golden Spike—is just northwest of Ogden. The railroad fundamentally transformed this place from a muddy Mormon outpost into "Junction City"—the nickname of this main stop for travelers heading across the country.

Today, Ogden resembles many midsized U.S. cities, especially former industrial towns in the eastern and midwest Rust Belt. There are the usual businesses and strip malls, office buildings, schools, churches, industrial areas, parks, some apartments and condos, and single-family homes. The west side, surrounding a downtown historic district, has a number of businesses—restaurants, grocery stores, and other offices and shops—that cater to its large Latino community.[9] In this area of town, there are many office buildings and factories. In contrast, its east side has more green space and parks, especially near the steep hill leading to a mountain range. The city's homes include a few larger residences, mansions even, in the central city and on the hills, but most are smaller brick bungalows. In many places, these would be "starter homes" for a single person or young couple. Ogden's residents tend to finish their basements, stretching them into three- or four-bedroom dwellings. This reflects the city's working-class character.

By national standards, Ogden is typical as a former industrial center—in this case, a railroad boomtown—that now struggles to redefine itself. The city has gone through hard times since the rail became less dominant in the mid-twentieth century. Downtown has a number of abandoned and decaying buildings—dismal monuments to past prosperity. But the city is not especially rundown, and residents talk about it being very much on the upswing. Its residents make a bit less income than the national average, and they have a bit less education. The nation's recent wave of immigration has also shaped the city. Almost a third of its population is Latino, and half of that community is foreign-born. According to the FBI, crime reports there fall near the national average (see Appendix). Each year, about five out of every one thousand people report a violent crime, and about five out of every one hundred people report a property crime. This too reflects the city's working-class character, as places with fewer economic resources tend to have more street crime. These characteristics of lower income and education levels, as well as higher crime, are unusual for Utah, but they are a fraction of the rates found in the most notorious areas of the United States.

Encountering this setting, you may form the mental image of a humble and charming, if a bit rough around the edges, city in the heart of Mormon country. It seems like a good place. Scanning news stories about Ogden found in national publications, you would not be alone in this assessment. In 2007, the *New York Times* ran a story that featured the city as an outdoor recreation magnet, attracting new professionals looking for skiing, hiking, arts, and entertainment.[10] Recent articles from the *Los Angeles Times* and *Newsweek* praise Ogden's lack of inequality, which allows for greater upward social mobility between generations.[11] *Forbes* called Ogden one of the best cities for raising a family.[12] *Sunset* magazine named it one of the five best medium-sized towns in the West.[13]

At the same time, describing Ogden as a good place is controversial. There is a longstanding battle over the city's reputation, and perceptions of Ogden vary widely. While some see the city as a beloved and welcoming hometown, with national-level assessments supporting this view, others view it as a frightening slum. A 2017 online survey by Ogden's local newspaper—the *Standard-Examiner*—asked people to "pick the first word that comes to mind when describing Ogden."[14] Out of more than seven hundred submissions, the third most common word—after "home" and "mountains"—was "ghetto." While this empirically questionable outcome may have been the work of pranksters, the newspaper certainly took it seriously. In accompanying articles, journalists asked if Ogden was indeed a ghetto, if its central city was in decline, what was Ogden's most dangerous neighborhood, and how the city's bad reputation is rooted in its history.[15] One resident stated, "Over the years, I have just seen [Ogden's] inner city deteriorate.... To me, it's like the inner city is getting worse and worse and worse."[16] Some people invoked race, as this resident also thought that the growing Latino population added to the area's decline. Another person described the city as "Tijuana North."[17]

Although greatly contested, Ogden's bad reputation is no secret locally. Negative views of the city, or neighborhoods within it, are popular among people in the area. In fact, Ogden has long been a, if not *the,* disreputable place of the state. The city's reputation makes it misplaced—"out of place"[18] in a region that, for many people, is a unique U.S. holy land. At the same time, the ambiguity found in varying understandings of Ogden reveals basic insights about the nature of urban reputations. Urban researchers who focus on disreputable places generally study the quintessential "ghettos" of large cities, seeing these examples as analytically pure and unquestionably authentic. Ogden's identity is embattled, but these very struggles over the city's image expose the factors underlying our perceptions of place. In areas with "obvious" bad reputations that are "obviously" connected to problems of deprivation and disorder, such processes tend to be obscured.

## RETHINKING URBAN REPUTATIONS

Urban research has long been tied to disreputable places through studies of "ghettos," "slums," "inner cities," and "the underclass"—centers of intense inequality and isolation. While hundreds of studies report how divisions between such communities and other places in the United States are especially entrenched, extreme, and grounded in racial inequality,[19] only rarely do they specifically consider perceptions of these maligned communities.[20] International research, concentrated in Australia and Europe,[21] as well as studies of "place marketing" and "nation branding,"[22] do analyze the reputations of places.

Whether focusing on reputations or not, researchers tend to understand a place's image as a problem, and they see the problem as stemming from material conditions. Predominant explanations of the development and maintenance of a disreputable place—"neighborhood effects" and "territorial stigmatization"—follow what I call an "internal disorder" approach. They strongly emphasize how economic and political circumstances shape the disrepute of areas.[23] Loïc Wacquant, who coined the term "territorial stigma," understands the low status of ghettos as emerging through the interplay between social class, race, and the state:

> To sum them up: repulsion into the black ghetto [in the United States] is determined by ethnicity (E), inflected by class (C) with the emergence of the hyperghetto in the 1970s and intensified by the state (S) throughout the century, according to the summary algebraic formula $[(E > C) \times S]$. By contrast, relegation in the urban periphery of Western Europe is driven by class position, inflected by ethnonational membership and mitigated by state structures and policies, as summed up by the formula $[(C > E) \div S]$.[24]

This research tends to assume that disreputable places, and their residents, more-or-less automatically gain a deviant status through powerful forces that deteriorate their communities.[25] The deprivation and disorder found there, as well as structural factors that create these concentrated pockets of disparity, generate the bad reputation of places.

Urban reputations do correspond with very real—even life and death—problems for those who they negatively affect. Disreputable places are isolated, reinforcing distance and inequality between people.[26] Those living in these communities are overwhelmingly the members of marginalized groups, especially by social class and race. These "insider" residents are concentrated into segregated neighborhoods far from wider social worlds.[27] They also are distanced from social networks and other resources that provide opportunities of education, careers, and wealth accumulation, while constantly facing neighborhoods with high levels of crime, repressive policing, environmental pollution, and health disparities.[28] In contrast, "outsiders" who live beyond these places overwhelmingly are the members of dominant groups, and they tend to avoid such problems. Admirably, urban studies expose the disordered environments, lack of opportunities, and governmental and commercial interventions that contribute to a community being disparaged. These are pressing concerns.

While there certainly is a link between the reputations of places and conditions within them, researchers and the general public alike go one step further and assume that these reputations *are the result of* conditions. People see their assessments of place as based on evaluations of features.[29] This includes the difference between safe areas—with nice, tidy homes and yards—versus high-crime areas filled with trash, graffiti, and abandoned buildings. We also imagine that places gain good reputations from the good people living there. These residents look out for one another and keep these communities safe, well kempt, and thoroughly respectable. Conversely, places gain bad reputations through rundown and dangerous conditions.

This well-organized image of the world has our signifiers closely approximating the signified. Policy makers and researchers hold this assumption as well, as Birgitte Mazanti and John Pløger state:

> When contemporary urban policy defines a deprived neighbourhood, one of the main criteria is a negative place identity. Urban planners consider the classification as a negative place to be the end result of problems such as high rates of unemployment, crime and drug abuse, all of which lead to other problems such as the absence of social networks and social cohesion.[30]

"Disorder" is a popular word among researchers, and theories of disreputable places focus on how it leaves communities and their residents stigmatized.

Yet, this clear connection between the conditions of a place and its reputation is questionable. As Robert Sampson and Stephen Raudenbush ask, "Is 'seeing' disorder only a matter of the objective level of cues in the environment? Or is disorder filtered through a reasoning based on stigmatized groups and disreputable areas? Simply put, what makes disorder a problem?"[31] A focus on internal disorder obscures how perceptions of place are collective understandings about the world that people shape. Although researchers note how various factors intervene between perceptions of a place and its conditions,[32] there is little sustained focus on the social construction of urban reputations. In the words of Ade Kearns, Oliver Kearns, and Louise Lawson, "two important aspects of neighbourhood reputations that rarely feature in existing research are, firstly, the content or meaning of reputations (what are they about?), and, secondly, the process by which they are created and sustained (how are they made?)."[33]

Urban reputations are indeed cultural symbols that people create and transform. They are ideas that shape our world, as Elijah Anderson outlines how the idea of "the iconic ghetto" "serves as a powerful source of stereotype, prejudice, and discrimination."[34] We also shape these ideas. Understandings of place are constructed and shifting "imagined communities"[35] that can vary widely in size, encompassing parts of town, neighborhoods, or streets, but also entire cities, regions, and nations. We demarcate the smallest of areas, even street by street or within a single block—such as the house at the end of the road that frightens neighborhood children.[36] We also designate huge areas as disreputable. Some people see the South of the United States as seedy and backwards. Internationally, a negative "nation brand" can cast a shadow on an entire country. Like many ideas, a reputation can be fragile and ethereal. Such designations of place radically change if we believe them to have changed. They stretch and contract, appear and disappear, and they can be simultaneously very real for some people and nonexistent for others. Current understandings, focused on internal disorder, turn these cultural processes—shifting symbols, meanings, and perceptions—into something structural—affixed to material conditions and resources.

Along with a neglect of *how* urban reputations are meanings that people create, also missing from understandings of disreputable places is *who* exactly is creating and promoting these ideas about the world, as well as *why* they do this. Disorder, deprivation, and the actions of institutional players definitely influence disreputable places, and government and business interests are unquestionably powerful. Yet, symbols of deviance and disrepute are not passive outcomes. People actively construct and deploy them.[37] Additionally, elites are not the primary people who do the symbolic work to define a place as deviant. While their efforts to sway an area's reputation can be successful, even the best directors of tourism and marketers—with ample funding—are constantly stymied.[38]

Instead, these definitions of reality require substantial acceptance by a wider community.[39] This community can fall at the international or national level, but generally, people living in surrounding areas construct and promote understandings of disreputable communities. For every Chicago, Las Vegas, or New York City that is evaluated on a world stage, there are dozens of places like Ogden, with little reputation beyond the regional level.[40] Ironically, local people define such places negatively despite how, because of their intense fear, avoidance, and stigma of disreputable places, this population is arguably the least well equipped to accurately assess them.

Current understandings neglect the influence of regional locals—the very people who are essential to the construction of most disreputable places.

Many studies completely leap over local contexts. They argue that disreputable places with similar characteristics dot the globe, detached from their local environments,[41] and they search for methods that standardize research between multiple disreputable areas.[42] Researchers simultaneously overlook these regional populations while unquestioningly embracing their understandings of place. They empirically record the challenges of insider residents, who overwhelmingly see their neighborhoods positively,[43] while analytically ignoring how such findings reveal the shifting nature of these cultural understandings.

In short, we tend to explain how places become disreputable through internal disorder. This collective hunch reflects the views of local outsiders, disregarding residents' counterclaims. In effect, researchers accept the assumptions of those with the least experience (people who actively avoid gaining any experience), and they dismiss the understandings of those with intimate familiarity. Instead of relying on these commonsense assumptions, we should distrust our perceptions and rethink our speculations. Far from being based on objective assessments of place, ideas of urban reputations shift between people. Not only this, these shifting meanings follow patterns that better explain who vilifies and shuns a place, who admires and embraces that very same area, and why these people do so.

## DISCOVERING OGDEN'S REPUTATIONS

Ogden does not have *a* reputation as much as it has *reputations*, as perceptions of place vary dramatically between individuals. In fact, reputations by definition are not conclusive. They are unverifiable, perpetually second-order understandings that people believe that other people believe.[44] A reputation, including the reputation of a place, would no longer be a reputation if everyone accepted it. This makes them not *things* but *processes* that people constantly negotiate and reinterpret between each other.

I wanted to study Ogden after noticing widely varying views of the city, including my own view. When first moving to the region from the center of Los Angeles, I found relentlessly negative understandings of Ogden very odd, as what locals saw as ominous seemed to me unthreatening and even quaint. Measures of disorder, such as crime rates, did not help to explain these perceptions. Ogden's crime rates are actually far lower than nearby Salt Lake City (see Appendix), which has a much better reputation locally. I wanted to understand why some people so feared and vilified this place, while I held such a different view.

Studies that focus on the images of places tend to analyze media representations or top-down interventions from government and business elites, often through comparisons between places. This study takes a different approach, intensively focusing on the case of Ogden and capturing the voices of its ordinary residents. I set about collecting and analyzing sixty-four in-depth interviews, given while residents traveled through the city's various neighborhoods. (I fully discuss the methods of the study in the Epilogue.) I use excerpts of them throughout the book to illustrate my argument, detailing what people who lived in Ogden thought about the city while immersed in its spaces, as well as what they thought that others thought about it.

This research captures the views of a wide array of Ogden's residents, supplemented by information and perspectives from various sources. I specifically sought out white and Latino residents, Ogden's two main racial groups, both Mormons and non-Mormons, a more-or-less representative number of men and women, and people across the age spectrum. Most of these people were native-born residents who had grown up in the United States, or they had moved there as young children. Others were foreign-born, often Latino immigrants. Interviews with residents provided insights into *what* people think about the city. Historical accounts, census reports, and other secondary sources about Ogden's past and present, coupled with urban studies and other academic research, helped me understand *how* and *why* people felt this way about Ogden. This dive into the local environment complemented the interview data, giving me further insight into Ogden's reputation.

I discovered a number of patterns by which different people understood the city. Locals from Northern Utah, but outside of Ogden's boundaries, tended to see the city as frightening, filled with crime, decrepit neighborhoods, homelessness, gangs, and other disorder. Ogden was the frequent target of jokes about the unintelligent, disheveled, and dangerous people who live there. A longstanding nickname for the city was "the armpit of Utah."[45] A Google image search of "Ogden, Utah" revealed, alongside the aggregate categories of "Downtown," "Map," "Mountains," and "Winter" at the top of the page, a tab marked "Ghetto."[46] A large and dominant population with more power to shape perceptions of the city than its residents, these local outsiders were the custodians of Ogden's bad reputation. They understood their views as reflecting established fact, and they often told Ogden's residents and visitors to be wary of the city.

This negative reputation, which separated the city from the surrounding area, was longstanding. It was entrenched in regional folklore, spread by generations of word of mouth and negative news reports.[47] It also coincided with Ogden's history of difference.[48] Compared to the surrounding area, Ogden's population was poorer, less Mormon, and contained a large number of native-born Latinos as well as Latino immigrants. This working-class, racially diverse, immigrant-heavy, and culturally varied population created an especially striking contrast to the higher-status and relatively homogenous areas surrounding Ogden. While large-scale economic shifts encourage new populations, especially Latino immigrants, to come to Utah, Ogden's unique characteristics explain how they came to settle in this specific place. The city's difference developed long ago with the establishment of a main railroad junction that set Ogden on a unique historical course, dramatically varying from the surrounding region. This key event was what I call a "historical echo." It reverberated into the present, shaping the city to this day.

Ogden's insiders—residents of the city—had a much different view than outsiders who lived in outlying areas. Most residents knew about Ogden's bad reputation, even if they disagreed with these sentiments. In defiance of views that Ogden was a disreputable place, they tended to embrace the city. They overwhelmingly saw Ogden as a good place, and they loved living there. They noted how local outsiders, not fellow residents, promoted the idea that Ogden had a bad reputation. They actively defended the city against these attacks, praising Ogden's small-but-not-too-small size, its outdoor recreation options (especially for hiking and winter sports like skiing), its historic downtown buildings, and its sense of community. They shared positive news stories, especially national articles that depicted Ogden positively.

At the same time, many of Ogden's residents mentioned disreputable areas within the city. Although they criticized outsiders for separating the city from the rest of Utah, claiming that such divisions were inaccurate and based on inexperience, these residents created similar designations within Ogden. They made "micro-differentiations"[49] between the city's good and bad places. These partitions also marked the boundaries between where different types of people—higher-class and white residents versus poorer, minority, and immigrant populations—tended to live. Like outsiders, they too relied on collective ideas spread by word of mouth, especially the understanding that a single road marked the line between reputable and disreputable places.

Speaking to Ogden's Latino immigrants (those who did not grow up in the United States) uncovered an additional pattern. Like other residents, their feelings about the city were overwhelmingly positive. Yet, they rarely mentioned Ogden's bad reputation. If they did, they nonchalantly dismissed it instead of defensively countering it, as other residents did. Also, unlike "native" residents (who grew up in the United States), these residents did not further subdivide the city into good and bad areas. They definitely noticed differences between various sections of Ogden, but they did not apply a moral framework to divide good and bad places, as well as good and bad people who inhabit these places. This was especially striking given how much of this population lived in areas that others considered the worst parts of Ogden. The residents of these neighborhoods, more than anyone, should know the horrors described by the proponents of Ogden's bad reputation. Yet, Latino immigrants spoke in glowing terms about their community, implicitly challenging those views. There was a clear difference between native residents' perceptions, regardless of their race, and those of Latino immigrants.[50]

Capturing residents' perceptions of an entire city, as opposed to some of its neighborhoods, as well as the regional contexts shaping their views, is a rare pursuit among urban researchers. They tend to study disreputable areas as carefully circumscribed, intimately tied to wider social forces while all but disconnected from surrounding areas. Yet, this focus on Ogden and its unique contexts, instead of limiting my understanding of how the reputations of places develop and continue, illuminated and expanded it.

## URBAN REPUTATIONS AS MORAL FRONTIERS

The main argument of this book is that urban reputations, including Ogden's reputation, are the result of a process of meaning-making that establishes or maintains "moral frontiers." Moral frontiers are constantly negotiated symbolic boundaries. They demarcate and preserve collective lines between what is good and bad, right and wrong, upstanding or dishonorable. They emerge through communities circumscribing what they are—and consequently, what they are *not*. This involves regulating their edges, determining spatial boundaries but also boundaries of membership and status—who is a good and respectable, or bad and vilified, member of a community.

There indeed is a moral quality to designations of place. People see disreputable places as dirty, disorganized, infamous, lawless, and dangerous. We invoke specialized language to describe them. They are "ghetto," "hood," "ratchet," "shady," "sketchy," "the wrong side of the tracks," and similar terms. Possibly the most popular word—which people frequently used when talking about Ogden—is simply "bad," as in a "bad neighborhood." We speak about disreputable places as separate from the good, invoking them in warnings, or punch lines, as ruined and filled with incivility. People often stigmatize anything associated with them, even when it is far removed from their borders.[51] We use the word "ghetto" to refer to a wide variety of things, including places but also identities, attitudes, lifestyles, speech, and aesthetics.

These boundaries are moral, but they also are designations of status. While people often relay a place's bad reputation through jokes, reputations—including urban reputations—are formidable symbolic weapons wielded on a field of competition between powerful and less powerful players.[52] Dominant groups, who overwhelmingly live outside of disreputable places, have a strong interest to demarcate the places where they live as good and the places where lower-status groups live as bad. Designations of places with bad reputations help them define and maintain their communities, securing their position as respectable members. These divisions reaffirm and protect outsiders' collective benefits—good neighborhoods, good schools, good air quality and other environmental advantages, and even residents' identities as good people—from encroachments by insiders wanting to reallocate some of these spoils and rise in status.

The dynamics that encourage higher-status outsiders to demean and avoid disreputable places operate in reverse for insider residents, encouraging these lower-status people to contest divisions and unify with a wider community. While some outsiders project their own treatment of insiders onto these populations, believing that lower-status communities are looking to dominate others and separate themselves,[53] insiders actually do less boundary work than outsiders. For example, while whites prefer to live in mostly white neighborhoods, people of color prefer integrated settings.[54] After all, insiders have less to gain from separation, and they can increase in status, opportunities, and resources by merging with the reputable. These boundaries are physical, social, economic, and political, but they also are moral. Insiders wish to discard their stigma and join the ranks of the good people who live in good places.

I built this perspective on insights from constructionist approaches to deviance as well as understandings of racial inequality. Sociological explanations of deviance from the social constructionist perspective, with variants called "labeling theory" and "societal reaction theory," have eclectic origins as a combination of Marxist, symbolic interactionist, and functionalist traditions.[55] The roots of this perspective are Emile Durkheim's functionalist theory of crime.[56] He argues that definitions of what is deviant do not come from those who are deviant. Instead of being intrinsically tied to any qualities of the deviant person (or deviant act), they are a collectively accepted understanding that can vary widely. They are the product of nondeviants who use definitions of the abnormal to reinforce what is normal, regular, and respectable. Durkheim concludes that crime and other deviance are not signs of chaos and pathology. Instead, these exceptions prove the rules. They are useful for a society, helping people define themselves and come together as a community.

Since Durkheim introduced his theory, researchers have further explored how people divide themselves through designations of the upstanding and the disreputable. Howard Becker argues that those on both sides of the line between what is deviant and nondeviant actively construct this boundary.[57] On one side, some people campaign to create and regulate standards of deviance (he calls them "moral entrepreneurs"), while others uphold these standards once they are established (the "rule enforcers"). On the other side, people develop and practice their deviance in groups that challenge, often deliberately, predominant ways.[58]

Similarly, Kai Erikson maintains that communities use definitions of deviance to designate who is a member and who is not.[59] Their boundaries circumscribe the center of a group, and battles for what is acceptable and unacceptable happen at their edges. The community designates those who they see as unacceptable as outside of these borders. The narrower and more restrictive a community's boundaries, the less it allows within its perimeters, and subsequently, the more falls outside of it. In other words, the more morally principled a community, the more deviance (and deviants) it creates. Things that people in a more permissive community would barely notice are scandalous in communities that are more restrictive.

Research on racial inequality complements as well as expands these understandings of the mainstream and marginal. Scholars of critical race theory and related approaches argue that whites—the dominant racial group—maintain their power in part through skewed and self-serving worldviews and justifications.[60] These higher-status people have the ability to shape and enforce understandings that make unequal divisions between people seem acceptable, rational, and even natural and inevitable. Thus, white people adopt elaborate defenses of unequal circumstances in order to sustain favorable ideas of themselves and their social positions.[61] Some even distort these relations to the point of inverting them—positioning themselves as righteous sufferers of the coercive and gluttonous residents found in disreputable places.

Compared to perspectives of deviance, theories of race especially emphasize power dynamics. Researchers of deviance tend to present marginalized populations as quirky outcasts who do not fit customary ways. This minimizes the extreme domination and disparities that often characterize such divisions.[62] Instead of "deviance," "terms like victimization, persecution, and oppression are more accurate descriptions of what is really happening," as Alexander Liazos states.[63] Perspectives on race more fully capture the inequality underlying relationships between dominant and marginal.

Although they may seem like a strange combination,[64] constructionist understandings of deviance, combined with the focus on power, oppression, and collective interests from perspectives on race, provide a useful theoretical foundation for analyzing urban reputations. Maybe most importantly, theories of deviance and race both divorce ideas of what is disreputable from any qualities of that thing. Just as the domination of racial minorities is not a result of their inherent deficiencies, there is nothing inherently disreputable about a place. Communities do not automatically gain bad reputations through their crime, graffiti, vandalism, trash, and other disorder. Instead, people actively create and promote these understandings through a process of collective meaning-making. Designations of the reputable and disreputable are intertwined with fundamental aspects of a society. Once firmly established, such divisions become solidified into ideas of the moral and immoral, pure and impure, and sacred and profane.[65] What we despise reflects what we value; who we exclude reflects who is included; and how some feel ostracized reflects how others feel connected.

Additionally, these perspectives contend that definitions of the disreputable emerge from those in the center of a community, not those on its margins. As powerful populations, dominant groups have more ability to shape and enforce meanings. Their collective interests, and the cognitive maneuverings to preserve them (including how they believe that they evaluate places), become folded into widely accepted perceptions of reality and obscured from their view.[66] Government policy, media reports, academic research, and other institutional players all tend to present viewpoints that uphold their worldviews. Whites often do not see themselves as a collective group with its own interests, even while denouncing the biases of other racial groups.[67] The self-serving understandings of dominant people are examples of what I call a "culture of abundance." While researchers have argued that lower-status people are embedded in a "culture of poverty" that further entrenches them into lowly positions,[68] a culture of abundance entails symbolic understandings that reinforce people's higher status.

At the same time, a moral frontier approach connects social divisions with physical ones, as theories of deviance and race both neglect the influence of space.[69] Social boundaries are intimately tied to physical boundaries.[70] Housing segregation is a prominent feature of cities, with lower-class people and especially racial minorities consigned to places with bad reputations.[71] When disreputable populations travel beyond where they live, outsiders view them as out of place and suspect, reinforcing difference and disparity.[72] We collectively define ourselves through spatial "boundary work"[73] to generate, maintain, or challenge ideas about good and bad people through designations of good and bad places.

Furthermore, the moral frontier approach challenges the internal disorder view. When understanding urban reputations as inextricably attached to disordered conditions, we not only confuse symbols of a place with its characteristics. We also misrecognize a place's bad reputation as a product of its residents, instead of local outsiders. Global capitalism and other social forces contribute to disorder in disreputable neighborhoods, but global capitalism is not committing street crime. Nor does it leave, or fail to clean up, litter and graffiti. When focused on internal disorder, we view insider residents—through attempts to gain resources and status in illegitimate ways, a lack of time, money, and willpower, or simply through (self) destructiveness—as those who primarily generate negative views of their own neighborhoods.[74]

Given such assumptions, an internal disorder view suggests that designations of disreputable areas are obvious, unambiguous, and best transformed by removing the clutter, crime, and (frequently) the populations underlying them. It has encouraged interventions to improve a community's image that focus on internal disorder, targeting the residents of disreputable places. These expensive and antagonistic policies further punish the victims of oppression for their deteriorated communities, and they level established cultures and histories through gentrification and displacement.[75]

Seeing reputations as tied to collective cultural understandings, instead of deprived and disordered conditions, opens up a universe of new ways of thinking and possible solutions for cities. While the residents of disreputable places contest dominant understandings, they face the powerful counterforce of outsiders who seek to reaffirm the maligned image of disreputable places. Currently, urban researchers also reaffirm these distorted images. They tend to unquestionably accept outsiders' views and largely dismiss the voices of those who live in disreputable areas.

## OGDEN'S MORAL FRONTIERS

Understanding urban reputations as moral frontiers, I argue that perceptions of Ogden reflect collective categories of people, rooted in long-standing divisions between these groups, and shaped by constant—if lopsided—struggles to justify and continue, or reassess and transform, these relations. Thus, Ogden's past and continuing difference from the rest of Utah, and boundary work—performed by outsiders and insiders alike—to separate themselves from a lower-status place and its residents, underlie the development and maintenance of the city's reputation. At the same time, these moral frontiers can change, especially through policies and practices that encourage unifying divisions.

People's perceptions of Ogden varied widely, but these were not simply the result of differences of personal opinion or varying reactions to the features of this place. Ogden's residents challenged negative views of the city, assessing it positively. These differing perceptions coincided with demographic differences that began more than a century ago. As a working-class place with many minorities and immigrants, the city has long been a local outlier from the rest of the area, which is largely higher class, white, and Mormon.

These divisions between insider residents and outsiders played out, on a smaller scale, within the city. The dynamics of people doing boundary work to separate themselves from a disreputable population, with that community challenging those designations, also happened among Ogden's own residents. Some did work to separate themselves from others and the places where they lived. This included their relationship with the city and its history. City leaders engaged in what I call "collective forgetfulness," as their marketing attempted to deemphasize and even erase Ogden's long-standing characteristics of difference. In contrast, other residents—namely, Latino immigrants—had the highest opinion of the city, and they did not divide the city and its residents.

Divisions between insiders and outsiders, as well as between different types of insider residents, reveal how differing views of place are patterns of status (see Table 1.1). The populations closest to the heart of Ogden, with the lowest status, had the most positive views of their community, just as local outsiders who lived beyond the city limits, with the highest status, had the most negative assessments of Ogden. Such conflicting views, and the patterns by which different people held them, reveal how there is much more to urban

Table 1.1. Perceptions of Ogden as Reflections of Residence and Status

|  | Appraisal of the city | Proximity of residence | Status |
|---|---|---|---|
| Outsiders | Negative | Peripheral | Mid to high |
| Native residents | Positive/Varying | Within the city | Mid to low |
| Latino immigrant residents | Positive | Central city | Low |

reputations than being a spontaneous outcome—a response to the stimulus of conditions. Ogden's reputation emerges from people constructing collective boundaries between themselves and lower-status populations.

This setting especially highlights the moral dimension of these dynamics. Designations of place as respectable or deviant connect with broader processes by which a community distinguishes between good and bad people, objects, actions, and ideas. Ogden is a place that regional people—often from communities with well-defined and carefully regulated religious principles—see as deviant. The clear moral standards that define Northern Utah are intimately intertwined with Ogden's bad reputation.

Like moral standards, reputations are continually evolving social constructions, grounded in fluctuating collective understandings. Although rooted in historical differences and upheld by symbolic work to maintain these divisions, people are constantly renegotiating moral frontiers. This suggests strategies to transform perceptions of places, including what I call "moral inversions." Ogden's residents could reimagine the maligned image of their community, turning their current feelings of hesitation and stigma into an embrace and celebration of their city's unique characteristics. Such symbolic transformations of disreputable places and people are central to the history of Utah. Between the 1800s and today, Mormons made an astounding transformation from a disreputable community to upstanding citizens. Centrally, this shift involved them becoming white.[76] When first coming to what today is Utah, Mormons were vilified outcasts—racial and sexual deviants who escaped persecution in the United States to settle on Mexican land. Today, these moral standards have become inverted. Mormons now see themselves as the respectable ancestors of this region, and many see a recent group of settlers—Latino immigrants—as disreputable invaders. Ironically, most of these new residents come from Mexico—the place to which Mormons originally fled. Understandings of which places, as well as people, are reputable and disreputable can blur and even invert over time.

Thus, the reputation of Ogden reflects a continual struggle between those within and external to a community to sustain or challenge its boundaries, which benefits some while being detrimental to others. To organize this argument in the remainder of the study, I focus on four interrelated issues:

- *Insiders and outsiders*
  How do the reputations of places reflect the characteristics of people—those assessing these places and those who live there?
- *Boundary work*
  How do people do symbolic work to generate and continue a place's reputation?
- *Contexts*
  What circumstances shape how these ideas about place develop and continue?
- *Maintenance and transformation*
  How are these spatial boundaries that divide people maintained, and how can they be reshaped to unify people?

Collective groups of people, their understandings of place, local and extra-local environments, and continuity and change are all central to understanding urban reputations. The following four parts of this book, and the chapters within them, consider these questions.

*How do the reputations of places reflect the characteristics of people—those assessing these places and those who live there?* Part One, which includes Chapters Two and Three, considers the relationship between urban reputations and insiders, who live within the boundaries of disreputable places, as well as outsiders, who live beyond them.

Chapter Two explains the linkage between spatial boundaries—which urban reputations circumscribe and reinforce—and social divisions between people. I review previous research on those who promote the bad reputations of places, higher-status outsiders, as well as the insider residents who challenge these views. Outsiders embrace and disseminate the bad reputations of places, even though they generally have little knowledge about these communities. This separation preserves their status, as divisions from disreputable places and their residents help them maintain their good neighborhoods, schools, identities, and other benefits. In contrast, insiders challenge these views, as contesting these boundaries lessens their stigma. Yet, insiders have little power to enforce this stance, and they often employ strategies similar to those of outsiders in order to distance themselves from lower-status residents within their neighborhoods. Some outsiders do challenge these divisions by moving into disreputable places, but their efforts often backfire, making such areas welcoming for other outsiders and hostile to insiders.

Chapter Three further illustrates, using the example of Ogden, how the boundaries of urban reputations reflect differences between people. I present demographic information to detail how Ogden residents contrast with people from the surrounding area. As a working-class city with much racial, immigrant, and cultural diversity, Ogden's reputation reflects its residents' dissimilarity and lower status compared to the rest of the region.

*How do people do symbolic work to generate and continue a place's reputation?* In Part Two, Chapters Four through Six, I draw from interviews with Ogden residents to explore how people, reflecting their attempts to gain or preserve status as members of collective groups, generate boundaries to both unify and divide areas.

Chapter Four analyzes how positive assessments and defenses against a place's bad reputation are efforts to lessen stigma and gain social status. I consider the perceptions of Ogden's native residents, those who have grown up in the United States. These people knew about their city's bad reputation, but they rejected it, assessing the community favorably. They also defended the city against its negative reputation, often by comparing it to other places. This unity of perceptions reflects a paradox, as insider residents' characteristics of difference united them through positive views of their community.

Chapter Five explores how residents of places with bad reputations attempt to gain status by separating themselves from, and physically and symbolically removing, disreputable populations. Native residents of Ogden hesitated in their embrace of the city. While criticizing outsiders for dividing Ogden from the rest of the region, they made similar "micro-differentiations" within the city. Areas within Ogden that they saw positively were predominantly white and higher-class parts of town, while disreputable areas were the homes of lower-class, minority, and immigrant populations. City leaders also showed this hesitation through "collective forgetfulness," presenting and marketing the city in ways that "magically" erased its diverse populations, their neighborhoods, and their histories.

Chapter Six considers how lower-status insiders understand their communities. In Ogden, these were Latino immigrants. Like native residents, they spoke very highly about their city. Unlike native residents, they rarely mentioned and casually rejected Ogden's bad reputation, and they did not divide the city into good and bad areas. They also did not engage in boundary work to divide themselves from a more disreputable population. Their low status makes them less likely to draw spatial boundaries between themselves and others. This also may be a result of their isolation from the wider culture, which learns a racial socialization associating Latino communities with disorder and disrepute.

*What circumstances shape how these ideas about place develop and continue?* Part Three, which includes Chapters Seven and Eight, considers the contexts shaping how Ogden's reputation developed and continues.

Chapter Seven considers the "historical echoes" of continuity and change that shape the varying reputations of places. I outline how Ogden's status as a regional outlier emerged and then continued to the present day. The establishment of a large railroad junction in the center of the city made Ogden a famous and worldly place. This event generated structural changes of an economic boom that attracted diverse communities and open vice. It also brought about cultural changes of a community of people with differing ways as well as the development of a notorious reputation. These past changes echo into the present. While places like nearby Park City experienced dramatic historical change, Ogden encountered historical continuity that maintained the city's extraordinary difference from the surrounding region, as well as its disrepute.

Chapter Eight focuses on how outsiders construct moral frontiers to circumscribe the edges of their communities. The higher status of locals living beyond Ogden's borders intersected with various characteristics, including race and culture. Whites—including those in Utah—preserve their status as good people by distancing themselves from disreputable populations and their spaces. Along with race, culture is another powerful force shaping these boundaries. Utah is embedded in a unique religious culture, and members of the Mormon Church have pressing concerns to remain morally upstanding in the eyes of their community. It advantages both whites and Mormons to avoid Ogden's perceived dysfunction and sinfulness. Dividing themselves from Ogden's residents helped them to maintain their status.

*How are these spatial boundaries that divide people maintained, and how can they be reshaped to unify people?* Part Four, Chapters Nine and Ten, considers the ways that people preserve as well as transform divisions between places.

In Chapter Nine, I explore how the boundaries between reputable and disreputable places and people are sustained but also blur. Ogden has instituted policies that target its disreputable populations, such as a campaign against gangs that was a "moral panic," reinforcing divisions between high- and low-status residents. Yet, these boundaries also have shifted and even inverted over time. While Mormons are undoubtedly dominant in Utah, their history blurs the line between oppressor and oppressed. This includes how Americans once vilified Mormons as a racial group. At the same time, dominant forces do not simply impose their will onto Latino immigrants. This community has their own agency, cultures, and historical legacies that only have cursory connections to whites and Mormons.

Chapter Ten focuses on how understanding urban reputations as moral frontiers suggests new interventions to transform meanings about place. The prevailing view of disreputable places inadvertently reinforces negative views of their residents, and interventions based on it have harmed these already marginalized people. In contrast to crusades against disorder within disreputable places, I suggest interventions that break down the boundaries between reputable and disreputable places, uniting these areas and their residents. This includes suggestions for the city of Ogden to do "boundary blurring," encouraging spaces and events where diverse communities interact, as well as invoking "moral inversions" that celebrate and promote difference instead of concealing it as shameful. Yet, I also question whether Ogden should be transformed. Although the city's bad reputation hurts its residents, transformations to Ogden that are not carefully considered and implemented may hurt them—and especially the most vulnerable citizens—even more.

The concluding chapter contains an overview of the main points of the study, as well as what it adds to understandings of urban reputations specifically and urban studies in general. I especially call for academic perspectives that evenly evaluate differing perceptions of places, instead of uncritically accepting outsiders' views.

The Epilogue and Appendix provide additional information and explanations. The Epilogue outlines the methods of the study as well as their benefits and limitations, while the Appendix presents reports of crimes in Ogden compared to other places.

# PART ONE

# INSIDERS AND OUTSIDERS

## 2

# PROMOTERS AND CHALLENGERS OF URBAN REPUTATIONS

Some of the safest sidewalks in New York City, for example, at any time of day or night, are those along which poor people or minority groups live. And some of the most dangerous are in streets occupied by the same kinds of people. All this can also be said of other cities.

—*Jane Jacobs*

There are people in the ghetto who have good, stable jobs, help their children with their homework, eat dinner together at a fixed hour, make payments on the car, and spend their Saturday night watching Lawrence Welk on TV—to their largely mainstream way of life we will devote rather little attention.

—*Ulf Hannerz*

*How do the reputations of places reflect the characteristics of people—those assessing these places and those who live there?* Although urban reputations are cultural, in the realm of symbols, meanings, and perceptions, researchers tend to explain them through structures—material resources and their unequal distribution between people. In this view, people create a place's disreputable reputation based on assessments of its internal disorder—the chaotic and lawless conditions within these places. While the features of a place definitely shape people's feelings about it, there is much more underlying these ideas. Urban reputations both reflect and shape our social world in profound ways, enveloping everything from who we welcome and embrace or shun and avoid to how we define our identities and even how we produce and maintain our standards of good and bad.

While differing evaluations of places are based on intimately personal tastes and opinions, they also are collective, reinforcing patterns by which people form groups. Underlying differing perceptions of place is a continuous struggle for these groups to maintain or gain status by either distancing themselves from others or uniting with them. The constant conflict between collective groups also means that these understandings shift, as people continually challenge the edges of such boundaries. They change over time, and loosening these firm divisions can lessen the inequalities underlying them.

In this chapter, I draw from previous research to give an overview of these promoters and challengers of urban reputations—the "outsiders" who create and maintain moral frontiers and "insiders" who contest them. The boundaries between good and bad places are intimately tied to ideas of good and bad people, lifestyles, activities, and other moral standards. While urban studies provide invaluable insights into this phenomenon, they also tend to reflect outsider understandings that places become disreputable through the actions of their residents.

## PROMOTERS OF A PLACE'S BAD REPUTATION

In most any urban area, those who live outside of disreputable places see it as sensible to avoid living in these communities or even traveling there. This is a main part of urban socialization. City dwellers quickly learn, and then teach one another, which areas are good and which are bad. A widespread understanding among outsiders is that you simply do not go to disreputable places, and if you do go, you should prepare for trouble from the people there.[1] Disreputable places and their residents face a stigma. Once labeled as "ghettos" or "slums," communities face uphill battles against further decline, leading to crime, graffiti, neglected properties, the loss of residents and businesses, and an overall lack of economic development.[2] Conversely, places that people label as good gain further benefits from positive assessments. Places thrive or deteriorate based on what people think of them.

This distance between disreputable places and other areas is built into the very fabric of cities. Outsiders maintain social and physical separation through segregated housing, schools, shopping and businesses, entertainment, and other settings that further insulate them from any sustained contact with these communities and their residents.[3] In the United States, freeway systems act as "boundary maintaining devices"[4] that allow middle- and upper-class residents to easily bypass disreputable places.[5] Entire areas of cities are "white spaces,"[6] where white residents can maneuver with little interaction with the people of color that disproportionately live in disreputable areas. Outsiders describe interactions where they actually meet those who are different from them, even simply entering a space where they are racially in the minority, as awkward and frightening. At the same time, they struggle to disassociate themselves from this isolation. Whites hold on to a "black friend"—often just an acquaintance depicted as a friend—as a prized symbolic resource that they invoke in order to show their ability to journey beyond this experience of separation.[7] After all, most like to see themselves as good people, and good people do not embrace this de facto racial apartheid.[8]

Outsiders gain many benefits and bear few costs from this isolation. They even are able to eat the cultural, economic, and political fruits of disreputable places without ever going near them or interacting with their residents. Well known disreputable areas of the United States are equally famous as places of deprivation—filled with residents who have limited opportunities and face arbitrary violence, increased health problems, and early death—and centers of culture. Blues, hip-hop, jazz, and Motown music, which fundamentally shaped the cultural landscape of the United States, originated in some of the country's most impoverished places—areas of the Mississippi Delta, the Bronx, New Orleans, and Detroit, respectively. Businesses sell millions of music recordings, films, television shows, and books from or about such areas and their residents to outsiders each year. Outsiders consume and appropriate these cultural products, listening to hip-hop music or performing "high fives" and "fist bumps," in settings far removed from the places where they originated. By embracing and legitimating the goods and practices from disreputable places, these consumers add to their sophistication and worldliness.

At the same time, outsiders treat most of these worlds as the opposite of sophisticated. Many see disreputable places and their residents as incompetent, alien, and threatening.[9] Even those who see themselves as "progressives" fighting for the underdog can believe that the marginalized people associated with disreputable areas are less moral and civilized—the products of a dysfunctional environment of neglect and negative influences. They see these residents as responsible for their disordered communities and corresponding bad reputations, learning and then passing on an oppositional and self-defeating "culture of poverty."[10]

Although there certainly are some unsophisticated and incompetent people living in these places, as there are in all communities, such understandings are mostly self-serving myths that justify social divisions. The idea that insiders have questionable principles is itself questionable. People from lower-status backgrounds are actually more morally attuned, with greater sensitivity to injustice and concern for others.[11] Yet, these collective myths about insiders certainly benefit outsiders, who embrace a "culture of abundance," accepting and promoting ideas that reinforce their higher-status positions.

Based on such understandings, outsiders carefully enforce these boundaries between good and bad, blurring the lines between disreputable places and disreputable people. They fight against "bad elements"—the people associated with crime and blight—infiltrating their own communities. They may watch and even contact the authorities at just the sight of "suspicious" people, those who live in disreputable areas, entering "their" spaces. The stigmatizing label of "ghetto" especially follows black people, no matter where they are, where they live, or where they grew up.[12] Latino immigrants, associated with disreputable places, face stigma as deviants—despite committing less crime than their native-born counterparts.[13]

The residents of disreputable places become shut out of numerous opportunities and resources when outsiders treat them this way, or if they reject this opposition and avoid the realm of outsiders. In order to navigate the frequently hostile world, they learn to code switch, incorporating "proper" and "professional" ways of speech and behavior that vary from those found where they live. They conform to the standards of outsiders, who do not need to perform this extra work.

Depictions of disreputable places from the mass media and other sources tend to reinforce outsider's negative feelings about these areas and their residents. News outlets, television programs, films, and books offer seemingly endless accounts of these communities' problems with very few counternarratives. Academic research also shares these tendencies. While exhaustively researched and excruciatingly detailed, many urban studies are narrow and one-sided in ways that exaggerate the negative qualities of these places. Even though they are clear that an unequal distribution of resources greatly motivates insiders' behavior, they focus on the most extreme neighborhood problems and the most extreme people there. In the words of Loïc Wacquant, "the most destitute, threatening and disreputable residents of the racialized urban core are typically made to stand for the whole of the ghetto."[14]

Such academic depictions are not made to denigrate this population. Just as medical doctors focus on the sites of disease instead of health, urban researchers devote great time and detail to pathology—the strange and exceptional of disreputable places—with the hope of illuminating and resolving problems. Still, researchers' constant cataloguing of drug users and dealers, gang members, the homeless, thieves, and other deviants buttresses outsiders' distorted and negative views of disreputable places and their residents, "creating one-dimensional caricaturized images of the urban 'other' and limiting our ability to systematically understand the populations we study," as Victor Rios puts it.[15] In effect, the research literature on disreputable places tends to mirror the negative focus found in other types of mass media. It too presents few counternarratives. It is filled with studies of the drug trade instead of church attendance, gangs instead of civic organizations, and violent confrontations instead of family picnics.

Such representations have the effect of strengthening boundaries between good and bad places and their residents. They greatly overemphasize the role of insiders, and underemphasize the role of outsiders, in the construction and maintenance of disreputable places. Researcher depictions focus on the attitudes and behaviors of rare outliers found in disreputable places, explaining their actions as responses to abstract and indirect "social structures." Such indirect explanations largely sidestep the direct role that outsiders play in maintaining boundaries between themselves and disreputable populations—and thus continuing inequality.[16]

Given this social and physical distance, the circuitous ways by which outsiders encounter and come to understand disreputable places and their residents, and how media depictions—including academic research—reinforce negative views of these places, it is not surprising that outsiders' understandings of disreputable communities are uninformed and inaccurate. Perceptions of neighborhoods often vary from empirical measures of the problems found there.[17] Outsiders' views of disreputable places can be extraordinarily disconnected, as Elijah Anderson explains:

> Outsiders typically have little direct experience with the ghetto; they gain their perspective from the media, from tales shared by friends, from fleeting glimpses of the ghetto's inhabitants downtown, or, in some cases, from having been threatened by racial succession themselves, with their own neighborhoods moving toward

becoming ghettos. Accordingly, they imagine the ghetto as impoverished, chaotic, lawless, drug-infested, and ruled by violence. Like most stereotypes, this image contains elements of truth, but it is for the most part false.[18]

Although outsiders have little involvement with or knowledge about disreputable places and their residents, this does not stop them from repeatedly—and even emphatically—accepting and promoting their bad reputations. There is a reflexive quality to urban reputations, as their very definition reinforces them. Understandings of disreputable places further discourage people from immersion into them or associations with their residents—deterring people from any firsthand experience that could reshape their views.

## CHALLENGERS OF URBAN REPUTATIONS

In contrast to outsider's negative assessments, the residents of even the most notorious places tend to think highly of their communities.[19] This is despite acknowledging that their association with these places is stigmatizing. Although they challenge the views of outsiders with positive assessments of their neighborhoods, insider residents have little power to have their views heard, much less adopted. They face an uphill battle against constant negative depictions and bias, as the reflexivity of urban reputations generates a circular logic that repels challenges. Insiders' counterclaims become folded into dominant frameworks and dismissed as further evidence of their antisocial ways. Those who openly love the ghetto are stigmatized as ghetto people. After all, "everyone knows" that these places are bad and to be avoided, so you would be foolish to embrace them.

Although they are stigmatized, the vast majority of those living in disreputable places are "decent people."[20] Many outsiders think that disreputable populations actively "stick with their own kind," separating themselves and preferring exclusion and dispossession. Yet, these populations, despite generations of marginalization and hostility from dominant groups, overwhelmingly share dominant values of faith, justice, and hard work. Even these residents' deviant activities, frequently interpreted as immoral pathology, are often attempts to acquire or maintain ordinary values—such as financial stability, fair and equal treatment, and individual independence, respect, and self-worth—within extraordinary circumstances of deprivation and isolation.[21]

For all of their efforts at respectability, they face a double victimization of being disproportionately the sufferers of crime and then regarded suspiciously as criminals.[22] As Elijah Anderson states, "It is a cruel irony that even residents of the black ghetto who resist the crushing economic and social forces at work there and live decently are victimized when they step outside the ghetto into the larger society."[23] Tellingly, the presence of racial minorities and lower-class residents in a place more accurately predicts people's negative assessments of it than any crime and disorder found there.[24]

Yet, the appeal of separating yourself from a disreputable place and its residents is strong. Even those who live in disreputable places practice it. They further subdivide themselves from disreputable areas, even block by block, and troublesome neighbors within their communities. This practice of "micro-differentiation" is a tool to preserve their standing as good people living in good places. As Matthieu Permentier, Maarten van Ham, and Gideon Bolt put it:

> Residents have an interest in micro-differentiations as a possible means to detach themselves from unwanted elements in their neighbourhood. Residents can associate with or disassociate from other parts of the neighbourhood. Residents of higher status areas within larger but lower-status communities will use micro-differentiations to emphasise the prestige of their residential environment.[25]

In order to preserve their status, insiders further carve out their neighborhoods into good areas, inhabited by the good people like themselves, and the bad places where disreputable people live.[26]

Such subdivisions of disreputable places end up reinforcing the very stigma that residents are attempting to escape. Micro-differentiation further separates residents, as they fail to recognize their shared dilemma of disrepute and work collectively. As Loïc Wacquant argues, they form

> an *impossible community*, perpetually divided against themselves, which cannot but refuse to acknowledge the collective nature of their predicament and who are therefore inclined to deploy strategies of distancing and "exit" that tend to validate negative outside perceptions and feed a deadly self-fulfilling prophecy through which public taint and collective disgrace eventually produce that which they claim merely to record: namely, social atomism, community "disorganization" and cultural anomie.[27]

After all, the practice of micro-differentiation operates by the same logic as broader condemnations of a place. Like outsiders, insider residents also wish to separate themselves from disreputable areas and their residents. Their scorn of those living in such areas neatly aligns with outsiders' negative views, if performed in a narrower geographical area.

Some people attempt to upend these social and spatial boundaries. They seek out disreputable urban areas as desirable places to live and work. Young residents, artists, or technology workers of the "creative class" or "neo-bohemia" are attracted to such neighborhoods.[28] These mostly white and young people from higher-class backgrounds, often highly educated and high-income workers, inhabit areas of town with ugly social problems, disorder, and danger. They partly choose these neighborhoods for their "authentic" urban characteristics—including historic, well-worn architecture but also "gritty" features like homelessness and street crime.[29] Similarly, some middle- and upper-class black residents choose to live in disreputable neighborhoods because they feel more connected with that community.[30]

By occupying places that others dismiss as uninviting and even dangerous, many of these "insider outsiders" are deliberately looking to undo this system of separation and the inequality that it fosters. Yet, these challenges to urban boundaries, much like the efforts of insiders to counter negative views and see their communities positively, usually become folded into dominant frameworks. The creative class and other spatial rebels may defy divisions between insiders and outsiders in the short term, but they often reinforce them in the long term. They can make up the leading edge of gentrification, when a neighborhood transforms from being inhabited by disreputable insiders into a place that is welcoming to outsiders.[31]

## OUTSIDERS, INSIDERS, AND URBAN REPUTATIONS

How outsiders, and some insiders, imagine the residents of disreputable areas as immoral and even criminal based on the reputation of where they live is not accurate. Although the reputation of a place affects all of its residents, stigmatizing them as disreputable, the majority of problems in crime filled areas are the result of a small number of individuals.[32] Outsiders' flawed perceptions are a logical error that confuses individual and collective levels of analysis. These are "ecological fallacies," the attribution of group data to the individuals within that group, such as assuming that the residents of areas with elevated drug arrests are more involved with illegal drugs than other people. Urban researchers struggle with this fallacy,[33] but individuals without a grounding of expert training and empirical findings constantly accept this faulty logic.

The imprecision and inaccuracy surrounding assessments of disreputable places are exactly what make them reputations. By definition, reputations are not grounded in systematic or empirical data.[34] Instead, they are based on scant, biased, or incomplete information. People know a reputation, not because they can factually confirm this belief, or even because they agree with it, but because they know that this is how others feel about it. Reputations are an inexact and unverifiable feeling, falling into the realm of gossip, rumor, and blanket generalization, about what people think that others think. We are frequently surprised, after gaining experience with a person, place, or thing, at how remarkably it varies from its reputation. Given this, it is to be expected that the bad reputations of places are primarily the product of those who know little about these communities.

These erroneous understandings of disreputable places are not simply flawed perceptions based on ignorance. They have a vicious, if unintentionally invoked, arrangement underlying them, as they play an active role in creating and maintaining separation and inequality. Such perceptions are greatly reassuring for those who promote a place's bad reputation. They can define themselves as good people who live in good places, confident that the bad people live somewhere else. This worldview is so totalizing that, when confronted with counterclaims pointing out how they are intimately involved with inequality and oppression, its adherents can react with defensiveness, angry outbursts, and even faltering incoherence.[35]

Ultimately, outsiders' status as the good members of a good place is tied to definitions of bad people in a bad place, and it hinges on reaffirming that they are not like these disreputable populations.[36] This involves creating and maintaining these moral frontiers, remaining socially and physically divided from "bad" communities and making them difficult to know. The more that people can imagine the residents of disreputable places as ill-mannered, incompetent, gluttonous, and violent strangers, the more it justifies their isolation and the advantages that come from that separation.

## 3

# A CITY DEFINED BY DIFFERENCE

In America, the dark ghetto stands similarly as the national symbol of urban "pathology," and its accelerating deterioration since the racial uprisings of the mid-1960s is widely regarded as incontrovertible proof of the moral dissolution, cultural depravity and behavioural deficiencies of its inhabitants.

—Loïc Wacquant

I don't really view Ogden as a bad place. It's like a village. It's just put together differently. The houses are different. Actually, there is a very large Latino portion of Ogden.... It's multicultural. It's not just like another concentrated area of Mormons that seems to be the popular thing around here. I mean, I'm sure there are Mormons here in Ogden but—I don't know. You just see a lot of strange things.

—Ogden resident, 24-year-old white male

Understanding urban reputations as moral frontiers—as primarily the result of external processes, as opposed to internal conditions—intimately ties them to collective groups, power dynamics, historical developments, and other contexts enveloping a disreputable place. Outsiders separate themselves from lower-status people through the symbolic boundaries of a bad reputation. Given this, Ogden has a bad reputation among outsiders, not because its *conditions* are *worse* than surrounding places (although they often are), but because its *residents* are *different*. The city's insider residents vary from outsiders, and this includes their differing perceptions of urban space.

Ogden's residents are indeed different. Here I draw from U.S. Census data and other measures to outline residents' characteristics and how they vary from the surrounding region. Ogden's citizens are similar in their working-class makeup, which is related to other collective categories, including race and immigrant status. At the same time, these similar demographic characteristics—as well as the strong pull of religion in the area—separate Ogden from the surrounding area, making this a city defined by difference.

## SOCIAL CLASS

Ogden has been, and continues to be, a decidedly working-class town. In an age where the service industry and careers with technology are dominant in the United States, replacing factory work and other blue-collar jobs, somewhere between 25 to 30 percent of Ogden's workforce is involved in construction and manufacturing (see Table 3.1). This is twice as high as state and national rates, despite the city having a large higher education school—Weber State University—based there. Although some of this business emerges from winter sports, the local area has many manufacturing plants that churn out products for aerospace, automotive, governmental, medical, and other industries. While such industrial work is a greatly diminished segment of the U.S. economy, Ogden bucks this trend.

The income of residents reflects this working-class level of relative prosperity. The 2016 American Community Survey estimates the median household income of Ogden residents at $42,482, well below both the Utah median of $62,518 as well as the national median of $55,322. Overall, household income hovers in the lower-middle income range (see Table 3.2). While about 16 percent of Ogden households make less than $15,000 a year, only about 8 percent of all Utah households make less than that amount. At the same time, while about a quarter of Utah households make $100,000 or more, only about one in ten Ogden households makes this amount.

Rates of housing and education also reflect Ogden's working-class character. More of the city's population rents their housing than the average U.S. resident, and they rent much more than the average Utah resident. In fact, less than 60 percent of Ogden occupants own their homes. This is despite inexpensive housing, with many three-bedroom homes selling for around $200,000. Regarding education levels, about 45 percent of residents who are 25 years old or older have a high school diploma or less, and another quarter of this population have some college but no degree.[1] These numbers are

Table 3.1. Percentage of Ogden Employment by Industry, 2017 Five-year Estimates, with Margins of Error)

| | Ogden | Utah | U.S. |
|---|---|---|---|
| Manufacturing | 19.7 (+/-1.4) | 10.7 (+/-0.2) | 10.3 (+/-0.1) |
| Educational services, health care, and social assistance | 17.8 (+/-1.5) | 21.9 (+/-0.3) | 23.1 (+/-0.1) |
| Professional, scientific, management, administrative, and waste management services | 11.2 (+/-1.5) | 12.1 (+/-0.2) | 11.3 (+/-0.1) |
| Retail trade | 10.9 (+/-1.5) | 11.9 (+/-0.2) | 11.4 (+/-0.1) |
| Arts, entertainment, recreation, accommodation, and food services | 8.9 (+/-1.0) | 9.1 (+/-0.2) | 9.7 (+/-0.1) |
| Construction | 8.6 (+/-1.1) | 6.7 (+/-0.2) | 6.4 (+/-0.1) |
| Public administration | 6.6 (+/-0.9) | 4.8 (+/-0.1) | 4.7 (+/-0.1) |
| Other services, except public administration | 4.2 (+/-0.7) | 4.4 (+/-0.1) | 4.9 (+/-0.1) |
| Finance, insurance, real estate, rental and leasing | 3.6 (+/-0.6) | 6.7 (+/-0.2) | 6.6 (+/-0.1) |
| Transportation, warehousing, and utilities | 3.4 (+/-0.6) | 4.8 (+/-0.1) | 5.1 (+/-0.1) |
| Wholesale trade | 2.2 (+/-0.5) | 2.6 (+/-0.1) | 2.7 (+/-0.1) |
| Information | 1.7 (+/-0.5) | 2.3 (+/-0.1) | 2.1( +/-0.1) |
| Agriculture, forestry, fishing, hunting, and mining | 1.3 (+/-0.3) | 1.9 (+/-0.1) | 1.9 (+/-0.1) |

Source: 2017 American Community Survey

higher than state and national rates. Again, this is despite the city having a large public university.

There is little difference between dwellings on Ogden's east and west side. The East Bench is filled with relatively modest houses, many far humbler than the historic mansions in the city's central areas. The eastern residences are

Table 3.2. Percentage of Household Income, 2017 (Five-year Estimates, with Margins of Error)

|  | Ogden | Utah | U.S. |
|---|---|---|---|
| Less than $10,000 | 10.2 (+/-1.1) | 4.4 (+/-0.1) | 6.7 (+/-0.1) |
| $10,000 to $14,999 | 6.1 (+/-0.9) | 3.4 (+/-0.1) | 4.9 (+/-0.1) |
| $15,000 to $24,999 | 10.2 (+/-1.0) | 7.4 (+/-0.2) | 9.8 (+/-0.1) |
| $25,000 to $34,999 | 13.3 (+/-1.2) | 8.5 (+/-0.2) | 9.5 (+/-0.1) |
| $35,000 to $49,999 | 16.7 (+/-1.2) | 13.0 (+/-0.2) | 13.0 (+/-0.1) |
| $50,000 to $74,999 | 18.2 (+/-1.4) | 20.7 (+/-0.3) | 17.7 (+/-0.1) |
| $75,000 to $99,999 | 13.0 (+/-1.3) | 15.2 (+/-0.3) | 12.3 (+/-0.1) |
| $100,000 to $149,999 | 8.0 (+/-0.9) | 16.5 (+/-0.2) | 14.1 (+/-0.1) |
| $150,000 to $199,999 | 2.0 (+/-0.5) | 5.8 (+/-0.1) | 5.8 (+/-0.1) |
| $200,000 or more | 2.3 (+/-0.4) | 5.1 (+/-0.1) | 6.3 (+/-0.1) |

Source: 2017 American Community Survey

priced higher than much larger and fancier homes just a handful of blocks to the west. There are a few sizable, ostentatious residences perched high on the eastern hills, but not many. Homes in this area are expensive, but they do not require great wealth to afford. Many faculty of the local university live there, and many do not make exorbitant incomes.

Reflecting the resources and tastes of this population, there are very few gated communities or other markers of wealth such as "luxury" stores and services catering to upper-class citizens. Some places do serve middle- and upper-class residents, such as boutique stores, restaurants, bars, coffee shops, nightlife, cultural events (especially through the university), and events like the seasonal farmer's market. You can find a slice of prosciutto or a buffalo burger with goat cheese in the city, but if you want to eat a gourmet meal, you will need to head south to Park City or Salt Lake City. Instead of being clustered into certain areas of upper-class companies and services, these businesses sit side-by-side with other establishments, and factory workers and other blue-collar laborers frequently visit them. An article about Ogden's small income gap quotes an Ogden resident: "When it's more equal, you can get along more equally. You feel pretty good to be neighborly."[2]

Still, there is class stratification. Much poverty is concentrated in the middle of the city, including the areas of downtown, central city, and West

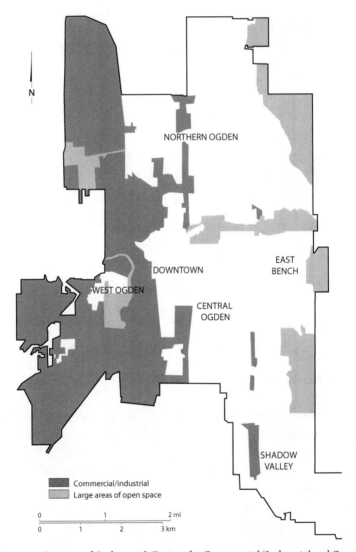

Figure 3.1. Regions of Ogden, with Zoning for Commercial/Industrial and Open Space. For clarity, the map does not outline smaller open spaces, as well as the mixed-use Central Business District surrounding downtown. Map courtesy of Bill Nelson.

Ogden. A look at the geography and built environment of the city alone reveals inequalities (see Figure 3.1). Ogden's western side is filled with commercial and industrial spaces, especially the airport in the southwest corner of the city. It also is low in elevation; what originally was swampland. A downtown factory produces dog food, filling the area surrounding it with a "unique" smell. As a news report on the city's West Ogden neighborhood from the 1970s puts it, these residents "have been given the slaughterhouse, the garbage, the industrial buildings and the unpleasantries of Ogden."[3]

In contrast, the east side of the city sits on hills that merge into picturesque mountains. The most upper-class neighborhood of the city—southeastern Shadow Valley—has larger homes valued at about $500,000. Some homes on the east side are hundreds of feet above their neighbors to the west, many with spectacular views of the towering mountains, the Great Salt Lake valley, or both. While they get the benefits of these views, they also have much more snow in the winter—even several feet more. In contrast to the west side's industrial areas, open spaces—parks and trail systems on the hills—dominate the east side where there are not residences.

Another indication of class inequality and poverty involves local and national interventions. Governmental and nonprofit organizations have focused on developing central and western areas of the city. Ogden receives federal funds from the Department of Housing and Urban Development (HUD) to provide quality and affordable housing, support homeless populations, make neighborhoods safe, and expand economic opportunities in the area. The project's Neighborhood Revitalization Strategy Area includes five census tracts in the center of the city. In these tracts, between 20 and 40 percent of the population are under the poverty line, and between 40 and 75 percent are minorities.[4] Another large project, Ogden United Promise Neighborhoods, is a collaboration between the local school district and several nonprofits, all headed by the United Way. It too focuses on the central areas of Ogden where poverty is concentrated. These and other efforts show how locals have reached out for support and development in central Ogden, and through external funding of such projects, government agencies acknowledge a pressing need for it.

## RACE AND IMMIGRATION

Another category reflecting Ogden's difference, and intersecting with social class, is the city's racial diversity. While research on disreputable places,

Table 3.3. Race by Percentage of the Population, 2010

|  | Ogden | Utah | U.S. |
|---|---|---|---|
| Hispanic or Latino | 30.1 | 13.0 | 16.3 |
| Not Hispanic or Latino | 69.9 | 87.0 | 83.7 |
| White alone | 63.5 | 80.4 | 63.7 |
| Black or African American alone | 1.9 | 0.9 | 12.2 |
| American Indian and Alaska Native alone | 0.8 | 1.0 | 0.7 |
| Asian alone | 1.2 | 2.0 | 4.7 |
| Native Hawaiian and Other Pacific Islander alone | 0.3 | 0.9 | 0.2 |
| Some Other Race alone | 0.2 | 0.1 | 0.2 |
| Two or More Races | 2.1 | 1.8 | 1.9 |

Source: 2010 U.S. Census

especially in the United States, has long focused on black communities, the setting of Ogden involves a different—although increasingly prevalent—population. In contrast to the United States' past color line that divided black people from whites, Ogden reflects an emerging racial picture that is heavily immigrant and Latino. This is what social scientists predict will define the twenty-first century, modifying or even replacing previous racial patterns.[5]

Latinos made up almost of third of Ogden's residents in 2010, making the city's Latino population more than double both state and national rates (see Table 3.3). These proportions were far higher than the numbers of other people of color, who more closely reflected Utah's low rates. About four out of five Latinos in Ogden identified as Mexican, and about half of them were foreign born—one out of every eight Ogden residents. One in five Ogden residents spoke Spanish at home. This community was especially concentrated into neighborhoods surrounding Ogden's downtown, what many people consider the worst parts of the city. Historically, this area included the segregated neighborhood where whites forced the black community to live.

Ogden has long had a substantial Latino population, and this community has seen a large boost in the past several decades. According to the U.S. Census, 30.1 percent of Ogden residents identified as Latino in 2010, numbers that rose from 23.6 percent just ten years before and 12 percent in 1990. This fits patterns of new immigration across the United States, where Latinos are a rapidly growing demographic. Previous Latino immigrants tended to settle in large gateway cities, such as Chicago, Los Angeles, Miami, and New York City. More recently, Latino immigrants have moved to metropolitan areas and small towns—known as "new immigrant destinations"—that are outside of these traditional settlement regions.[6] Researchers have been scrambling to record and understand the impact of these dramatically changing demographics, where large numbers of immigrants are reshaping established social relations.

Not coincidentally, this city with a bad reputation is home to a large Latino population, and historically Ogden has had much racial and immigrant diversity. As I discussed in the previous chapter, assessments of places are closely tied to the demographics of their residents. Outsiders feel that it is in their interests to separate themselves from those with a lower status. They see such disreputable populations as threatening to their jobs, their housing values, their safety, their language, and even their ways of life and identities.[7]

## CULTURE

Religion is a central presence in the region, shaping most every aspect of life. Unsurprisingly, it also shapes Ogden's reputation. Utah has a deeply entrenched religious culture. Along with winter sports, Northern Utah is most famous as the heart of the Church of Jesus Christ of Latter-day Saints. Locals frequently shorten this name to "LDS," although "Mormon," while initially used as an insult, is the most popular term for the church and its members. The majority of Utah's residents are members of this church. On a wider scale, Utah is part of what researchers call the "Mormon culture region,"[8] an area of the United States with a large population of LDS Church members. While this region includes areas of Arizona, California, Idaho, Nevada, and Wyoming, the state is undeniably its center. Salt Lake City contains the headquarters of the church. It is where Mormons settled after violent confrontations with midwestern locals drove them west.

The Mormon culture region has unique characteristics that mirror but also extend beyond official church teachings, making the area especially saturated in social and cultural standards. Mormons speak about Utah as a "Zion" of the United States. Zion being "the place for the pure of heart," a promised land where those who are righteous and wholesome gather.[9] The church's members embrace and celebrate well-defined moral principles, conformity, and restraint. They greet eccentricity and social change with wariness and even indignation. This homogeneity and guardedness about difference surpass religion to encompass the regional culture, its politics, as well as its racial dynamics. Utah's population is one of the most politically conservative in the country, and its residents are just over 80 percent white, far higher than the national average.

In the center of this uniquely American holy land sits Ogden, which historically diverged from the rest of Utah. Unlike measures of the city's lower class, minority, and immigrant communities, it is difficult to know Ogden's rates of religious adherence. The Mormon Church holds membership information close to its organizational vest.[10] While other measures do not narrow their focus down to the city level, they do reveal much lower rates of adherence at the level of county. Weber County, of which the city of Ogden makes up more than a third of the population, contains substantially fewer Mormons than the state overall, and counties adjoining Weber have between 25 to 50 percent more Mormons living in them.[11] Historically, Ogden has been less Mormon than the rest of Utah,[12] and there is a popular belief, mentioned frequently in interviews with Ogden residents, that the city is far less Mormon than adjoining towns (that are all within Weber County). This, coupled with the county level data on religious adherence, strongly suggests that Ogden has markedly fewer Mormons than the surrounding region.

This makes Ogden different, not only by social class, race, and immigrant status, but also by its status as a cultural outlier. Further amplifying Ogden's disreputable image is its setting in the center of this Mormon holy land. Ogden has a history of diverse populations, cultures, and moral standards, in great contrast to the surrounding region's characteristics—and celebrations—of homogeneity and conformity. Through Ogden's long-standing tendencies toward diverse people and their varying ways of thinking and acting, it is a local challenger to this dominant culture. It pays a high price for this difference through its bad reputation and the corresponding lack of status and resources that it brings. Sitting in the center of an area defined by homogeneity and adherence to established moral codes, the city continues to be controversial.

# PART TWO

# BOUNDARY WORK

# 4

# DEFENDING A WORKING-CLASS PLACE

Some identities have consequences for claimants. Not only are these reputations firmly established, but in their solidity, a powerful moral evaluation has been established. A person who pushes for a reputation that is sharply opposed to the consensual perspective can be stigmatized by that claim.

—Gary Alan Fine

*Interviewer*: So, you talked about the lower-class people living down in central Ogden, the middle-class people living in Shadow Valley—so, where do the high-class people live?

*Respondent:* Park City.

—Ogden resident, 46-year-old Latino male

*How do people do symbolic work to create and maintain a place's reputation?* Researchers have long noted how people's assessments of a place differ, as well as how these perceptions vary from measures of crime, disorder, and other problems found there. In her 1961 study of a New York City neighborhood, Jane Jacobs argued that the area was safe, contrary to widely held beliefs about it.[1] Longtime residents knew this, but outsiders avoided this place, even though they had little experience with it. This is because reputations are not assessments of objective fact, or even public opinion, as much as they are "beliefs about beliefs."[2] People imagine them to be accurate representations of reality, they believe that others believe them, and they often adjust their behaviors in light of them. Still, those who invoke reputations generally cannot attribute them to any specific proof, and they may not even accept the reputations' claims as true.

Thus, reputations act on the world even while they are unverifiable. In fact, a reputation is by definition outside of the realm of confirmable fact. As Isaac Pinyol, Jordi Sabater-Mir, and Guifré Cuní state:

> *Reputation* refers to other's evaluations and therefore is considered a meta-belief, that is, a belief about other's belief. This brings us some important consequences, since accepting a meta-belief does not imply to accept the nested belief. Assuming that target agent A has some given *reputation* means that it is reputed with more or less goodness, and that such evaluation circulates on the society, but not necessary implies to share the evaluation itself. So, *reputation* refers to what is said, not what is true.[3]

Although urban reputations are not accurate representations of reality, they still have very real effects on places and their residents.

Researchers distinguish between "internal" views of places, held by insider residents, and the "external" views of outsiders.[4] The perceptions of insiders, Ogden's residents, differed from those of outsiders who lived beyond the boundaries of the city. These variations are intertwined with differences between people. Ogden's residents were living in the same place, but these spatial similarities intersected with demographic similarities, which contrasted with the surrounding region. Through such mutual connections, they united in positive feelings about their community, and they defended it against challenges to this view. These were collective attempts to improve their status by challenging boundaries between Ogden and the rest of the region.

I also found differences among Ogden's residents, especially by immigrant and native-born status. While resenting how outsiders separated themselves from Ogden, higher-status insiders constructed similar symbolic boundaries to separate themselves from low-status residents within Ogden and the neighborhoods where they lived. Like divisions between the views of insiders and outsiders, these spatial subdivisions also reflect social difference. "Native" residents—those who grew up in the United States—separated themselves from areas where Latino immigrants lived, and those immigrants had remarkably different views of Ogden than natives.

Drawing from interviews with Ogden's residents, this chapter considers how insiders challenged outsiders' negative views, the following chapter analyzes how residents made divisions among themselves, and then Chapter Six analyzes the perceptions of Latino immigrant residents.

## UNITING OGDEN

As insiders, residents of Ogden frequently mentioned how outsiders thought badly about their city. Reputations are a vague yet influential idea, as opposed to being based on an empirical majority (if more than 51 percent of people adhere to them) or other verifiable measure. If reputations are "beliefs about beliefs," then native residents of Ogden believed that other people believed the city to be blighted, chaotic, and dangerous. At the same time, their views align with multiple reports about Ogden's bad reputation in the region.[5] Yet, Ogden's residents overwhelmingly challenged these negative assessments. Such positive views united them, defying popular understandings of the city's bad reputation.

Native residents constantly invoked the city's bad reputation while discussing it in interviews. When asked what he liked least about Ogden, this 43-year-old white male answered:

> That it is a dump. It has turned into the biggest crap hole ever! ... Yeah, I mean a lot of the people—they don't take care of their yards. It looks like crap! People don't care. I mean, it's like slum city almost anymore.

Ogden's bad reputation is a robust idea, persisting through any changes—boom and bust, crime wave or decline. It has been passed down between generations for many decades, and it is told far and wide to people in the region as a hegemonic truth.

Although a few respondents agreed with wholesale negative assessments of the city, responses like those of the resident quoted above were rare. Native residents, such as the following respondent, saw such views as coming from those who lived outside of the city:

> *Respondent (24-year-old white male):* Most people who call it ghetto typically don't live in Ogden.
>
> *Interviewer:* They're outsiders?
>
> *Respondent:* Yeah. I mean, they just live in cleaner-kept suburban areas.

Ogden's bad reputation is largely regional, but one respondent, a 31-year-old white male, mentioned how people in other areas also invoked it:

> I went to Texas to a meditation center, a Buddhist meditation center for like two weeks. And some of the people there were like, "Oh, you're from Utah? Have you been to Ogden before?" I'm like, "Yeah, of course. I grew up there." They're like, "Oh, Ogden sucks!" I'm like, "Why?" They're like, "It's dirty. Weird people. Just ugh, Ogden!" Like some people call Ogden the armpit of Utah.

Although I found little evidence, other than this example, that Ogden's bad reputation extends beyond Northern Utah, this respondent was confronted with the reputation of his hometown even when traveling far from it.

Most residents did not share negative views of Ogden, even though they were well aware of the reputation. In fact, while residents acknowledged negative views of Ogden, they tended to have the opposite opinion. They loved the city, as this 46-year-old Latino stated:

> To me what makes a city? Well, you have everything you need in one place. Um, we have a hospital. We have a mayor, county building. We have a city council building. I mean it's in the same building, but it is a different thing. We have DMV department. What else do we have? We have everything—everything a city needs. Also, police department, which is not the best, but we have a police department. Um, what else? For a lot of people, we have something interesting, which is a mall. A small one, but we have a mall. We have a university.

Like the residents of most cities,[6] they had a strong connection with the place where they lived, and for many Ogden was their hometown. This was, after all, a biased sample of people who had, for the most part, chosen to live in Ogden.

These respondents often spoke of Ogden's size as a great benefit. They could easily travel around the city; it had the "small-town" feel of a close community; and it contained everything they needed in this relatively small geographical area. A 32-year-old white male answered what he liked most about the city with the following:

I like how the city was meant to be able to be traveled through. So there are lots of things that are close and lots of different ways to get there. So, like, the grocery store is always close; downtown is pretty close; and the mountains are close. The river is close. I like the proximity here. The convenience.

As a 39-year-old Latina put it, "I just like Ogden, cause it's not too big and it's not too small. Um, everything is so close. You don't get overwhelmed with a lot of people, or overwhelmed with a lot of traffic." Native residents also praised the historical architecture, downtown's entertainment options, as well as scenic mountains and their opportunities for outdoor recreation. Indeed, city leaders promote outdoor activities as an attractive feature of Ogden. This mirrors the feelings of these residents, who greatly valued such assets. For some, the mountains and their trails were just steps from their front door.

## DEFENDING OGDEN

When praising the city, native residents often felt the need to defend it against those espousing its negative reputation. Occasionally, these vindications of the city emerged from actual attacks. They recounted examples of people who had disparaged the city, and they relayed the responses that they had made (or had wanted to make). Respondents spoke about friends and family members stating negative positions and warning them about how unsafe they were. Yet, more often, these were one-sided arguments, with the respondent simply assuming a commonsense "folk theory"[7] that "everyone knows" the bad reputation of the city.

The following respondent, a 36-year-old white male, defended Ogden against an unstated argument that it should "sketch him out":

I don't know, but the bottom line is Ogden doesn't sketch me out at all. It's a really nice area. It's got a lot of cool features. It's just—I like it, I think it's cool. It's got a ton of trees and nature. It's a really clean city.

Another respondent, a 32-year-old white female, stated that "everybody" told her that the city had a bad reputation:

The thing about it is that I was really nervous moving here because everybody was like, "Oh, Ogden has this really bad reputation of being a really unsafe city." And truthfully, I came down here, and I was on 25th [Street]. And they have this whole different restaurant district. There's people walking around, and you don't see a lot of homeless people, or, you know, straggly looking people. It looks like it's very clean, and it's kept up very nicely. And it's really neat to see. And not—I don't think a lot of people understand that. And I didn't either, until I found it one day.

These examples show how a place's bad reputation, although unsubstantiated and unstable, is also a powerful force shaping our relationship with urban space. This respondent, who did not grow up in Ogden, noted how she thought of the city negatively until she experienced it firsthand.

This squaring of Ogden's bad image with firsthand knowledge appeared in multiple responses. Several native residents had difficulty reconciling the idea of Ogden's bad reputation with their experience, even while they drove around the city during the interview. The following 28-year-old white female had safe experiences in Ogden, even while she defined it as an unsafe place: "I've never really felt not safe here, I guess, but in my head I don't think of it necessarily as a safe city. It seems weird." A second respondent had difficulty resolving his negative view of West Ogden, especially as a gang-infested area, with what he was witnessing while doing the interview:

*Respondent (36-year-old white male):* My perception of West Ogden has always been really poor. I've always envisioned a gang-riddled— and maybe I'm just not seeing a lot of the local inhabitants.

*Interviewer:* The "flair"?

*Respondent:* Yeah, the flair. But it's always been a gang-riddled area. I don't feel that here. I've been in places where there's a strong gang affiliation.

These seem to be examples of "cognitive dissonance," where individuals hold inconsistent or contradictory thoughts that inhibit their ability to form a coherent picture of reality. The pull of the idea that Ogden—or parts of Ogden—has a bad reputation, so engrained in the worldview of these residents, competed with their lived experience to the point that they had difficulty believing what they were seeing with their own eyes.

Respondents admitted to the legitimacy of complaints against the city to varying degrees. Some saw the bad reputation as largely unfounded, some admitted to certain amounts of crime and disorder, or crime and disorder in some places but not others. A resident described seeing the aftermath of a stabbing during a downtown holiday event:

> *Respondent (27-year-old male):* I spend a lot of time around here during the Christmas time too because they do the lights. That's actually one of the things—when my wife and I were dating, we'd come here and walk around the light all the time.
>
> *Interviewer:* Yeah, that sounds good. I think I've done that before too, last year. They have a parade that goes by. It's pretty cool.
>
> *Respondent:* Yeah, they have a parade. Although last year when I went to the parade, it was kind of interesting. Somebody got stabbed.
>
> *Interviewer:* Oh [*laughs*].
>
> *Respondent:* [*Laughs*] Right over there.
>
> *Interviewer:* Ah, man!
>
> *Respondent:* When we got done with the parade, we turned around, and there was this handprint on the wall. Like, is that a bloody handprint? Nah, it can't be.
>
> *Interviewer:* That's crazy!
>
> *Respondent:* Turns out somebody got stabbed during the parade and [was] trying not to die, I guess.
>
> *Interviewer:* Wow.
>
> *Respondent:* That's the fun part of Ogden, I guess.

Despite this story, native residents rarely mentioned even such indirect connections to crime in Ogden, although they frequently expressed fears of it.

When defending Ogden, several respondents connected Ogden's reputation to the local religious culture. One respondent saw the city as moving in cycles of development and decline that he attributed to "some people of certain religions that kind of dominate the area":

*Respondent (36-year-old white male):* I think the bad rap that it gets, I think it gets stuck in growth cycles. That's probably what I like least about it. At one point, people want to invest money, and look into new growth, and get cleaned up. Then it will stop and slide back a couple of years. Then it becomes a dump. And then suddenly people get excited about it again, and start fixing things up. So, what I like least about it is, um—you know, I guess, the thing I like least is there's a certain stereotype with some people of certain religions that kind of dominate the area.

*Interviewer:* You know you can say it.

*Respondent:* The Mormons drive me nuts.... The Mormons drive me crazy. Well, they don't drive me crazy. They can become stuffy sometimes. Because even downtown Ogden—that's just part of growth. Having been in Phoenix, if you go to the bad parts of Phoenix, it's— Ogden is still really nice.

This respondent seems wary of even mentioning Mormons and their "stuffy" relationship with the city as a reason for its stagnation, even though the religion dominates the region. Others who mentioned religion often spoke in similarly reluctant and guarded ways, possibly to show respect for others' beliefs.

## COMPARING OGDEN

Many respondents defended Ogden through comparisons. One way that this happened was across time, with native residents relating the current city with its past. As a 27-year-old male said:

I don't remember how long ago it was now, at least some time in the last ten years, there used to be a mall down where that big empty lot, next to the [Mormon] temple. That used to be Ogden City Mall, but it was like the worst mall in the world. Like, nobody went there to do anything besides hang out and steal stuff. And downtown wasn't a supergreat place to hang out. The city over the years has done a lot to bring in stuff. Like, the Junction [mall] is new within the last ten years. And not just the city. Businesses around here have done a lot to invest in that part of town to hopefully make it nicer and a little bit more livable.

Many residents compared Ogden with a past version of the city, sharing this feeling that things were better today than they were in the past.[8]

Another respondent mentioned witnessing a shooting as a child to explain how the city has changed:

*Respondent (32-year-old white male):* I grew up here, although my neighborhood has changed dramatically from when I was a little kid. When I was a little kid, I was sitting in my dad's kitchen, and [I] saw a drive-by.

*Interviewer:* Oh geez.

*Respondent:* But it was one neighbor. One neighbor was like a magnet for trouble, ya know. And then as soon as they were gone everything got better, ya know. I think that can probably happen no matter where you live, possibly.

While recounting a traumatic past crime, he also defended the city by minimizing the incident, stating that it was one troublesome neighbor and the neighborhood where he grew up had changed since then. Many native residents echoed the idea that Ogden has less crime today. Yet, FBI reports show that, while property crimes have greatly fallen, rates of violent crime have remained largely constant for the past several decades (see Appendix). Present-day ideas shape our memories of former times.

Along with comparisons across time, there also were comparisons across space. Residents defended the city by comparing it to their experience living in, or traveling to, other places. These other cities functioned as makeshift control groups that they used to evaluate whether Ogden *really* was as bad as people thought it. Many compared the crime and disorder in Ogden to other places. As a 36-year-old Latino stated, "I honestly, aside from that one couple of houses—and I know a lot of stuff that happens in those few houses—I have not felt that one area is remotely poor compared to other areas in other cities."

The same respondent compared his experiences in Ogden by relating them to an incident in Southern California:

*Respondent:* From what they were saying, the majority of the gang activity [in Ogden] takes place on 26th [Street]. But I have yet to drive through Ogden and see a gang member. Have you ever seen a gang member in Ogden?

*Interviewer:* Probably not knowingly.

*Respondent:* It's not like driving through—I remember one time we went to Disneyland. We were running out of gas, so I took the first exit I could, and we pulled up to get gas. And it was Compton gas station.

*Interviewer:* Ah.

*Respondent:* Yeah, I was like, "Alright, well—"

*Interviewer:* There are areas down there where—no white boys allowed.

*Respondent:* I was terrified, actually. My mother-in-law didn't know what Compton was.

*Interviewer:* That's probably a good thing.

*Respondent:* I said, "Stay in the car, everybody quiet. I'm putting my head down, we're getting gas and getting out of here."

*Interviewer:* Longest five minutes of your life.

*Respondent:* It really was. Dude, it was sketchy. It felt like they were going to pull in and I could see the doves come flying. Like, sending out signals: There's a white boy in Compton. And I'm brown, but still. I was like, "Oh shit, I don't want to be here." It gave you a sketchy feeling.
*Interviewer:* That's an interesting point, there. Even the locals give Ogden a bad rap, but you go to a place like that, it's no joke.

*Respondent:* It isn't no joke.
*Interviewer:* Your life is in danger.

*Respondent:* I didn't want to flash the wrong color. I didn't want to look into anyone's eyes. I just wanted gas. We only put, like ten bucks in and got out of there.

This respondent compared Ogden to a place that he understood as having legitimate danger, although that other city's negative image also shaped his feelings. He initially frames the story as being about gang members, and he conveys a palpable and vividly recalled sense of discomfort. Yet, his description is lacking any specific encounters or interactions, and he never mentions facing any actual problems with this place or its residents. Instead, the response simply recounts feelings of threat and imagined possibilities of danger. His main concern seemed to be simply being in a place with a notoriously bad reputation—Compton, California—and seeing nonwhite people there.

One respondent, a 27-year-old white male, invoked Chicago in comparison to Ogden:

I've dated a girl for a while that lived in North Ogden. It was only just ten minutes from her place to mine, and North Ogden is a much different demographic from Ogden proper. It's much wealthier and pretty much predominantly Mormon. But even her, going up to Weber High: "Oh you know, is it as bad as they say?" What do you mean, is it as bad as they say? "You know, like people get shot, stabbed and what not." No, no, it's not that bad. Then I stopped to think about it, and well, actually—I mean, that thing did go down yesterday. Like, my senior year, someone got stabbed in front of the seminary building and stuff like that. Okay, maybe it's a little rougher than I thought. But you know, it's normal, not a big deal. It's not like it's Chicago or anything.

Along with the comparison to Chicago, this respondent shows great hesitation in how he perceives the city. His views reverse three times, from "No, no, it's not that bad" to "Maybe it's a little rougher than I thought" to "It's normal, not a big deal." I explore this hesitation more fully in the next chapter. This response also shows how those living just a short distance from Ogden fully embraced its bad reputation. As another example of this, some residents of North Ogden protested a proposed extension of Monroe Boulevard in 2015, "expressing concerns of linking Ogden and North Ogden bringing more crime into the city."[9]

Another respondent compared Ogden to his experiences in Denver by giving an account of staying at a hotel there:

*Respondent (24-year-old white male):* There's bad parts of Ogden, but you'll still drive through them 'cause you don't really care. 'Cause it's really not that bad. Like, my warning level went from like a one to a three, but it's still no big deal. But when I drove through Denver, it just went straight up to an eight! Like, fuck! Like, when we first arrived there to our hotel, there was a half-burned couch sitting in the middle of the intersection, and people laying on it. And the light was broken. It looked like it had been broken for months, just nobody wanted to fix it. Then there's like this group of bums sitting on a half-burned couch in the middle of the intersection right across the street from our hotel. And the hotel and everything had like gates all around it. As soon as you go out there, there's just like trash everywhere. Everybody asks you for money every three seconds.

*Interviewer:* So in comparison, Ogden's not bad?

*Respondent:* No! Ogden's definitely not bad. I think most people who try to play it off like it's really bad are just younger kids. Like, somebody who goes to school in Layton [a nearby city], or like goes to Weber State [University] all the time and then finally transfers to the Applied Tech [Ogden-Weber Applied Technology College], who never visited Ogden that much, or doesn't have friends here, just isn't in the area that often, will go and have a bad—because their initial impression of the area is some kind of ghetto place. They'll try to act more ruthless or kind of play the part.

These descriptions of traveling into the heart of disreputable areas of the United States read like war stories. The respondents confront danger and chaos in environments where civility has broken down, and they have lived to speak about it. In contrast, they see Ogden as relatively sedate.

Along with various cities across the country, a main place to which these respondents compared Ogden was nearby Salt Lake City. Historically, Ogden has had a rivalry with this place. Associations between these two cities, with Ogden viewed as decidedly worse, are about as old as the cities themselves. Historian Val Holley quotes the *Salt Lake Tribune* from 1889:

> There is no rivalry between Ogden and Salt Lake City except a generous one.... Ogden has one advantage: Its people are wickeder than ours, and wicked people as a rule are different from those who get all their punishment in this world.[10]

This slow-simmering competition between two of the biggest towns in Utah probably dates back to the coming of the railroad in 1869. Brigham Young, Mormon prophet and founder of Salt Lake City and the region in general, was publicly outraged by the decision. Ogden city leaders later renamed city streets, changing names celebrating Mormon leaders to the names of U.S. presidents. As an example of this animosity, Young Street—named after the Mormon leader—became Grant Avenue. Ulysses S. Grant had led a crackdown on polygamy in Utah.[11]

This contention continues today. Many native respondents did speak positively about Salt Lake City. The very things for which people praised Ogden, a smaller city with an intimate feel, also meant that it was missing the features of nightlife and other resources found in this much larger city to the south. Yet, most preferred Ogden. When comparing the city favorably to Salt Lake City, native residents felt as if they were taking a position that they knew others would reject out of hand. This 37-year-old white male defended the city against "what gets said," a passive-voice construction that omits the speakers of these criticisms:

> You gotta realize, when you have been here for a long time, there is a stigma of Ogden in general, not that there should be, not that

it's warranted, but there is. It's compared to Logan, compared to Provo, compared to Salt Lake City. It has a reputation as being in a rougher, more blue-collar city. And sometimes what gets said about Ogden, I get very defensive, 'cause a lot of it isn't true. There is crime in Ogden. I wouldn't say there is more crime in Ogden than there is in Salt Lake City.

This respondent passionately defended the city, attempting to convince a hypothetical audience that disagrees with him.

Many comparisons between Ogden and Salt Lake City revolved around the amount of crime and safety in the two cities. As this 32-year-old white male stated:

Yeah, [Ogden's] got a bad image. It's kind of weird because houses are cheap. And this is not something that I know for sure, but I don't think the crime rate is all that high, especially if you compare it to Salt Lake, or ya know—but for some reason people just think it's terrible here.

A second respondent, a 24-year-old white male, described Salt Lake City as "trashy":

I go to Salt Lake a lot. I think that it's worse than Ogden [*laughs*]. That's where a lot of my friends are. Now that's some serious trashy place [*laughs*]. That's where you have like complexes filled with everything like meth-heads. And here you'll get the one or two tweaked-out people in a complex but most people are pretty calm and stuff.

These residents challenged perceptions of Ogden as having much crime, understanding Salt Lake City as far more dangerous and disordered. Empirical reports support these claims (see Appendix).

While native residents saw Ogden's reputation as a misrepresentation of their city, they also noted its power for attracting business and other resources to Salt Lake City—and away from Ogden:

*Respondent (43-year-old white male):* I can't figure out why Salt Lake just keeps growing and growing and Ogden cannot—

*Interviewer:* Can't get over the hump?

*Respondent:* Yeah, or like plateaued. We just can't seem to expand.
*Interviewer:* Why do you think that is?

*Respondent:* I, for the life of me, cannot figure out why. Salt Lake is only thirty miles away. It shouldn't make that much difference if I set up my distribution center in Salt Lake or here in Ogden. It shouldn't make a difference for Adobe, Intel—I mean eBay is huge down in Salt Lake now.

*Interviewer:* Hmm, I didn't know that.

*Respondent:* Adobe just built a huge complex down there. Intel has one of their facilities, and the NSA building at Camp Williams.

*Interviewer:* I know that stuff's really coming online down there.

*Respondent:* But I don't know why that stuff stays down there and none of it gravitates up here.

While these residents saw their city as clearly better than its reputation, and better than Salt Lake City in many ways, they also realized that they were at a disadvantage to convince others of this. For them, Ogden's reputation among outsiders hung like an anchor, keeping the town from soaring with prosperity.

Native respondents mentioned that another loss to Ogden was the lack of visitors, especially regional locals. Residents have a popular saying that Salt Lake City is thirty miles from Ogden, but Ogden is three hundred miles from Salt Lake City. This expresses the feeling that Ogden residents frequently travel south to Salt Lake City, but Salt Lake City residents rarely travel north.

*Respondent (32-year-old white female):* I love it [Ogden]. I'm totally happy with it. So yeah, that's the thing. It's so funny because no one wants to come up here and visit. I'm like, why? It's really nice! Everybody's so scared of Ogden down in Salt Lake. It's so funny.

*Interviewer:* It's funny too 'cause just wait til spring and summer, the trees start blooming and the mountains—it's gorgeous.

*Respondent:* I know!

*Interviewer:* People down in Salt Lake don't know what they're missing.

Another respondent, a 37-year-old white male, spoke of Ogden positively in terms of geography, the mountains and their trails, by comparing them to those in Salt Lake City: "Like these mountains is such a treasure. I feel like we got the best mountains in Ogden. I think they're better than Salt Lake City mountains. And you got these awesome hiking trails here." While such statements express local pride, this loss of potential visitors also means that the city is missing out on a fortune in tourist money.

## THE PARADOX OF UNITY

This chapter has analyzed how Ogden's "native" residents united in their views of the community, despite the city's bad reputation. They defended Ogden against real and imagined attacks, often by comparing it to other places. There are two dynamics at play here. One is how Ogden's residents shared a unified positive view of the city. They embraced their community, despite the pull of its bad reputation. This reflects their insider status as residents, but this status is coupled with similar backgrounds of difference, especially in their social class, that separate them from the surrounding region.

A second dynamic is how others evaluate these spaces based on their residents' characteristics of difference, assessing places as disreputable by the disreputable people who live there. While thinking that they are considering disordered conditions, people tend to judge a place by the people there. In an experiment where researchers asked subjects to evaluate different videos of the same neighborhood streets, some with white residents in front yards and sidewalks and others with black residents there, subjects judged these places as more desirable when whites were present.[12] What we think of as objective assessments of place instead rely on previous assumptions and unconscious bias—especially bias against residents from marginalized groups.[13] Another way of saying this is that the very presence of disreputable populations *is itself the disorder* that brings down the status of places.

Together these two dynamics created a paradox, as the very thing that united Ogden's native residents in positive views of their city, their similar characteristics of difference, also reinforced the bad reputation of their community. Yet, residents' attempts to boost their status did not only happen through unification but also through division, which I detail in the next chapter. While they collectively united in order to protect their status from outsiders' counterclaims, they also engaged in "micro-differentiations" of Ogden's spaces in order to separate themselves from the city's lower-status residents. Both of these practices of unity and division had the same goal of guarding their social standing against challenges, either from outside or within the city.

# 5

# A HESITANT COMMUNITY

Nations may have brands—in the sense that they have reputations, and those reputations are every bit as important to their progress and prosperity in the modern world as brand images are to corporations and their products—but the idea that it is possible to "do branding" to a country (or to a city or region) in the same way that companies "do branding" to their products, is both vain and foolish.

—*Simon Anholt*

If you were to ask people from Salt Lake what they think about people from Ogden, they would probably think it's an armpit. And the thing I like about Ogden is, when you're from Ogden, there's kind of a sense of—there's pride. You know, you're proud to be from Ogden. You grew up in these areas. You knew everybody. It's got history. It's got style. Not all of Ogden.

—*Ogden resident, 36-year-old white male*

Reputations are difficult to change. In the words of Gary Alan Fine, they are "sticky."[1] A reputation actively shapes associations, interactions, opportunities, and the overall health of a place.[2] New residents, businesses, and entire industries are attracted to areas with good reputations, creating pockets of growth and prosperity that spur further opportunities.[3] Conversely, a bad reputation does not necessarily reflect poverty, crime, and danger in a place, but if enough people embrace the idea that such things exist there, they may as well. A place's bad reputation also can amplify and even create these problems, as well as stunting new residential growth, tourism, business development, and other measures of success.

Disreputable places face problems that are directly related to the success of more highly regarded areas. Internationally, the extravagant wealth found in centers of industry and innovation, such as technology in Silicon Valley or fashionable clothing in Paris, is intimately connected to the appalling conditions found in places on the other side of the world that produce, or dispose of, these goods. On a smaller scale, disreputable areas of cities are often dumping grounds where unseemly problems such as homeless populations, polluting industries, prisons, and airport noise become concentrated. Higher-status people work to keep such problems far away from the places where they live, even as they benefit from them. Many happily travel to disreputable places in search of goods and services—from gambling, strip clubs, and loud music venues to illegal drug sales and prostitution—that they would not tolerate in their own neighborhoods.

An additional negative effect of a disreputable place involves the identities of residents. People living in places with good reputations tend to understand their status as the result of their hard work, intelligence, and other personal choices and traits. This addition to their lives comes at the cost of subtraction from the lives of the poor, people of color, immigrants, and others who live in disreputable places.[4] As Robin DiAngelo states about the places that white people occupy:

> The quality of white space being in large part measured via the absence of people of color (and Blacks in particular) is a profound message indeed, one that is deeply internalized and reinforced daily through normalized discourses about good schools and neighborhoods. This dynamic of gain rather than loss via racial segregation may be the most profound aspect of white racial socialization of all. Yet, while discourses about what makes a space good are tacitly understood as racially coded, this coding is explicitly denied by whites.[5]

Higher-status populations receive a double benefit. They gain material advantages from where they live as well as an elevated self-worth that comes with not acknowledging how those benefits are the result of an unequal system.

Just as residents of so-called good neighborhoods receive this boost in identity, the residents of disreputable places often face a "spoiled identity."[6]

The bad reputation of their community generates or reinforces their "territorial stigma."[7] Instead of recognizing their disadvantaged positions as imposed from outside forces, residents can internalize their marginality as personal shortcomings—the result of a lack of responsibility or willpower or even the sign of inherently evil selves.[8] People embrace their communities, but they know that these same places lower their status, stigmatizing them.

Although Ogden's native residents saw their city positively, there was a hesitation to how they embraced their community. They applied caveats to positive assessments. While overwhelmingly happy with the city, native residents also divided Ogden into good and bad areas. These coincided with places where residents of different social class, racial, and immigrant status lived. Additionally, how Ogden officials presented and promoted the city—engaging in a "collective forgetfulness" of its unique and diverse characteristics as well as promoting "magical solutions" to the city's image—also shows this hesitation. These views reveal how, although native residents rejected Ogden's bad reputation, they still felt stigmatized by negative perceptions of the city, and this stigmatization shaped their assessments.

**DIVIDING OGDEN**

Ogden's native residents, who saw their city so positively, also generated boundaries by which they divided it into good and bad areas. This created a spatial and social hierarchy where they valued some regions within the city, and their residents, more than others. These divisions spanned from east to west, with people most appreciating places on the east end of the city, and they disparaged those on its west side. Native respondents often saw Shadow Valley and the East Bench—elevated areas near the picturesque mountains—as the most desirable neighborhoods. One interviewee referred to the East Bench as "the Bel Air of Ogden." On the opposite extreme, the least desirable areas of Ogden sit below these inclines, surrounding its downtown. When asked what he liked least about downtown, a 43-year-old white male answered, "It is kind of a ghetto! It's a shit hole."

In their discussions of the city, as well as their defenses of it, native residents drew boundaries between different areas. This respondent, a 32-year-old white female, drew lines between reputable areas and places with homeless populations and youth detention centers:

It's so funny, 'cause when people found out I was moving to Ogden, they were like, "Why are you moving to Ogden? It's so bad!" And I'm like, "Well, I'll just move to a good area." I mean, there are some parts where you kind of have to watch out for. With some places downtown I've noticed you—there's a lot more homeless people. Which really shocks me that there's so many homeless people in North Ogden, or Ogden anywhere in general, because it's freezing in the winter. But you know, they have the youth detention center down there and all that stuff, and it doesn't necessarily freak me out. But there's problems like that everywhere. And there's always going to be sketchy parts of town in every city you go to. So, you just have to, you know, avoid it or try to make it better. There's nothing you can really do about it.

This respondent understands divisions as inevitable, always appearing in cities. After saying that people can "try to make it better," she quickly adds, "There's nothing you can really do about it." Her response is to live on the good side of the line between good and bad places.

In their creation of boundaries within Ogden, many native residents spoke of "the Harrison divide." This was a symbolic line along Harrison Boulevard, which runs north to south across the city, thus dividing the city into eastern and western halves (see Figure 5.1).[9] East of Harrison was the East Bench and Shadow Valley. A respondent spoke of this divide in terms of race and class, distinguishing between Latino manual laborers and those with "desk jobs":

*Respondent (52-year-old black male):* I think what lives below Harrison is, and it's just me guessing, from what I see population-wise, this to me, and now that we've crossed Harrison and now that we're in Ogden, you can kind of see a little bit of the difference. I think this is where the temporary population lives. Um, Hispanics moved here because there are jobs here. There's construction here, so to speak. Um, you can kind of tell. I'm looking at vehicles and things of that nature. They're not bad vehicles, but they're for daily use. There were a lot of, um—where we were [the East Bench], there were a lot of vehicles, but they were the Audis.

*Interviewer:* BMWs.

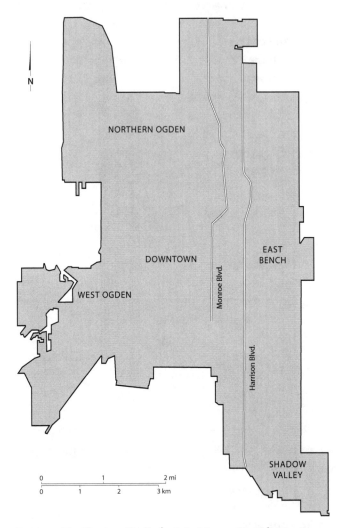

Figure 5.1. The Harrison Divide (and the Monroe Divide). Map courtesy of Bill Nelson.

*Respondent:* Yeah, business.

*Interviewer:* Yeah, nice ones.

*Respondent:* You can tell there's a business life up there. They had desk jobs. This is the manual labor, uh, like I said, temporary population that either—Vegas crapped out. There are jobs here. There's construction going on here. They were doing the I-15 corridor, which you and I were on. It used to be only two lanes but they expanded it. When they did that, a lot of doers, a lot of construction workers that were Hispanic were being hired that you could see all in this neck of the woods, so to speak.

Interestingly, he portrays the Latino community as the "temporary population." This may simply be a reference to the impermanent nature of much manual labor, but it also implies that these residents are less legitimate than higher-status residents.

This same respondent understood the Harrison divide as a boundary of safety. For him, it was a line between carrying a gun or not:

*Respondent:* And that's where, this is where it kind of changes like night and day. 'Cause we're—it's the bench portion of Ogden, and when you get back up in here with benches, you'll see that it's kind of nice, like North Ogden, but then we're at, basically, on Harrison. 'Cause Harrison is like a divide.

*Interviewer:* Yeah.

*Respondent:* And then you have, you'll be on the benches. And we're on Harrison now, but as you cruise down Harrison and you go this way, towards the bench of Ogden, you'll see a lot of older homes. They're nice, just like Ogden, not as much land or property, but it's really a nice area. Then, again with Harrison, once you go this way down, once you go west off of Harrison, it starts getting rough. And the night thing that you asked me—

*Interviewer:* Um hm.

*Respondent:* If I go out at night in that portion of Ogden, I'm packing. I'm bringing weapons, arms. 'Cause I just don't—it—I guess if I'm walking, if I'm in my car, I would only go in that area via car, and I don't really recommend it at night for anything else. Plain and simple.

Many native residents mentioned this spatial division, as well as how east of it was respectable, while the west was suspect. As a 32-year-old white male put it, "Harrison is kind of the divide. If you live that way of Harrison, you're in a less good neighborhood. If you live that way of Harrison, you're in a good neighborhood. Not exactly sure how that works out, but that's the way it works out." These were moral frontiers—spatial boundaries between the good and the bad.

Many native respondents used terms like "shady" or "sketchy" to describe certain Ogden neighborhoods or their residents, including this 24-year-old Latino:

I used to not be a big fan of Ogden, just 'cause, I don't know, I never came here very often, and some of the people I saw, you know? It's weird when you're not used to seeing people walking down the street and then you do see them, and they're like shady-looking characters, you know what I mean? Like they're probably just normal people, and I'm just judging.

Another respondent divided Ogden into "shady" and "nonshady" areas:

*Respondent (28-year-old white female):* Yeah, I guess there's kind of stereotypes of Ogden.

*Interviewer:* Yeah?

*Respondent:* Above Harrison and below Harrison, it's kind of the cutoff, it seems like, for shady and nonshady areas.

*Interviewer:* Ah. And which one would be which?

*Respondent:* Above Harrison is nonshady, below Harrison starts to get shadier.

The word "shady" is not describing the amount of cover from trees or dark alleyways in these areas. It is referring to people and their activities, and it is not too much of a stretch to connect this word with the skin tone of neighborhood residents. While probably not consciously invoked as a racial expression, this language holds a double meaning, performing a linguistic sleight of hand where people are speaking about the qualities of these spaces on one level, but they also are drawing boundaries between spaces filled with, and designated for, white and nonwhite—as well as higher- and lower-class—people.

These residents defined space by the types of people in it, whether fitting categories like white or Latino, lower or upper class, or criminals like gang members or drug dealers. Native residents divided between "good" and "bad" areas of Ogden corresponding to categories of people:

*Interviewer:* So what was the, like, main reason you chose to move into this part of town?

*Respondent (28-year-old white female):* Um, probably the stereotypical, this being the nicer part of Ogden, I guess.

*Interviewer:* You have like, does like, safety or anything or anything like that come into—

*Respondent:* Yeah, definitely. It's definitely advertised as a safer section of Ogden, I guess. And being a single white female, that was necessary.

This respondent linked where she should live with the category of "a single white female."

A second native respondent connected West Ogden with gangs, although he feels a gang injunction instituted by the city largely curbed their activity:

*Respondent (48-year-old Latino):* I like West Ogden. There are some gang members out here too, though. I don't remember the names, though. Got some weird names.

*Interviewer:* The gangs themselves?

> *Respondent:* Yeah, there are two or three different gangs in Ogden. OVG—Over the Viaduct Gangsters. West Side Players. I don't know what all else. Like I said, with the injunction it really helped eliminate a lot of that.
>
> *Interviewer:* Yeah.
>
> *Respondent:* Those kids were wanting to opt out of it, because they are getting older and have families and stuff.

This description links types of people, in this case gang members, to entire neighborhoods within the city.

Talk about gangs and gang members was directed at the central and west side of the city, especially West Ogden. When asked what she liked least about Ogden overall, a 37-year-old white female emphatically answered, "The gangsters!" She also placed the gangs geographically, admitting that she was apprehensive about traveling through West Ogden:

> *Respondent:* Now, as we get further into West Ogden, it starts making me feel a little nervous, because I used to hang out with the gang members.
>
> *Interviewer:* Nice [*sarcastically*].
>
> *Respondent:* I had friends that were in the gangs here, and this isn't the area where I would technically want to be hanging around by myself, or with anybody, for that matter. A little freaky.

Another respondent, a 22-year-old Asian male, when asked what he liked least about central Ogden, gave this reply:

> Um, I, I think that the only thing that stands out is, there's sometimes the stigma that it's not the greatest area. Um, potential gang activity and stuff like that. I don't know how much of that is currently going on, but that's probably one of the negatives.

These residents associated the western areas of Ogden with gang members, even though they made up a miniscule percentage of its population.

Both native whites and native Latinos tended to perceive areas of Ogden through this lens of disorder, crime, and danger grounded in types of people. The following Latino respondent described negative changes to central Ogden as the result of "a lot more minorities":

*Respondent (48-year-old Latino):* Back in the mid-eighties, early nineties, anything above Monroe [Boulevard] was good. Anywhere between 12th Street and 20th and Monroe wasn't too bad. But not anymore.
*Interviewer:* So you think people have gotten rougher in those areas?

*Respondent:* Oh yeah, there are a lot more minorities.

*Interviewer:* But you're a minority.

*Respondent:* Yeah, I know. That's how I know.

Other native Latinos stated that the central and west areas of Ogden were "the ghetto of Ogden" (21-year-old Latino), "scary" (39-year-old Latina), and a 20-year-old Latina blurred the categories of gangs and Latinos when defining the area negatively:

I think more violence happens down here [west]. Like, below [west of] Monroe or on Monroe. Just 'cause you have the originators of the gangs. There's gangs that mostly, like, live here I guess. Gang members. I don't know. It could also be that I think that way because this is where a lot of Hispanics live.

Interestingly, neither of these respondents placed the racial and class divide at Harrison, as others residents did. Instead, they put it at Monroe Boulevard, which runs parallel to Harrison about a half mile west. This minor variation in spatial boundaries was the only substantial difference between the views of native whites and native Latinos. Like other native residents, Latinos did relay that central and west Ogden had a bad reputation. Even while acknowledging the self-deprecating nature of their views, they too connected this negative image with the Latino population living there.[10]

## COLLECTIVE FORGETFULNESS

Just as native residents, through divisions of their community, expressed hesitation at fully accepting this place, Ogden's city leaders also were torn between embracing and feeling ashamed of it. The city of Ogden, as a governmental organization, maintains city spaces, promotes them, and presents itself to the world. Attempting to improve Ogden's bad reputation and market it to tourists and prospective residents, city leaders sought to reimagine the city. In doing so, they erased a substantial segment of its population, even the majority, from past and present representations. These portrayals stripped Ogden of its lower-class, minority, and immigrant residents. The idea of "collective memory" considers the ways that people reenact, memorialize, and identify themselves by invoking history.[11] City leaders, in their maintenance and branding of Ogden, were not engaging in "collective memory" as much as they were practicing "collective forgetfulness."

There is much potential for development, marketing, and tourist money from visitors to Ogden and new residents alike. Indeed, millions of people live a short drive from the city, and many thousands of tourists come to the region each year for skiing and other winter sports, as well as when passing through on their way across the country or when visiting the area's many national parks. The city has boutiques, bars, and restaurants, as well as entertainment and cultural events like outdoor concerts, parades, an auto show, and a summer farmer's market.

Yet, this potential for visitors is not even close to realized. For the most part, downtown's 25th Street attracts only modest foot traffic, even from residents, and regional locals shy away from the area. Many downtown businesses close by five or six in the evening, and most restaurants and bars there are only moderately full on Friday and Saturday nights. Additionally, large portions of its storefronts are empty (a problem "solved" by a deal with Coca-Cola to add colorful advertisements). Although there is much recent development, abandoned downtown buildings still linger as historical residue of past times.

In an attempt to erase its negative stigma and gain status, city leaders did symbolic work to actively forget its long-standing difference and diversity. National news articles about Ogden, encouraged by a city marketing campaign,[12] rarely mention its historically entrenched working-class, minority, and immigrant populations, even as they laud the low cost of living that is very much the result of these communities. Instead, they present Ogden as an outdoor and winter sports epicenter, privileging its east side communities of the white and higher class. These representations reimagine the city as a haven for retirees, a "college town" for students, and a winter wonderland for sports enthusiasts.[13] As Roger Brooks—a consultant hired to study and promote the city—stated, "While we replaced bootlegging, prostitution, and gambling with skiing, kayaking, and mountain biking, Ogden's soul will always remain untamed."[14] Museums in downtown Union Station barely reference the unique, diverse, and notorious history of its downtown. Instead, their focus is on the comparably safe subjects of railroad operations, classic cars, and gun manufacturer John Browning. In fact, the city has treated Union Station, this iconic geographic and historical focal point for the city, with neglect that approaches open contempt. For more than a decade, a former mayor completely cut city funding to this almost one-hundred-year-old building.[15]

Certainly, the mountains, trails, and winter sports near the city are local gems that the municipality should publicize. Yet, such promotions of the city "magically"[16] reimagined this working-class manufacturing town filled with Latinos as almost the opposite of what it was. This disavowal treated the city's unique characteristics, which could have been hugely attractive to people, as shameful deficits and defects.

Places that are similar to Ogden have capitalized on their unique features and even their bad reputations. Downtown 25th Street was a concentrated and historic area of entertainment and vice, much like Fremont Street in Las Vegas, Beale Street in Memphis, or Bourbon Street in New Orleans. In fact, Ogden even held a summer Mardi Gras celebration in 1890 that included a troupe from New Orleans.[17] Las Vegas embraces its label of "sin city," and it has promoted itself as a scandalous place where "What happens in Vegas stays in Vegas."[18] Similarly, historic centers for people of color—such as areas of Mexican culture like Olvera Street in Los Angeles, Old Town San Diego, and the San Antonio Riverwalk—are thriving.

Unlike these places, which are international tourist destinations that produce large amounts of revenue, Ogden was largely quiet about its unique downtown and its heritage. If its residents and city leaders would abandon their hesitation and magical solutions, Ogden could promote itself as an Old West town where celebrities and dignitaries visited, women and people of color were tough-as-nails business owners, and historic buildings still reflect this bygone age.

## MICRO-DIFFERENTIATION AND CONTINUED SEPARATION

Ogden's native residents subdivided the city into reputable and disreputable areas based on the populations that lived there, and the city marketed itself in ways that disavowed the very existence of Ogden's past and present diversity. Both of these practices of "micro-differentiation"[19] cracked the unity of their positive assessments. By seeing some areas of Ogden as indeed disreputable, native residents partially validated the city's bad reputation among outsiders. While marketing has the aim of accentuating the positive and minimizing the negative, what city leaders' branding efforts accentuate and minimize are telling about what, and especially *whom*, they see as reputable and disreputable. They seem ashamed of the city and its people, longing to dismantle much of Ogden and replace it with something different.

These moral frontiers reflect struggles between collective groups. How native residents dispute the boundaries that separate Ogden from the region, as well as how they draw boundaries within the city, has the same goal of gaining status. Native residents sought to enhance their standing through challenges to local outsiders' views of the city. They also did this by distancing themselves from the disreputable populations concentrated in the center of the city. This process of maintaining boundaries led to surprising results. Some residents had difficulty reconciling their negative views of the city with what they were experiencing firsthand, and native Latino residents disparaged Latino communities as "bad," "ghetto," and "violent." City leaders distanced themselves from these marginalized communities as well. They reimagined Ogden in order to separate the city from associations with its disreputable populations. In their portrayals of Ogden as similar to surrounding areas that are predominantly white and higher class, city leaders attempt to unite with outsiders by ignoring their difference from them.

Given that techniques to challenge their disreputable position and further subdivide the city have the same goal of raising people's status, it is not surprising that Ogden leaders' promotion of "magical solutions," covering the foundation of the city with a coat of symbolic whitewash, have not been successful at changing its local image. The city's attempts at collective forgetfulness are an unworthy opponent to more than one hundred years of entrenched ideas about this diverse working-class town and its bad reputation, grounded in racial and class difference, division, and disadvantage.

In fact, these strategies actually reinforce outsiders' perceptions. They accept the view of the regional outsider, championing the higher-class, as well as racially and culturally homogenous, standards that surround the city. Accordingly, city leaders treated Ogden's diversity and difference, a potential source of pride, celebration, development, entrepreneurship, and tourist dollars, like a dirty secret to hide from view. Most of Ogden's residents should be pleased that such marketing failed, as it had the potential to fundamentally transform the city that they embrace—or even drive them from it. Instead of further moral frontiers separating reputable and disreputable places and people, a more effective strategy for transforming a place's bad reputation would involve breaking down these spatial and social divisions.

6

# IMMIGRANT PERCEPTIONS OF PLACE

Among the public, policy makers, and even many academics, a common expectation is that the concentration of immigrants and the influx of foreigners drive up crime rates because of the assumed propensities of these groups to commit crimes and settle in poor, presumably disorganized communities. This belief is so pervasive that in our Chicago study the concentration of Latinos in a neighborhood strongly predicted perceptions of disorder no matter the actual amount of disorder or rate of reported crimes. And yet immigrants appear in general to be less violent than people born in America, particularly when they live in neighborhoods with high numbers of other immigrants.

—Robert Sampson

Here it's as if you are entering in another place. I don't know. As if, the Old West, like if you transport yourself to another place on this road. . . . I love that. I pass often by here. I like it a lot. I like to walk by this road a lot. It is as if you are transported to another era because of the old buildings that have been here. It is good that they haven't destroyed them. It is good that they remodel them and maintain them. It is nice.

—Ogden resident, 54-year-old Latina

Perceptions of urban areas follow patterns that correspond with different types of people. In addition to differences between insider residents and outsiders, a person's social class and race, combined with the social class and race of those who occupy a place, influence whether they are attracted to or repelled by an area.[1] What residents living in majority white and middle-class areas of town see as trashy and seedy, or gaudy and ostentatious, can be perfectly acceptable and even celebrated in lower-class minority neighborhoods. For example, people who embrace European-based standards of well-manicured lawns and carefully managed gardens may find the Mexican American aesthetic of "rasquache"—which includes adorning one's house and yard with brightly colored secondhand items—a junky affront to their tastes.[2]

Immigrants also shape perceptions of place. While researchers report how people's perceptions of immigrants negatively shape urban reputations, we know little about what Latino immigrants to the United States think about the places where they live.[3] The previous chapters have considered how native residents—whites, Latinos, and others who had grown up in the U.S.—understood their city. This chapter explores the views of Ogden's Latino immigrants. When initially planning this project, I focused on whites and Latinos—Ogden's two main racial groups. I noticed how one early interview in particular stood out from the others, and this Latino respondent was an immigrant. Pursuing a hunch that there may be differences between how people raised in the United States and those raised abroad saw their community, I sought out more interviews with the immigrant population. I indeed discovered striking variations between how native residents understood the city and the views of Latino immigrants.

If positive assessments of a disreputable place reflect one's insider status, Ogden's Latino immigrants were probably the most insider of all residents. Geographically, they were concentrated in the center of the city. Demographically and culturally, they varied the most from the higher-status people who live in surrounding areas. In her study of Ogden, Cassi Meyerhoffer found that white residents greatly preferred black residents, who they saw as more "authentic" Americans, to Latinos.[4] Often living in poverty, leaning Catholic—not Mormon, and a politically controversial population residing in conservative Utah, Ogden's Latino immigrants were an especially stigmatized subset of people of color. Not surprisingly, they reflected fellow insiders in their glowing assessments of Ogden.

What surprised me was how, in great contrast to native residents, Ogden's Latino immigrants seemed either uninformed about or uninterested in Ogden's bad reputation. Additionally, unlike native residents, they did little, if any, boundary work to divide the city. Thus, the views of Latino immigrants, a very low-status population who had few people more disreputable than them from whom they could divide themselves, further illustrate how urban reputations emerge from the struggles of collective groups to divide themselves from lower-status people and unite with the higher status.

## IMMIGRANT OGDEN

Between 1990 and today, Ogden has undergone enormous shifts to its demographic makeup. Census data from the past fifty years reflects the change but also continuity of Ogden's minority populations (see Table 6.1). Even before recent growth, the Latino community was long established in Ogden. It surpassed the numbers of black residents—the next largest minority group—at least forty years ago.[5] This population was about 8 percent of all residents in 1970, between two and three times the size of the black community. It then rose and greatly enlarged between 1990 and 2000, growing to almost five times its size between 1970 and 2010. In fact, the city of Ogden was declining in population between 1960 and 1990, and the influx of Latinos spurred growth. Between 1990 and 2000, Ogden added 20 percent to its population, and 80 percent of that gain came from Latinos. In contrast, the numbers of Ogden's black population changed little in the fifty years between 1960 and 2010.[6]

Much of the Latino community's recent growth, and therefore Ogden's growth, came from immigrants. Most of Ogden's new Latinos are immigrants. According to the U.S. Census, the number of foreign-born Ogden residents more than tripled between 1990 and 2010. Immigrants made up about 8,000 of the roughly 10,000 Latino residents added to the city between 1990 and 2000. By 2000, about 40 percent of Ogden's Latinos were foreign-born. More than three-quarters of this population did not have citizenship. This does not necessarily mean that they were undocumented, although many certainly were.[7] Compared to other residents, this foreign-born population was especially concentrated in construction, manufacturing, and "arts, entertainment, recreation, accommodation, and food services" industries for their work.

Ogden's huge influx of these residents mirrors recent increases in Latino, and especially Mexican, immigration to the United States. The city is what researchers call a "new immigrant destination," a recent setting of immigrant growth outside of traditional gateway areas such as California and Texas.[8] While Audrey Singer specifically identified nearby Salt Lake City as

Table 6.1. Race of Ogden Residents, 1960–2010

|  | 1960 | 1970 | 1980 | 1990 | 2000 | 2010 |
| --- | --- | --- | --- | --- | --- | --- |
| White | 95% (67,726) | 96% (66,406) | 89% (57,498) | 87% (55,885) | 79% (61,016) | 75% (62,318) |
| Hispanic, Latino, or "Spanish" | - | 8% (5,506) | 10% (6,324) | 12% (7,669) | 24% (18,253) | 30% (24,940) |
| Black, African American, or "Negro" | 2.4% (1,666) | 2.7% (1,881) | 2.7% (1,723) | 2.7% (1,741) | 2.3% (1,785) | 2.2% (1,821) |
| Total | 70,197 | 69,478 | 64,407 | 63,909 | 77,226 | 82,825 |

Source: U.S. Census

a "pre-emerging gateway,"[9] Ogden seems to be facing even stronger shifts in its population. The rising numbers of Latinos have lowered the relative percentages of all other racial groups. In 2010, the percentage of whites living in Ogden was almost 4 percent less than ten years earlier. There already was a larger-than-average Latino population in Ogden, and this established populace is now being "replenished"[10] with new generations of residents.

A combination of changing national policies and international economic shifts greatly influenced the growth of this immigrant population. New policies drove a huge surge in non-European newcomers that peaked in the 1990s, and it has only recently receded. The 1965 Hart Celler Act revised previous law, and the Immigration Reform and Control Act (IRCA) of 1986 further reformed immigration policy. Current laws follow a type of quota system that only allows a certain number of immigrants from each country. This is meant to allow a diverse mix of immigrants, with no one nationality dominating in numbers. In effect, it makes legal migration from a nation where there is a high demand extraordinarily difficult. This, coupled with the decimation of opportunities for lower-class workers, violence, and other instability in home countries, along with relatively high wages in the nearby United States, creates a strong incentive for poorer Mexicans and Central Americans to travel north. The result is undocumented immigration.

Immigrant populations have been—and continue to be—controversial, marginalized, and stigmatized. Historically, immigration to the United States has been intimately linked with racial animosity, as laws restricting immigration show.[11] The United States had no immigration laws until they banned convicts and prostitutes in 1875, followed by another disreputable population—the Chinese—in 1882. Native workers' fears that immigrants were competing with them economically, as well as warping the country's culture, inspired these restrictions. In 1921, the country instituted quotas that favored European immigrants, especially those from Northern Europe, and severely restricted nonwhites.

Despite the great demographic shift brought on by these new residents, Ogden's Latinos are inconspicuous, and even invisible, to others. Studies of new immigrant destinations have found that immigrant populations are socially but also spatially marginalized, as they tend to live in the obscure outskirts of cities.[12] In fact, they are often invisible to other residents and visitors. As Katharine Donato, Melissa Stainback, and Carl Bankston state, "the greatest problem facing Mexican immigrants in U.S. society may be that the parts they play occur off the public stage, unheard and unseen."[13] Ogden's Latino community, concentrated in the very center of the city, does not fit patterns of spatial isolation found in other new immigrant destinations. Still, this large population is largely invisible to others. Many native residents are surprised when they hear about Ogden's high percentage of Latinos. This population also is greatly underrepresented in politics, business, and other positions of power, as is the case for similar immigrant destinations.[14] As I mentioned in the previous chapter, marketing by city leaders includes little, if any, representation of Ogden's large Latino community.

The marginalization of Ogden's immigrant community mirrors long-standing feelings of many natives that these populations are disreputable. Yet, this is more of a collective myth, reinforcing long-standing boundaries between native and immigrant populations, than fitting any empirical reality. The massive increase of immigrants to the United States during the past few decades has coincided with *lower* crime rates, and cities where there has been an increase in immigrant populations tend to have the same or reduced amounts of crime as before their arrival.[15] Undocumented populations, while greatly stigmatized, fill important economic niches, including seasonal agricultural work and other low-paying, temporary, and dangerous jobs that native residents find unappealing. Although this issue is politically controversial and greatly contested, the benefits of undocumented immigrants seem to equal or exceed losses that they take from the country.[16] Tellingly, places within the United States that have heavily cracked down on undocumented immigration have suffered negative economic consequences.[17] While specific arguments against immigration change over time, many native residents' same feelings of threat and animosity—and their subsequent construction of boundaries—remain.

Although invisible to many, Ogden's immigrant community is well established and thriving. Grocery stores, restaurants, and other businesses serve the specialty tastes of these residents. There is a clear divide between Mexican restaurants that cater to native residents and relatively new businesses catering to immigrants. More established eateries—some founded by previous generations of immigrants—feature much melted cheese, tomato-based salsa, "hard" deep-fried tortillas, and Tex-Mex dishes like nachos and enchiladas. In contrast, Ogden's more immigrant-friendly restaurants feature carne asada, tomatillo salsa, "soft" tortillas, and dishes such as birria, menudo, and tortas. Their customers prefer "paletas," Mexican popsicles, over ice cream. The settings of these eateries are different as well. While restaurants tailored to native residents are storefronts and buildings, those for immigrants occupy brick-and-mortar spaces as well as food trucks and food carts. I also have heard of clandestine restaurants, catering to immigrants, run from within the homes of Ogden residents. Reflecting the city's homogeneity of social class, where businesses catering to upper class and working class are found side by side, most of these businesses occupy the same area surrounding downtown.

The demographic revolution hitting Ogden has been a quiet one, with little open conflict, but the isolation of the city's Latino immigrants also maintains long-standing divisions between dominant populations and marginalized communities. Native residents' belief in spatial boundaries between the city and surrounding areas, as well as their boundaries within the city between good and bad areas, reflected these divisions. Not coincidentally, Ogden's "bad" areas were where immigrants lived.

## NO HESITATION

In interviews, Latino immigrants' responses had many of the same characteristics as those of native residents. Immigrants overall liked the city, and they too praised its mountains, intimate size, and feeling of a small community. Although for them, the community may be smaller and more geographically bounded to central areas of the city, as this 38-year-old Latina immigrant explained:

> *Respondent:* You can see in the middle of Ogden there is a "Little Mexico" in there, you know. We have people that they don't see the need of speaking English or trying to go and, I don't know, and pay the bills or making commercial transactions or something like that in another language. Because everything is in the middle of Ogden, so why do I need to try to speak English if I have, you know, the access or the opportunity to speak my language and do all this in the middle of Ogden? Why do I need to go to Salt Lake City and maybe go to one of the activities they have over there if I have the same activity in the middle of Ogden, maybe in Spanish? So is, like, they create their own comfort area, you know, is a—how can I explain?
>
> *Interviewer:* They create, like, their own culture within a culture?
>
> *Respondent:* There we go! They create their own culture in the big culture, and they feel so comfortable enough there is no reason for, you know, mixing myself. Is no any reason for, let's see, and explore how the big culture lives. Let's go to be part of their activities, part of their holidays because they don't see the need. Because everything they need to do is in the middle of Ogden. So there is nothing for them to say, I need to take the risk and see what happens. Let me live in my comfort circle.

This respondent saw the resources of central Ogden, including bilingualism in "Little Mexico," as comfortable for the Latino immigrant population. In fact, the community was too comfortable for her tastes. Several immigrant respondents felt similarly dismayed that people in their community were not learning English and engaging with the larger culture. Such responses downplay the extreme risks that immigrants, especially those who are undocumented, face from journeying outside of their "comfort circle."

While appreciating this ethnic neighborhood and how it catered to them, immigrants also spoke about embracing—or attempting to embrace—the wider community. As a 66-year-old Latino said, "It takes some work for me to be able to define what is middle class in the United States because in Mexico, middle class doesn't exist anymore. There is only low class and high class."

Immigrant respondents mentioned how they preferred some cultural practices to those of their home country. A 44-year-old Latina, originally from Chile, spoke positively about how people frown upon littering:

> Having lived fourteen years in this country, you start to adapt to the culture. Because you are not going to throw something out the window or any dirty thing. You will save it in your pocket or, I don't know, and then you will find the opportunity to throw it away. If you see someone do that, it frustrates you, and it makes you want to say, "Hey! What are you doing?"

Other respondents appreciated social controls, such as citations for messy yards and traffic tickets, that tempered the more freewheeling practices that they experienced in Mexico and other countries.

As these examples show, Ogden's Latino immigrants, much like native residents, overwhelmingly embraced the city. At the same time, the responses of native residents and immigrants had clear differences. One big difference was a lack of the hesitation that defined native residents' assessments of Ogden. Consider a 48-year-old Latina's view of Ogden's center:

> In all of the areas, you can see the same development and growth. I mean, I have seen that it has expanded much more. There is construction of more houses, construction of more shopping centers, because I remember when we first got here. You could find Sam's or Lowe's, only in Ogden. I mean, big stores where you could buy—Walmart. So now, lately I have gone to other cities, other areas, and I see that there is also a Walmart here. There is Lowe's here. These places also are advancing. And I say, oh, that's good because now people don't have to go a long distance to acquire what they need every day. So, it is advancing in home growth, but it also has grown commercially. You can see it because I say, oh wow, this store wasn't here before, and there's this. Oh, and now they built this, and you can see—you can notice the difference a lot, but without losing its essence of being a town with a lot of vegetation. A town that cares for the vegetation, the trees, the water, the river, the lakes—what they have. In the parks, I have seen that the city puts a lot of effort into maintaining them, so that we don't lose those breathing lungs of nature while the town is growing. It's what I admire about Ogden. They keep maintaining their nature.

This response is characteristic of descriptions by immigrant residents. Like native residents, they love this small community with all of the amenities that they appreciate, including much green space.

Yet, such responses are remarkable for the absence of what was typical in others. They are missing the defensiveness and divisions that filled native residents' responses. They point out both positive and negative features without invoking the city's bad reputation or tying negative features to disreputable populations. Nor do they defend Ogden against negative attacks, communicating how aspects of the city defy its bad reputation among outsiders. The above respondent did not defend her experiences in the city against the monolithic idea of Ogden's bad reputation.

In fact, most immigrants seemed to be either unaware or unimpressed with the very idea that Ogden had a bad reputation. Native residents mentioned its existence as an undeniable fact, even as they believed it to be in error, and they defended the city against it. Their responses are saturated in talk about it. In sharp contrast, the responses of this population rarely mentioned Ogden's bad reputation. As a 20-year-old Latino said, "It is a calm area. It's not a very dangerous place. It's not a big city, but it also isn't a small city." When they did mention it, they seemed unconcerned about it. As a 66-year-old Latino stated, "I have heard that it is—there are some areas in the center, downtown, something unsafe, and with the criminality, it is more notorious above all. . . . Well, in personal experience, I have not had any problem."

While immigrants were certainly worried about safety, Ogden's bad reputation did not influence their evaluations. A 44-year-old Latina mentioned that, to assess the safety of places, she checked an online sexual offender registry. She said about central Ogden, a neighborhood greatly maligned by native residents, "It is very beautiful. The houses are old, but the area is very nice. And yes, I would move to live here, but only when I know that it is safe." Instead of relying on ideas of the "Harrison divide" and other folk beliefs, she sought out empirical verification.

Even when an interviewer—defying my instructions to remain neutral and not steer the conversation—specifically asked about the city being dangerous, the following respondent dismissed that idea in this telling exchange:

*Interviewer:* Are there any parts of Ogden that you don't like going to? Like it is dangerous?

*Respondent (38-year-old Latino):* No, until now I haven't been anywhere that would give me fear. I have felt fine everywhere.

*Interviewer:* There are many people that think of Ogden as being dangerous.

*Respondent:* Only when I am out drinking I try to watch myself, but besides that I feel fine here.

Despite the interviewer twice interjecting that Ogden is "dangerous," the respondent still assessed the city positively, although he did mention concern for his safety ("I try to watch myself").

Latino immigrants saw their neighborhoods far more favorably than native residents. While native residents discussed disorder, crime, and threatening populations of the homeless and gang members as problems, this 38-year-old Latina's biggest complaint about the city was a lack of winter activities for her children:

> I know the thing that I don't like the most about Ogden is that there's not much to do in the winter as a family, especially with kids that are teenager years. I'm kind of experiencing that when my kids were younger the hotspot was the McDonald's Playground. You know [*chuckles*] and that was kind of easy because they just go play with other kids. But now that they're older and I try to find stuff for them to do, it's kind of hard, without them being stuck in front of their electronics.

A 2013 community survey of over seven hundred people in central Ogden, given through the United Way's Promise Neighborhood project, supports this claim.[18] Non-English-speaking respondents (and researchers only administered the survey in English and Spanish) were significantly less likely to see crime, violence, gang activity, substance abuse, and noise as problems in their neighborhoods. They also were significantly less likely to report feeling discriminated against, threatened, or treated disrespectfully, and they were significantly more likely to report feeling that their neighborhood was close-knit.

## REFINING AND INVERTING DIVISIONS

Along with not hesitating in their embrace of the city, another difference between the responses of immigrants and native residents was how Latino immigrants refined and even inverted many native understandings. While native residents divided the city in ways that corresponded with the social class and race of their residents, the views of immigrants did not contain such boundaries. Immigrants definitely recognized differences between various areas of Ogden in terms of crime, social class, race, home values, and other variations between neighborhoods. Yet, their responses had more refined nuance and specificity than those of native residents.

Native residents tended to paint entire areas with a broad brush, especially partitioning physical space to divide the city into distinct good and bad areas. The apparent precision of this line—cut by the exact border of a roadway—belies how this was a more-or-less arbitrary division of space based on a folk belief. Some native residents put this divide at another street—Monroe Boulevard. Instead of labeling areas as tainted by the people living there, Latino immigrant residents presented a more detailed approach to understanding the city that focused more on specific activities, involving specific people, and happening in specific places. For example, this 47-year-old Latino discussed gang activity in Ogden as involving infrequent incidents in a carefully circumscribed area:

> In the north area it is rare, very rare, to see gangs. But in the specific area of 24th, 25th Streets between Wall and Monroe, maybe you can extend it to 27th and 22nd between Washington and Monroe. This is where you see most of the gang activity, and you do hear about random cases of drugs or assaults on people. But it's mostly about how they took a bike from the front yard of a house, or they broke a car window and stole the stereo. You hear these occasionally, very occasionally. That is where you see the so-called gang members—in the streets, in the cars. That is the area that they frequent the most.

As opposed to portraying an entire area as disreputable, he mentioned how crime only happened occasionally ("it is rare, very rare"). He also pinpointed its occurrence to certain blocks, not entire neighborhoods as many native residents did. Additionally, he did not link their instigators to a broad category of people, nor did he speak about these places and people through morally tinted language. Missing from his description were negative words, such as "bad," "ghetto," or "sketchy," that native residents used. Immigrant responses did not have a clear separation between good and bad places, with good and bad residents inhabiting them.

Some responses even contained an inversion of the boundaries of good and bad described by native residents. The following statement by a 48-year-old Latina reversed Ogden's reputation for crime in the region. She instead saw the city as safe in comparison to other local cities:

> So, I think that the city of Ogden has worked a lot in maintaining the serenity and security of people, of the families, of the children, and more than anything I see, I have seen that they have managed to control drugs being sold. That is very strong, and I admire the police a lot. Because in comparison to other cities like Midvale [or] Salt Lake, you hear it in the news a lot that they steal or assault. Thank goodness we do not see that here. There are rare situations of vandalism that present themselves.

It seems that, by not having their perspectives distorted by the idea of a bad reputation, these residents did not hesitate in their embrace of the community. They also were able to give more accurate and nuanced evaluations of crime and other problems in these places. Compared to those of native residents, Latino immigrant perceptions of Ogden and Salt Lake City aligned more closely to empirical numbers of crime reports, which find much more crime in Salt Lake City than Ogden as well as much higher rates of property crime than violent crime in Ogden (see Appendix).

In another example, a 38-year-old Latina spoke positively about Ogden in comparison to her home country:

> When I first came from Mexico, I missed Mexico a lot. It was different. It was difficult for me to adapt because of the language and the customs. But with time, I saw that now, in Mexico, security has changed a lot, and I see that it is more calm here. There's a big difference, especially because there is safety here. You can go walking. You can go in your car. You can leave your car door open, and you can go to the store and leave your car door unlocked. And no one comes to break your window. No one comes to give you a flat tire or commit mischief against you. Compared to other cities or Mexico, there is a big difference.

While this response is similar to how native residents compared Ogden to other places, she is not using this comparison to defend the city against attacks based on its reputation.

Latino immigrants also inverted the boundaries that native residents established by being much more critical of neighborhoods where higher-status people lived. They were definitely aware of the safe, tidy, and peaceful environments of higher-status areas. As a 54-year-old Latina said of the East Bench, "Normally, the Americans are very clean. Um, because they are born here, they know the rules and laws. So, normally they are clean. There are people who have no manners, so maybe they are very dirty. But in this area, it is very nice. It is very clean. It looks good. Good houses."

Yet, they also leveled criticisms of the places that native residents uncritically accepted as good. Many of these focused on the weather and elevation in higher-status neighborhoods. A 44-year-old Latina criticized the high amounts of snowfall in these elevated areas: "I like the landscape, but yes. In the summer, it must be beautiful, but I say now, in winter, when those storms come and they say, 'Wow! Five feet of snow fell.' Honestly, I wouldn't like to live by here so much." Another 62-year-old Latino was wary of the eastern areas of town because "I have heard of people saying that there could be an avalanche of snow on the houses that are close to the mountain." A 48-year-old Latina spoke of the East Bench as a place for "people who want to live peacefully and who don't have high blood pressure," stating that the elevation there could affect people with that medical condition. In contrast, native residents rarely criticized these areas. For them, these were the most desirable parts of the city, and living there was a marker of status and accomplishment.

Several respondents also spoke of these areas as isolated—cut off from resources and other people. A 38-year-old Latina stated about Shadow Valley, the most upscale area of the city, "I don't see there's much here for me that, you know, other than what I already have down in the area where I live." Another 47-year-old Latino called the East Bench "lonely":

> In this area, you see little traffic. It looks clean, but at the same time, it looks lonely. When I say lonely, I mean you don't see people on the streets compared to the area that we were in a few minutes ago in the center, in the heart of the city, where you always, always see people walking. Or you see people working. You see human activity.

Unlike the overwhelmingly positive views of native residents, immigrant respondents criticized higher-status eastern neighborhoods for lacking the movement and street life found in the center of the city.

While researchers argue that such constant activity gives urban areas vitality and safety,[19] native residents seemed to interpret the energy of central Ogden very differently. As I reported in the previous chapter, one said, "It's weird when you're not used to seeing people walking down the street and then you do see them, and they're like shady-looking characters, you know what I mean?" The vibrancy of this area may have seemed to native residents like disorder and even a dangerous threat. For them, it signaled trouble. Latino immigrants interpreted this street life very differently.

## EXPLAINING IMMIGRANT PERCEPTIONS

Generally, the residents of a disreputable place are well aware of their community's status, as well as how that status stigmatizes them. In fact, the pull of this moral geography is so strong that those living in places with bad reputations also adopt it, further dividing themselves from the disreputable places, and their residents, within their communities. Given how previous research links disreputable areas with the stigma of their residents,[20] Ogden's Latino immigrants should have been the most aware of their community's vilification and how they were hurt by it. Yet, their responses do not fit these patterns.

While Latino immigrants certainly mentioned crime in central Ogden and other divisions of social class and race, they were much more evenhanded in their assessments of the city. They mentioned the positive and negative aspects of all areas. They also did not employ morally saturated boundary work to divide the city into good and bad halves defined by good and bad residents. Maybe most tellingly, Latino immigrants seemed to be overwhelmingly unimpressed with Ogden's bad reputation. This was very different from native residents, who invoked it eagerly, often, and spontaneously—with no prompting. Even when directly prompted, immigrant residents were dismissive of this idea.

This raises the question of why the perceptions of Latino immigrants varied so remarkably from those of native residents. I anticipate that many readers will see these differences as the result of immigrants' ignorance to the realities of the city and the palpable dangers that its reputation reflects. We often think of those with such knowledge as being "street smart"—savvy and astute negotiators of cities.[21] Yet, such a view does not fit this data. Overall, the responses of Latino immigrants, compared to those of native residents, show a more nuanced and detailed picture of Ogden that fits more closely with empirical findings. In contrast to the crude collective assumptions on which many natives relied (such as the "Harrison divide" and gang threats), immigrants' views are more grounded in experience and even—in the case of the woman who checked sex offender registries—data. There is more to the views of immigrants than an absence of knowledge and good judgment.

Here I present three possible explanations, with each one probably being a factor. Given the main argument of this study, a first explanation involves moral frontiers. The different perceptions between immigrants and natives make sense given how urban reputations are the result of boundary work. Ogden's native residents had a collective interest to defend their city from outsider attacks, protecting their status, but they also had an interest in dividing themselves from lower-status people who lived west of Harrison (or Monroe). Ogden's Latino immigrants were some of the city's most vilified and controversial residents. They had little possibility of gaining status by distancing themselves from anyone below them. Instead, they gained standing by unifying with surrounding areas and their residents, making their views of the city much more tempered.

A second explanation is that these immigrants' views reflect their separation from other residents. Because of their cultural, social, and physical isolation, Latino immigrants did not know the great significance that Ogden's reputation holds for others. Defused of its hegemonic power as an entrenched idea that "everyone knows," the reputation weakened and withered in their minds. If they had heard anything about it, they seemed to dismiss this idea as not fitting their experience. This does not mean that the bad reputation does not negatively affect them. Others still adhered to it, bringing many negative consequences. What this does mean is that immigrants approached the city with much less fear and hesitation than other residents. In contrast to research that links disreputable places with a stigmatized identity, their senses of self did not seem to be negatively impacted by living in this place. Stigmatization is not an automatic result of living in a disreputable place.

A third, and related, explanation involves socialization. Compared to other countries, people in the United States especially associate places where people of color live with disorder, crime, and other problems.[22] Immigrants may not have developed these racialized mechanisms for evaluating place. As people who primarily grew up in Mexico and other Latin American countries, these respondents would not see other Latinos as threatening. On the contrary, they find Ogden's "Little Mexico" to be welcome and comforting in this foreign land. Along these lines, these residents' overall positive views of Ogden may have to do with the small percentage of black people living there. Although their racial socialization is different, many immigrants do enter the United States viewing African Americans—and African American neighborhoods—negatively.[23] Ogden has few black residents that might sour their feelings about the city's spaces.

Also, Latino immigrants' feelings about central Ogden may be shaped by their socialization with Latin American cities, which are organized differently than those in the United States. While U.S. "inner cities" are often infamous as concentrated centers of poverty and segregation, city centers of Mexico tend to be the most desirable areas, and its outskirts contain the slums.[24] Given the perspectives of these foreign-born residents, they may see living in the center of a city as an advantage, and even a privilege, instead of a liability.

While Latino immigrants were much more unified in their assessments than native residents, these extremely positive assessments of Ogden may be short-lived. Isolation is a common feature of Latino immigrants in new destinations because of their separate communities, poverty, housing segregation, cultural and language barriers, and fear of authorities because of their legal status.[25] Ironically, the more that immigrants become integrated into the wider community, the more they will assimilate and learn the cultural codes of the United States. This includes learning to scorn and fear the places where minority populations live.[26] Then they will rise to a level of status where they too can divide themselves from disreputable populations, seeing those who look like them as problem residents and dangerous threats.

# PART THREE

# THE CONTEXTS OF URBAN REPUTATIONS

# 7

# HISTORICAL ECHOES

People benefiting from the existence of a given complex will devise means of perpetuating it even after it has outlived its uses or the original set of factors accounting for it.

—*Orlando Patterson*

*Respondent (32-year-old white male):* Right here there used to be a big cattle auction place, and that might have been what happened to this neighborhood too. Ya know, it smells like cows all the time. Maybe? I don't know.

*Interviewer:* Just the smell mixed with cow and landfill.

*Respondent:* Yeah. I honestly think that it's mostly just like your reputation. Ogden just, for some reason, has this stigma.

—*Ogden resident, 32-year-old white male*

*What circumstances shape how ideas about place develop and continue?* Past characteristics of cities—including their reputations—shape their varying paths, influencing who moves to them, who visits them, and who avoids them.[1] These differing destinies arise from multiple historical factors, including activism, culture, demographics, economics, and politics, that shape the present. Orlando Patterson argues that historical change or continuity happens through pivotal events that shift historical trajectories, structural factors such as economics and race, and cultural factors—the taken for granted beliefs and activities that make up our everyday lives.² Through a combination of these three dimensions, places gain unique characteristics that further shape their paths.

Given this, Ogden's history is important for explaining differences between the city and the region, including views that it is a disreputable place. The city has a unique past that has and continues to make it an epicenter of social class, racial, and immigrant diversity. Patterson's framework is useful for explaining Ogden: a key historical event shifted the city's path, transforming its economic and demographic structures, and leading to cultural changes—including the development of a bad reputation—that continue to shape the city. These are "historical echoes," as incidents from more than a century ago reverberated into the present, influencing current perceptions. Such contexts molded the unique path of this place, just as other circumstances shaped surrounding areas in much different ways.

## THE COMING OF THE RAILROAD

By all historical accounts, the origins of Ogden's difference, and the city's bad reputation in the region, began more than one hundred years ago with the coming of the railroad. Although long gone, this event—bringing with it dramatic economic and cultural transformations to the city—has shaped the city to this day.

In 1869, locals and national onlookers at Utah's Promontory Summit witnessed the Golden Spike Ceremony, where the future founder of Stanford University drove in the last railroad spike, connecting the East and West Coasts of the United States by rail. Officials soon established a permanent junction just southeast of there, in the nearby town of Ogden. Almost equidistant from Los Angeles, San Francisco, and Portland, the city became a main stop along the transcontinental railroad. The choice of Ogden had much to do with geography, as a nearby canyon pass made for a natural route through the city. Yet, it also conspicuously missed the nearby (and much larger) Salt Lake City. Eight months later, an additional rail line connected Ogden with Salt Lake City. Mormons considered this decentering of their flagship city to be a snub. This event may have started a slowly simmering rivalry between the two cities. Although Salt Lake City had its own prostitution district and no shortage of vice, locals soon began contrasting the piety of Salt Lake City with the sinfulness of "Junction City," as people came to call Ogden.³

With the establishment of the rail, the town quickly grew from a sleepy fur trading and agricultural area into a thriving junction for travelers during this era, which lasted from the late 1800s into the mid-twentieth century. As historians F. Ross Peterson and Robert Parson put it, before the railroad Ogden was "a small Mormon town on the edge of the desert. Its population of 1,500 people lived mostly in adobe or log houses, and its sole claim to fame was that, in rainy weather, it had the muddiest streets in Utah."[4] After 1869, the city became "a booming transportation hub and commercial center that was Utah's portal to the world. Its saloons, hotels, and eateries added an air of rowdy excitement unknown in most Utah communities, and its gentile [non-Mormon] and ethnic communities brought a rich diversity in culture and politics."[5] Ogden's population ballooned from 1,463 people in 1860 to 12,889 in 1890.[6] This transformation to the city was so great that, by 1870, 72 percent of those who lived in Ogden in 1860 had moved out of the city.[7]

The decision to place the railroad junction in Ogden forever shifted the city's historical trajectory. Surrounding cities remained quiet, small, and culturally homogenous Mormon outposts. In contrast, this external, national event fundamentally transformed Ogden, blossoming it into a vibrant and cosmopolitan city—for a long time the second largest in Utah. This event also led to economic and cultural openings that a diverse population, which would not have been there otherwise, filled.

## ECONOMIC BOOM AND DIVERSE COMMUNITIES

The railroad brought huge economic and demographic changes to Ogden. Downtown's 25th Street—nicknamed Two-Bit Street—became a booming center for travelers. Another consequence of the coming of the railroad was much greater diversity, especially when compared to the surrounding region. As economic opportunities encouraged people of color and immigrants to come there, Ogden became a temporary or permanent home for many Asian, black, and Latino workers. This injected the city with ethnic but also cultural diversity in an area where the hegemonic center was and remains the Latter-day Saints Church.

As people who were the last to be hired and the first to be fired, rates of racial groups and immigrants in Utah rose and fell dramatically with employment opportunities.[8] Just as immigrants helped to build other large-scale projects throughout the United States, people from China, Mexico, and multiple European countries worked to complete the intercontinental railroad. From 1900 through the 1920s, there was further growth in the immigrant population.[9] In 1923, 20 percent of rail workers were *traqueros*—Latinos who

Table 7.1. Race of Weber County Residents, 1870–2000

|  | 1870 | 1880 | 1890 | 1900 | 1910 | 1920 |
|---|---|---|---|---|---|---|
| White | 7,833 | 12,291 | 22,525 | 25,087 | 34,484 | 42,608 |
| Hispanic | | | | | | |
| African-American | 21 | 17 | 87 | 51 | 204 | 270 |
| Chinese | 3 | 33 | 106 | | 93 | 95 |
| Japanese | | | 4 | | 391 | 490 |

Source: Perlich (2002)

laid and maintained the railroad tracks.[10] While the Great Depression lowered the numbers of minorities dramatically, the wartime boom of the 1940s and 1950s (and, in the case of Chinese immigrants, an end to restrictions on immigration) followed this era, creating a resurgence of these populations.[11] Economic opportunities intersected with the racial hierarchy of the United States. While new immigrants and people of color with a higher racial status had their preference of jobs over those lower on these rungs, some workers replaced more established groups by working for lower pay. Many people of color first found themselves in Utah as strikebreakers.[12]

During its railroad era, Ogden also had a substantial number of immigrants, and the current influx of Latinos mirrors these past patterns. After the coming of the rail, the city quickly filled with residents from other nations, as Lyle Barnes colorfully illustrates:

> In 1890, one out of every 3 or 4 residents of Weber County was an immigrant to the area from some distant country. Assuming this ratio would remain nearly the same on 25th Street, a traveler could expect to see, in every 100 people on the Street, about seven from Canada, two from England, two from Denmark, two from Sweden, and one each from Germany, Holland, Ireland, Scotland and Norway. On a larger scale, in every 150 people that the traveler passed, he would also see one person from Wales; in every 300, one from China; and in every 400, one from Italy.[13]

| 1930 | 1940 | 1950 | 1960 | 1970 | 1980 | 1990 | 2000 |
|---|---|---|---|---|---|---|---|
| 50,831 | 55,942 | 81,281 | 107,809 | 122,315 | 135,522 | 146,550 | 172,339 |
|  |  |  |  | 5,864 | 8,570 | 11,042 | 24,858 |
| 233 | 351 | 1,106 | 1,738 | 2,073 | 2,350 | 2,446 | 2,748 |
| 83 |  |  | 79 | 114 | 165 | 226 | 343 |
| 533 |  |  | 795 | 840 | 660 | 817 | 703 |

By 1900, foreign-born residents made up 24 percent of Ogden's county.[14] Along with immigrants, a modest population of minority residents dates back to the 1800s (see Table 7.1).[15]

Other residents reacted to these diverse populations by enforcing separation and inequality. Ogden's minority and immigrant communities grew in a restrictive environment, living in segregated neighborhoods south and west of downtown.[16] Originally swampland, this was some of the least desirable land, as it contained factories, the stockyard, and the local garbage dump. The rail and nearby downtown businesses were some of the few places where black people could work, and central Ogden was one of the few places where these residents could live. Authorities restricted black residents to neighborhoods within a six-by-three-block area just south of 25th Street.[17] 25th Street was itself segregated, with black residents only allowed on its southern side. Even before the coming of the rail, authorities instituted such racial-spatial divisions. City leaders named Wall Avenue, which intersects with 25th Street at the railroad's Union Station, after a planned—but never completed—security measure against the threat of Native Americans.[18] Ironically, the area within this proposed wall, meant to protect settlers from people of color, would later become home to its minority neighborhoods.

With economic boom and residential segregation came a thriving entertainment district that catered to rail travelers and workers alike. Much like Bourbon Street in New Orleans or Beale Street in Memphis, Ogden's 25th Street encompassed several blocks filled with bars, music, and hotels. It also included legal and illegal alcohol, drug use, gambling, prostitution, and other deviance, often operating under the watchful eye of police and city officials. People engaged in this vice, and open street crime—including public murders on 25th Street—took place in downtown Ogden.[19] Harman Peery, Ogden's mayor in the 1930s and 1940s, pursued a policy of openly allowing vice (and its financial windfalls).[20] A report of the American Social Health Association from 1949, Peery's last year in office, proclaimed: "It can definitely be reported that matters are looking up in Ogden. The corrupt mayor, Harman Peery, is still in office and the houses of prostitution continue to flourish. BUT, the mayor is up for re-election this Fall and there is good reason to believe he will be defeated."[21]

A newspaper description from 1890 highlights the moral divisions between the "bad," "evil," and "lewd" people who "decent" people saw as overtaking Ogden:

> Liberal ascendency in Ogden a year ago last winter was followed by an in rush of bad women and gamblers. . . . Houses of prostitution multiplied and the names of the keepers were conspicuously exposed on the doors, as if the business were lawful and conducted under the protection of the municipal government. The police authorities were appealed to suppress the evils, but only smiled at the decent people who protested against the city being converted into a brothel. It was claimed by the city authorities that gambling houses and houses of prostitution were essential to the material prosperity of the town: that if the lewd women and gamblers were driven out enterprising men would follow them and the city would suffer.[22]

According to this account, authorities tolerated and even encouraged vice in Ogden many decades before the era of Mayor Peery.

Ogden's very active downtown brought some people misery and disgrace, but it brought others opportunity and achievement. Diverse communities profited from Ogden, as a healthy number of businesses owned and run by immigrants, minorities, and women sprouted there. People of color and immigrants were involved in legitimate as well as illegitimate operations, as Asians ran the opium trade and Mexican traffickers brought in marijuana to 25th Street.[23] The era of Prohibition also was a time when many immigrants made and sold illegal alcohol.[24] Women also ran several prostitution businesses. This was a place where marginalized people could flourish.

It was only in the 1950s when authorities seriously cracked down on vice, ending 25th Street's time as a semi-official vice district. Lessening the hold of decades of entrenched criminality on 25th Street, and its openly authorized support, did not happen quickly or smoothly. As county attorney Maurice Richards stated about a campaign against prostitution:

> For months I had calls threatening death or broken legs and arms. Many were by phone. Some were by letter and quite a few were in person on the street, or the court house and three were at my car after work. In each of these cases, one of the law men helping me made a "house call." Never in the history of this country did so many pimps in a month's time have so many broken arms, legs, noses and heads.[25]

In the late 1940s, after a crusading sheriff's deputy confronted Rose Davie, who ran 25th Street's Rose Rooms brothel, she explained that she already had paid the police for the month.[26] The transformation of 25th Street emerged from the efforts of law enforcement, but it also coincided with rail travel becoming less popular, leading to the slowing of Ogden's economy.[27] The financial incentives for legitimating vice had greatly declined.

## CULTURAL TRANSFORMATIONS

The coming of diverse communities to Ogden, emerging from structural changes to the city that began with the railroad, also brought cultural transformations. Workers on the railroad attracted minority-owned businesses that catered to the unique tastes, traditions, and activities of immigrants and other diverse peoples. In the 1890s, Chinese immigrants established restaurants and laundries in downtown Ogden.[28] Early twentieth-century migrant workers living in Northern Utah traveled to Ogden for Catholic Mass and other religious ceremonies.[29] Black entrepreneurs opened the Porters and Waiters Club on 25th Street from around 1916 until 1960. The business offered food, lodging with ninety-three beds, and entertainment for black railroad workers—especially, fitting its name, porters and waiters—and other customers.[30] Anna Belle Weakley, a black woman who gained the nickname "the Queen of 25th Street," ran the establishment from 1947 until its closing.

The populations restricted to central Ogden certainly faced, and still face, exclusion and vilification. As James Gillespie summed up the treatment of black residents in the region, "In Mississippi they'll kill you, in Utah they just starve you to death."³¹ Yet, divisions emerging from segregated neighborhoods and other exclusion also concentrated these residents into accepting and supportive places.³² As James Carr notes:

> Segregation can reinforce close-knit societies and provide a supportive environment to residents. It can help preserve cultural heritage and build children's sense of self-respect and dignity. In many communities, particularly in ethnic enclaves, it can reduce such challenges as language barriers and provide a social network for people to find jobs, acceptance, and responsibility.³³

Minority and immigrant populations found such an accepting environment in central Ogden, an oasis in a desert of cultural homogeneity and scorn.

Ogden's open deviance, coupled with its diverse communities and the unique cultural resources catering to them, also brought about Ogden's bad reputation. The entertainment and vice found downtown, perennially controversial in the United States and only allowed in carefully circumscribed ways, was especially countercultural in the heavily Mormon region surrounding the city. Indeed, a conversation with Ogden madam Belle London in 1911, recounted by a displeased local woman, illustrates this extreme clash of values. From different perspectives, prostitution is "reform" or her argument is "witchery":

> "It is easy to be misunderstood and misrepresented in this world," continued the hostess with the witchery of her specious reasoning, "and no woman in the world has ever been wronged in this way than I have been in Utah. When you know me and the grand work of reform that I am doing, you will hold me high in your esteem."³⁴

While open deviance and crime is largely a thing of the past, the city's cultural divergence from the surrounding area, as well as its reputation as a notorious place, continues.

## HISTORICAL CONTINUITY AND CHANGE

While historians and others who research the past tend to focus on large-scale, dramatic shifts, the flow of history is more about the day-to-day reproduction of social reality than a march of grand events.³⁵ Much social change takes place gradually through small drifts, the addition of new forms of activity, and other forms of subtle transformation.[36] At the same time, many aspects can remain relatively stable, even over long periods of time (as the saying goes, "history repeats itself"). Without cultural, demographic, economic, or political forces pushing the image of a city in another direction, it will tend to remain steady.[37] Such places will faithfully reproduce the features that give it unique characteristics, even after the original conditions that created them have long disappeared. Some places tend more toward historical continuity, keeping them much the same over time, while others experience historical change that fundamentally transforms them.

While the city of Ogden is currently changing, even dramatically, such shifts have largely reproduced its historical path of difference and disrepute. Current demographic and cultural transformations, brought about through a large number of Latino immigrants, may be as radical a historical event as the coming of the railroad one hundred and fifty years ago. Yet, this large shift is currently folding into long-standing negative perceptions of the city, which are connected to its difference. As historian Gene Sessions put it, "Utah is a pretty lily-white place, but Ogden has a pretty diverse racial makeup. . . . There's no doubt that ethnic diversity led people to think of Ogden as a rough or lower-class place. It's all related to good, old-fashioned racism and classism."[38] Ogden had diverse populations consistently from 1870 to the present day. Additionally, this former railroad town has retained its working-class population.

Historically, immigrants and people of color pursued work in Utah, and the region benefited greatly from their cheap, and often exploited, labor. This pattern continued, as a 1985 newspaper series on migrant labor documented. Local agriculture relied upon these workers—many of them undocumented Latinos—to pick their crops. When reforms threatened to curtail this practice, an Ogden farmer responded, "I'm in the business of making a profit, not checking to see whether the workers are legal or illegal. . . . We need the cheap labor."[39] The region gained this economic support at the literal cost of these worker's lives. Paid little, living in dire conditions, and largely invisible to the wider community, migrants faced stigma and discrimination.[40] In 1984, their life expectancy was 49 years, compared to a national average of 72.[41]

Fitting past patterns of segregation, Ogden's immigrant and minority populations remain concentrated in neighborhoods surrounding downtown, although today their larger numbers have greatly expanded this footprint. As resident James Gillespie explained in 1999, the black community continued to live there, and real estate agents steered them into it.

> You'd see in the newspaper, "House for sale—nice location for porters or waiters." Most Blacks lived between 24th and 30th Street, west of Grant, and still Blacks live between 24th and, I would say, 30, 30 west of Washington. Very few Blacks have moved out of area. If you want a house, you go to real estate man. The real estate man tells Blacks where to live. Blacks still live in areas with Black people, and I don't see anything wrong with it. But I don't want a real estate agent telling me where to live.[42]

Segregation also continues today in the city's "Little Mexico," where many Latino immigrants live in the same neighborhoods where previous generations of immigrant and minority populations resided.

Along with its continued demographic characteristics, the city's bad reputation also has endured through the decades to the present day. The city abandoned policies of tolerating vice after post–World War II decline, but locals continued to see downtown Ogden as a rough place. As Lyle Barnes states, "In talking to many people in the late 1960s that were familiar with the earlier times and the place, they reported their fear of [25th] Street and exclaimed that they never went near it, on foot."[43] A 1972 article in the *Salt Lake Tribune* stated, "Twenty-fifth Street still has its bootleggers and some prostitutes—and its reputation for violence. No rapes have been reported on the street this year, but it has the distinction of being the only street in Ogden where there were three homicides in a single month."[44] Such attitudes reflected, but also reinforced, deteriorated conditions in the city's downtown. By the 1970s, many historic buildings on 25th Street became hollowed out and dilapidated. Crusading preservationists saved many from destruction, but only because the city was so depressed that authorities could not enact plans for large-scale demolition and redevelopment.[45]

An incident in 1974 further amplified Ogden's reputation as a center of crime intertwined with racial difference. The "hi-fi murders" rocked the city, as two black men, robbing an audio store (hence the name "hi-fi"), shot five white people after raping one and torturing them all. Two of the victims survived and testified against the men, and the local media graphically detailed their descriptions of the crime, traumatizing those in the region and sending waves of racialized fear through the area.[46] Police sought out others who may have been involved, "prompting whites in the community to suspect and ostracize black residents at the time as well as advocates accusing police of racially targeting the suspects," as Andreas Rivera reported.

These conditions of crime, economic decline, and dilapidation continued from the end of the railroad era until recent decades. In the 1980s and 1990s, people continued to avoid Ogden and especially its downtown, despite attempts at revitalization. As a recent newspaper article stated, "until the early 1990s, 25th Street deserved its notorious reputation."[47] A downtown mall, opened in 1980, struggled to attract both customers and businesses, especially after a similar mall opened nearby. Unlike the historic buildings on 25th Street, the city did have funds to demolish it in 2002.[48] The open-air mall that replaced it in 2007—the Junction—is thriving. This suggests a slow recovery to the area.

Today, fear of Ogden's downtown seems to be lessening. There is a growing fascination with Ogden's notorious past, which connects some residents and outsiders alike to this place. While most histories of the city focus on the dignified topics of leaders and key events, such as a book commissioned by the city about "its governmental legacy,"[49] a number of histories focus on the seedy details that are either missing or underemphasized in those works.[50] Local interest in Ogden's infamous underbelly goes beyond historians' accounts. Just as people overstate Ogden's current depravity, recollections and reimaginings often exceed historical verification to romanticize and exaggerate past crime and other wild doings. After all, Ogden's area of vice covered just a few blocks, and it mostly catered to travelers passing through the city. Still, many locals embrace this unverified mythology. A popular rumor is that Chicago crime boss Al Capone said that Ogden was "too wild for my taste." Numerous locals also swear, despite a lack of evidence, to the existence of elaborate downtown tunnels that they say criminals once used to transport alcohol and drugs.[51] While we do not know the origins of this urban legend, it may be connected to Ogden's Chinatown, which used to be located downtown at 25th Street and Grant Avenue. There are similar rumors of tunnels running under the Chinatowns of numerous U.S. cities, linked to stereotypes of Asians as secretive and nefarious.[52]

Those interviewed for this study overwhelmingly expressed appreciation and great comfort with visiting Ogden's downtown and 25th Street. While some did mention homelessness and other problems, many saw downtown as an absolute gem; it was their favorite thing about the city. This suggests that 25th Street may be losing its long-standing association with disreputable populations, pulling Ogden's downtown away from the neighborhoods surrounding it, which many residents still perceive as threatening.[53] Yet, this shift seems to be limited to Ogden's residents. Respondents also conveyed how local outsiders are still wary of the city. While Ogden may be changing, it mostly retains continuity with its past as a maligned community of working-class, people of color, and immigrant residents.

In great contrast to Ogden's historical continuity, nearby Park City is an example of dramatic historical change.[54] A mining town during roughly the same era that Ogden was a railroad town, from the 1860s until the 1950s, Park City faced similar economic hardship when the silver industry collapsed. Yet, it abandoned its working-class and industrial roots in the 1960s, transforming into an upper-class skiing and tourist center.[55] As a history of the area explained, "In 1950, if a person had asked a group of Park City residents to describe their town in the year 2000, it is unlikely that even those with the wildest imaginations could have come close to divining the future of their struggling little mining town."[56] While Park City does have a large Latino population, this is actually a reflection of the city's changes, not its continuity. This population performs service work for affluent clients.[57]

In great contrast to Park City, Ogden retains many of the same characteristics of difference that separated it from the region more than a century ago. This has massive drawbacks but also some benefits for its residents. The bad reputations of places have disastrous consequences, including lost revenue and opportunities, repressive interventions against crime and disorder, negative impacts on identities and civic pride, and the maintenance of divisions between social classes and races and their corresponding inequalities. Ogden reflects all of these outcomes. At the same time, these very features preserve such places as an acceptable—and even welcoming, given the responses of Ogden's Latino immigrants—environment for marginalized communities. Today, Park City has a higher-class population with pronounced stratification between service workers and wealthy clients. In great contrast, Ogden maintains much of its past characteristics of difference and disrepute, and it remains a welcoming place for some of the most marginalized people in the region. In many ways, its residents are unified through these traits.

# 8

# THE MORAL FRONTIERS OF OUTSIDERS

Unfortunately there can be no doubt that man is, on the whole, less good than he imagines himself or wants to be. Everyone carries a shadow, and the less it is embodied in the individual's conscious life, the blacker and denser it is.

—*Carl Jung*

Ogden is probably less LDS [Mormon]. Probably more—more of like the Hispanic population. Trying to sound politically correct. Don't want to say "the poor population," but the disadvantaged are more down in this Ogden area, it seems like. So there's probably less LDS people down here.

—*Ogden resident, 31-year-old white male*

Ogden's bad reputation developed through a unique historical trajectory that separated it from the rest of the region. While the city's open drug use, gambling, prostitution, and other vice are largely of the past, what does continue is Ogden's difference from local outsiders as well as its negative image in the region. The city's residents do not subscribe to the idea of its bad reputation, nor do they promote it. On the contrary, they embrace their community, even while some disparage areas within the city. In contrast, outsiders establish and maintain the edges of these moral frontiers separating themselves from the people of Ogden. They vilify the city, avoid it, and they give warnings about the safety of those who live there or visit.

According to Gary Alan Fine, bad reputations develop and continue through those with the power to label a person (or thing) negatively, and those who do this labeling can greatly benefit from this definition, as it creates or maintains influence and control over others.[1] These designations also reestablish moral boundaries between good and bad. Politicians and others who hold power, who Fine calls "reputational entrepreneurs,"[2] generate or perpetuate reputations in ways that consolidate their influence and draw lines that separate themselves and their communities from the bad.[3]

While Fine focuses on individual reputations, as well as individual reputation makers, entire communities also do work to maintain boundaries of status and morality.[4] Constructions of deviance—including the deviance of a bad reputation—are integral to how the nondeviant, those on the other side of this equation, circumscribe and maintain their own communities.[5] People define criminals and other bad people as a way to establish themselves as noncriminal and good. As Kai Erikson puts it, "the deviant and the conformist, then, are creatures of the same culture, inventions of the same imagination."[6] Negative designations are intertwined with positive definitions of morality, respectability, and other characteristics that are a community's fundamental bedrock.

The boundaries between respectable and deviant are also tied to identities, as their maintenance is connected to collective definitions of a respectable life. Generally, a person on the good side of these boundaries fits customary standards of success. This includes holding a good job and living in a good house in a good area of town with good schools. It also involves being a moral person, with concern for others and clear ethical principles. Like most everyone else, higher-status people tend to see themselves—and want others to see them—as upstanding, conscientious, and helpful. Many make efforts to care for the poor and disadvantaged, doing their part by supporting charities and engaging in volunteering and activism.

Yet, this collective group faces a dilemma, as fortifying the edges of their communities involves excluding what is deviant. Their definition of being a good person involves the contradictory goals of helping the downtrodden while simultaneously enforcing distance from them and status above them. If these good people were to move to a disreputable place, or their neighborhood were to transform into one, they could face real or perceived threats to their financial, social, and moral status—including lowered property values, worse schools, criminal activity, competition for employment, and stigmatization through their association with disreputable people. Dominant populations meet wide-scale "invasions" of marginalized people with fears that their communities, cities, regions, or nations are declining, as well as fears that they no longer have a place in them. They generate ideas, a "culture of abundance," that explain and justify their isolation from others.

The outsiders who shape Ogden's bad reputation, higher-status locals, separate themselves from the city. Multiple dimensions of difference are at play in the division between Ogden and the region, including social class, race, immigrant status, and culture. Although all of these are interrelated, here I focus on race and culture. Ogden's native residents openly spoke in racial terms about divisions between the city's reputable and disreputable places, and these same dynamics circumscribe the boundaries of difference between the city and the region. As in the rest of the United States, white people have long been Utah's dominant population. They are higher in social class than most other racial groups, reaping the vast majority of financial, educational, political, cultural, and health benefits that emerge from this inequality.

Ogden residents also mentioned how Utah's unique religious culture shaped the city's reputation. Even though they are a fringe presence in other places, Mormons are unquestionably a dominant group in Utah. Like whites (and the vast majority of them are white), they tend to have higher than average incomes.[7] Along with this elevated racial and class status, Mormons have an additional interest in maintaining a cultural status as thoroughly conventional and morally impeccable. One way to uphold these standards is by separating themselves from Ogden's difference and perceived disrepute.

## WHITES' SENSE OF GROUP POSITION

Creating and maintaining ideas of good people necessitate definitions of bad people, deviant populations that fall outside of the boundaries of a community. Ogden varies greatly from the surrounding area through many markers of difference. The city has an especially large population of lower-class residents, immigrants, and racial minorities. Not coincidentally, many see Ogden residents as the bad people of Utah, placing themselves outside of the boundaries of Ogden, or certain neighborhoods of Ogden, that they see as disreputable, disordered, and even dangerous. The drawing of racial lines was one way that they evaluated the city, its residents, and its reputation.

These power relations emerge from long-established social divisions, with their corresponding interests. Our allegiance to racial groups, and our collective interests in maintaining (or dismantling) disparities between them, shapes our perceptions.[8] As Eduardo Bonilla-Silva states:

> Since actors racialized as "white"—or as members of the dominant race—receive material benefits from the racial order, they struggle (or passively receive the manifold wages of whiteness) to maintain their privilege. In contrast, those defined as belonging to the subordinate race or races struggle to change the status quo (or become resigned to their position). Therein lies the secret of racial structures and racial inequality the world over. They exist because they benefit members of the dominant race.[9]

Whites develop perceptions that uphold and justify their collective racial interests, and they promote ideas that are tilted in their favor, even while thinking of them as unfiltered reflections of the world. Thus, Herbert Blumer argues that racial divisions are not grounded in prejudice and bigotry. Instead, they emerge from a "sense of group position."[10]

Feelings of group position among white communities involve staking out racial territory that they claim as their own. As a higher-status group with its own collective interests, white people actively enforce these divisions, especially when they feel that lower-status challengers are upending established racial boundaries. Aggressive boundary maintenance, instilling repression and fear against marginalized groups, has been a feature of race relations throughout U.S. history. Once one system of division weakens, dominant populations have replaced it with a new one. Following the end of slavery's stark, legally sanctioned, and harshly enforced racial divisions, whites of the Jim Crow era sought to restore these boundaries, and one strategy that they used was brutal violence and terrorism. They lynched thousands of people, many at public events where onlookers proudly watched and even bought commemorative picture postcards of mangled bodies, while law enforcement made little effort to interfere or investigate.[11] Today, the criminal justice system, especially fueled by drug laws, imprisons people in numbers that far exceed those of other countries. While different populations are involved with illicit drugs at similar rates, these actions disproportionately target people of color, making this—following slavery and then Jim Crow—the modern version of racially based repression.[12]

Cultural understandings fortify these structural systems of dominance. Throughout every era, whites tend to sustain the idea that they are good people. They obscure their extreme efforts at boundary maintenance behind justifications that these arrangements are normal, reasonable, and even necessary. They do not see themselves and their views as shaped by a collective special interest. Many understand themselves as holding no racial bias, being neutral and "colorblind," as they have long understood their worldviews as grounded in the "objective" and "rational" dictates of Western logic.[13] They continually see themselves as righteous and even superior people. They can become exceedingly upset and defensive at even the suggestion that this may not be the case.[14]

Yet, their views are actually *more* distorted, skewed to favor their interests, than those of subordinate groups.[15] Although inaccurate, the ideas upheld by dominant groups are especially influential for shaping perceptions. These groups have the power to perceive and promote their views as normal and even natural.[16] That people of color—including Ogden's native Latinos—also internalize these racial understandings, seeing themselves and their communities as inadequate and rightfully subservient,[17] shows how ever-present and unquestioned they are.

As whites in Utah live in a place with few people of color, they often have little experience with racial difference.[18] This can translate to a refreshing openness, acceptance, and helpfulness, but it also results in patronizing and insensitive microaggressions, denial of the very existence of racial inequality, and outright exclusion and discrimination. Examples abound. In 2008, state senator Chris Buttars apologized after criticizing a pending bill by saying: "This baby is black, I'll tell you. This is a dark, ugly thing."[19] *Utah Valley Magazine* made national news in 2012 by labeling a photo of their white staff, dressed in bright clothing, as "Women of Color."[20] Regional racial insensitivity continues despite national notoriety and even anticipatory warnings.[21] A local term describing people who do such acts—"Utards," a combination of the words "Utah" and "retard"—perfectly sums up the depths of this problem. It denounces this open insensitivity with a term that itself is openly insensitive.

Whites tend to embrace justice and equality in a vague sense. After all, these are treasured values of the United States, and being a good person includes subscribing to them. Yet, they also want to protect their benefits against adjustments to their standard of living that would come from a more equitable apportionment. They may celebrate small changes that do not impact them very much or even enhance their identities as defenders of racial equality, such as the advancement of a limited number of elites from marginalized groups, while angrily dismissing more sweeping changes (affirmative action policies, school desegregation, reparations for slavery) as extreme, unpractical, and even unfair. They walk a delicate line between maintaining their identities as compassionate people and protecting their status. Many acknowledge how this constant symbolic juggling is exhausting. They long to be freed from the restrictions of "political correctness" and other standards of behavior for good people, as these practices keep them from publicly expressing their collective interests.

## THE MORMON BUBBLE

Along with splits between whites and people of color, higher and lower classes, and native and foreign born, a further boundary between Ogden and the surrounding region falls along cultural lines. The righteous and wholesome values of Mormonism deeply contrast with Ogden's "notorious" image as well as its historical embrace of diverse perspectives and behaviors. As Val Holley explains:

> What did set 25th Street apart from other American vice districts was its ironic emergence in the heart of a Mormon city. Nowhere else was there such a configuration of contenders: a dominant, but beleaguered, religion fighting to retain political control of a city whose economic lifeblood, the railroad, was leveling the playing field.... In such a context, the decadent pastimes along 25th Street were always somewhat more threatening to locals than in other cities.[22]

Mormons triumph values that reject the drinking, gambling, sex, and other vices that embodied historic 25th Street.

Yet, Mormons' aversion to this place runs much deeper than simply the avoidance of sinful activities. All communities have standards of membership, with guidelines for those within them. By defining these boundaries of membership and their acceptable standards, people create categories of nonmembers and the unacceptable by default.[23] As Gary Alan Fine states, "Boundaries are strengthened by the communal creation of moral exemplars who typify what the society should value or who serve to warn of the dangers of socially recognized threats."[24] Mormons in the area have developed a unique culture, separate from the rest of the United States—even separate from Mormons who live in other places. Researchers call it the "Mormon culture region."[25] I have heard it informally called "the Mormon bubble," a term that better captures this community's tight-knit, insular ways as well as their clear boundaries between members and nonmembers.

For Utah's Mormons, these boundaries are well defined and carefully enforced. Those in the bubble see it as important, and even mandatory, to fit the standards of the religion in order to gain and preserve their status as a respectable member of the church. The church provides a pathway for clearly distinguishing the acceptable from the unacceptable, giving members well-regulated principles and direction for how to live their lives. For many, the truth of the church is unequivocal, indisputable, and officially verified with references to divine sources. There is a bureaucratic character to how Mormons meticulously organize, catalogue, and cite mystical revelations and other transcendental matters with the skill of a reference librarian. Members reach self-fulfillment through prayer, introspection, and personal development, but the importance of closely fitting these codified standards tends to dwarf such practices. Not only is the unexamined life worth living, but it is a worthy way to live, shielding one from trespasses of thought and behavior. Many Mormons in Utah are openly uncomfortable with ambiguity, debate, and dissension.[26]

Unlike many churches, Mormon membership is not accomplished simply through a ritual of joining and then adding one's name to the organization's roles, making contributions or withdrawals the voluntary choice of members. Adherence is crystalized by earning and then keeping a "Temple Recommend," proof of good standing in the church. Additionally, church representatives keep in regular contact with members. Until recently, they visited members for "home teaching," now called "ministering." As the official church website described:

> As part of their responsibility to watch over the members of the Church, home teachers visit their assigned families at least once each month to teach and strengthen them. Home teachers establish a relationship of trust with these families so that the families can call upon them in times of need.[27]

Temple Recommends and constant contact with members are thoughtful efforts to make members feel included and intimately connected to the community, their well-being continually considered. Family is very important to Mormons, and these arrangements extend the family and its tasks of care and inclusion to a broader community. Through such activities, members can feel comfortably enveloped in this lifestyle. Furthermore, they provide members with a clear identity, giving their life meaning, direction, and structure.

Yet, the bubble extends far beyond the official dictates of the church organization. At times, it is even in conflict with them. The bubble is exclusive and near totalizing, as "dense concentrations of Latter-day Saints, coupled with intergenerational family ties, fuse church and community norms, and make good standing in the church a marker of social respectability around town."[28] Church culture can be deeply immersive, fundamentally coloring any external influences, lifestyles, and beliefs. Even activities that are largely secular in other places become enveloped into it. For example, college-bound Mormons can avoid interacting with nonmembers by enrolling in the local (and prestigious) religious school—Brigham Young University. Most of Utah's colleges are "commuter schools," lacking the large dormitories, fraternity housing, and other places where young people live together without close supervision. Although it is home to a large university, Ogden city has regulations against more than three unrelated people living together.

Recently, the standards of the bubble have become more homogeneous and restrictive. Compared to other religious groups, Mormons have extremely low levels of interfaith marriage.[29] Politically, Mormonism has become almost synonymous with conservatism. While older generations were a mixture of Democrats and Republicans, young Mormons are more and more identifying as conservatives.[30] The religion has a member—Mitt Romney—who was the 2012 Republican presidential candidate. Being a good Mormon has become tied to being a good Republican. Such isolation and polarization are even apparent in the popularity of quirky names. Their unusual spellings (Kinzee for Kinsey, Jaymz for James) and inventiveness (Decken, Jenedy, Zaylie) show how Mormons have developed an insulated culture that extends beyond the teachings of the church.[31]

These tight-knit social networks provide countless opportunities for connections and benefits among members. The bubble is a community that, in addition to religious services, offers business contacts, dating and marriage prospects, friendship, social support, and recreation. In political circles, it is especially advantageous. While about 60 percent of Utah's population is Mormon, they have a far greater representation in the state legislature. A 2012 newspaper poll, answered by about a third of legislature members, found their numbers at 77 percent, although "some lawmakers estimated that 90 percent of the 75 Utah House members are LDS, and that 27 of 29 senators are."[32] The bubble has a sweeping political influence in the state.

While being a part of the bubble provides great benefits for upstanding church members, there are great disadvantages for those who breach its boundaries. Mechanisms that tie Mormons to each other are also a powerful form of social control. Traveling outside of the bubble's social and moral boundaries, or even the appearance of such trespasses, can be a scandalous act. As the church actively monitors members, they are held accountable for violations of participation, behavior, and belief. Church authorities can withhold membership status from those who do not fit these standards. In extreme cases, excommunications occur, especially following the open conflict or protest that both leaders and members despise. As membership in the church is tied to one's family, friends, and even career, being ostracized can mean having the foundation of your identity stripped from you. Without a Temple Recommend, people are barred from many key activities with their wider Mormon family.

In answer, shunning contamination from anything beyond the limits of membership—disreputable thoughts, actions, and associations—is a sure way to avoid dings to one's reputation. Some Mormons are quick to cut ties with the wayward, even immediate family members. Utah has a high rate of homelessness among LGBTQ teenagers that Mormon families have rejected.[33] Even some church members are circumspect, outside of the bubble's boundaries. Mormons who move to Utah communicate how, even though surrounded by fellow church members, they feel outside of the culture.[34] They express how their treatment by "Utah Mormons" is much different from their experience with church members from out of state.

Given the tremendous benefits that whites receive from their separation from others, as well as Mormon standards of virtue and constant attentiveness to them, having a strong evasion to Ogden is reasonable—and even advisable—for these collective groups. Whites have a lot to lose from associating with lower-status people, from housing values to quality schools, feelings of security, and even their identities as respectable people. They often juggle protecting their collective resources with holding identities as good people. Likewise, Mormons preserve their privileged place in the social (and celestial) order by avoiding disreputable things, people, and places. They celebrate and otherwise affiliate themselves with disreputable places and their residents at great personal risk to their social standing.

Ogden has been, and continues to be, the flip side of the coin for white and Mormon Utah. It is the symbolic threat that these communities use to define their boundaries and reinforce social benefits. It is the devil that necessitates God; the danger that legitimates distance, control, and restraint; and the outsider that defines the insider.

# PART FOUR

# TRANSFORMATION

# 9

# BOUNDARY MAINTENANCE AND BOUNDARY BLURRING

The practice of discursive redlining sets the stage for targeted policing practices and criminal-civil hybrids like gang injunctions, which have the consequence (unintended or otherwise) of encouraging the displacement of young men and their families from the neighborhood through eviction, incarceration, or mandatory exclusion (for example, stay-away orders are a condition of probation). In short, when newcomers to an area think of the ghetto as something that *people carry with them*, then institutionalized efforts to get rid of the ghetto are naturally tied to getting rid of the people who are seen *as* ghetto.

—*Nikki Jones and Christina Jackson*

Having placed so much wilderness between them and the dangers threatened in the past, hope once again reached the hearts and minds of the people as they settled on the west reaches of the Rocky Mountains where they built up a great city in the desert—Salt Lake City. Their new prophet, Brigham Young, called groups of people to settle in every direction to colonize the wilderness. For most of these settlements, all hopes were rewarded as communities sprung up in the Utah Territory, and other surrounding territories.

For those who settled in Ogden, however, once again they would be invaded by individuals that would seek to destroy their peace and tranquility.... The railroad was a Pandora's Box. It was the first great highway to tie a nation together, but it made Ogden accessible to all the base elements of society. The misfits and dregs of society seemed to thrive in the frontier where law enforcement and controls might be more relaxed. The longer these elements remained without social controls, the more difficult they would be to eradicate.

—Lyle Barnes

*How are the spatial boundaries that divide people maintained, and how can they be transformed to unify people?* Divisions between high-status and low-status populations contribute to boundaries that separated, and continue to separate, Ogden from the rest of Utah. Along with cultural understandings, institutions also enforce, formally or informally, these divisions between reputable and disreputable places and populations. One such institution is law enforcement. When people view bad reputations as primarily grounded in graffiti, trash, and street crime, they develop interventions that discourage this internal disorder. While on its surface a sensible way to help the people living in disparaged places, such solutions have created circumstances for their residents that are arguably worse than the original disorder. Perceptions of crime and other problems in disreputable places, even if the uninformed views of outsiders, underlie and justify expensive and repressive interventions that further maintain divisions between people.

Yet, these boundaries also can blur, shifting and even inverting definitions of disreputable places and their residents. Like an internal disorder view, a solely critical view—pitting monstrous dominator against victimized dominated—also reinforces and even naturalizes these divisions under the guise of resolving them. Ironically, it makes the powerful the center of the universe. Treating marginalized communities as stigmatized sufferers, battered in the seas of waters created and controlled by external forces, ignores their accomplishments and self-determination, negating their agency and choices. It also can make these shifting dynamics seem like historically embedded inevitabilities. Power is subtly, continuously, and precariously negotiated, with the symbolic, social, and physical boundaries between people constantly changing.

Through ongoing relationships between powerful and marginal, domination is normalized and entrenched—but it also can be challenged and transformed.

## BOUNDARY MAINTENANCE

The boundaries dividing reputable from disreputable places reinforce unequal treatment and further inequalities. While open, legally sanctioned racism and prejudice have mostly disappeared in the United States, discriminatory practices continue to maintain these divisions in less visible ways. Various institutions reflect the collective interests of dominant groups and uphold these divisions. Housing discrimination is still rampant, even as "redlining"—officially dividing areas by race—is illegal.[1] Public health campaigns operate under standards that define marginalized communities as deviant threats.[2] Similarly, the criminal justice system continues to be a main vehicle by which inequality continues, even as racial bias is officially outlawed.[3]

Underlying such practices are taken-for-granted assumptions about the world, including ideas about a place's reputation and its relation to the conditions found there. A perspective that closely links perceptions of places with disorder, James Wilson and George Kelling's "broken windows theory"[4] has been astoundingly influential on law enforcement and public policy. It also epitomizes the internal disorder view. The theory argues that people develop feelings about places based on cues from the conditions there. If a place has disordered features, not only will its residents think less of their communities, they also will further neglect them, leading both a place's reputation and its conditions into a downward spiral. According to this theory, we can reverse bad reputations by curtailing disorder. When conditions are cleaned up—everything from murders to the eponymous broken windows—residents will see their neighborhoods more positively and act in ways that improve their reputations. Interventions based on this theory focus on intensively curtailing disorder within these places, especially small "quality of life" infractions like graffiti, littering, loitering, and public drinking thought to breed further decline.

Based on this idea, cities across the United States have devoted millions of dollars to campaigns, such as "zero tolerance" policing, that aggressively battle disorder within disreputable places with the hope of improving their images. Implementing changes based on broken windows theory, police and other authorities in New York City—followed by urban areas throughout the United States—began vigorously punishing "quality of life" matters in the 1990s. This included the practice of "stop and frisk"—where police could detain, question, and search residents without probable cause. Such interventions had questionable effects on crime rates, while disproportionately subjecting the people of color living in disreputable places to intense scrutiny.[5]

This has helped create a dramatic rise in incarceration rates and other outcomes that limited their life chances.

Such policies not only reinforce inequality but also actively generate it. Some of the disproportionate crime rates between places are the result of this intense scrutiny that people from disreputable places (namely, poor and especially minority populations) face from law enforcement. For example, black people—who disproportionately live in disreputable places—and white people in the United States report that they use illegal drugs at about the same rates, but you are far more likely to be stopped, searched, arrested, prosecuted, and sentenced to jail time for a drug offense if you are black.[6] Police, backed by "tough on crime" politicians and public praise, subject people in disreputable places to aggressive anticrime campaigns, including continual and frequently arbitrary stops and searches. All the while, those in middle- and upper-class settings happily sell, buy, and consume drugs with little fear of punishment.[7]

Such interventions become self-fulfilling prophecies, unevenly targeting certain populations, and then using their heightened involvement in the criminal justice system to justify further interventions. These practices of constant surveillance and punishment, disproportionately affecting people who live in disreputable places, operate under the logic that they encourage people to "straighten up and fly right." Yet, they often have the opposite effect. Police, schools, and employers label people from disparaged communities—formally and informally—as tainted deviants, and immersing them into the criminal justice system especially dampens their future opportunities.[8] When we treat those thought of as disordered and dangerous, and the places where they live, much more harshly than others, we then confirm assumptions that they are more prone to crime and other troubles.

This labeling goes far beyond wrongdoers, or even those accused of wrongdoing. The people that these interventions target become intertwined into a bundle of negative "neighborhood effects" that sustain and amplify problems—including school dropouts, unemployment, health problems, and even the disordered conditions that they seek to alleviate.[9] Communities are stripped of their men, through high unemployment and incarceration rates, and then outsiders blame them for not upholding values of family and responsibility. Simply from their residence, people living in disreputable places—from gang members to Sunday school teachers—face a stigmatized status of being morally suspect and regularly denied opportunities.[10]

Along with aggressive law enforcement, another popular solution for reducing disorder that is disastrous for the residents of disreputable places is when a neighborhood "turns around" through gentrification.[11] These "up and coming" areas can and do change their reputations for the better, attracting new growth and business, but this often happens by replacing "problem" populations with those of higher status. The injection of these new residents, who initiate shifts of lower crime rates, rising home values, and other improvements, is far more effective at transforming places than any law enforcement techniques. But like policies influenced by the broken windows theory, gentrification also is an attack on established residents. Most cannot celebrate this positive turn of events, as these vulnerable populations are subjected to rising rents, evictions, and displacement.

Wishing to appease the fears of outsiders and residents alike and boost the city's reputation, Ogden's city leaders have instituted repressive law enforcement techniques. These include a gang database that has grown to include more than 1 percent of the city's population[12] as well as a gang injunction that the Utah Supreme Court ruled unconstitutional.[13] The city has also instituted policies that encourage gentrification. They introduced incentives to convert downtown dwellings from multiunit apartments into single-family residences.[14] This was done with the openly expressed hope of pushing out lower-class residents and attracting higher-status homeowners, who they hoped to entice through marketing campaigns that reimagined this working-class and heavily Latino city as a haven for them. While such interventions seek to target crime and other nuisances in Ogden, they negatively affect the city's most marginalized communities.

### OGDEN'S MORAL PANIC AGAINST GANG THREATS

Interventions against Ogden gangs are especially revealing as an exercise in maintaining the boundaries between reputable and disreputable populations. Robert Durán, who studied Ogden, argues that they were not grounded in fighting crime as much as repressing young Latinos.[15] This fits the characteristics of a "moral panic," where officials and the mass media exaggerate or even invent a crisis in order to benefit themselves and suppress a disadvantaged population.[16] As Durán explains, authorities began cracking down on Ogden's gangs following the 1992 Los Angeles race riots and consequent reports of gangs moving from Southern California to Utah. It is probably no coincidence that, also during this time, Ogden was beginning to see its large influx of Latino immigrants.

Interventions against gangs became especially harsh in 2010, when the city instituted an injunction against gang members, forbidding them from associating with each other in public. Authorities applied it to most areas of Ogden, restricting more than four hundred people. While the Utah Supreme Court struck down this policy as unconstitutional in 2013, a gang database continues. It is easy to be labeled a gang member or associate, and difficult to be removed once entered onto this list. Many of the criteria, such as "resides in or frequents a gang area," consist of being in a region defined as gang territory and knowing or congregating with people who have been labeled. In other words, simply being a member of this community, especially as more and more of its residents were added to the list. As of November 2015, the gang database contained 898 people—slightly more than one out of every one hundred people living in Ogden.[17]

An ironic consequence of moral panics is that their instigators often amplify the very phenomenon that they claim to be stopping. Ogden's gang crackdown subjected young minorities, whether they were affiliated with gangs or not, to regular and intense scrutiny. As Durán explains:

> At the inception of the Gang Unit in 1992, there were 250 listed gang members and associates in Ogden, which was slightly larger than the number originally recorded in Salt Lake City. These numbers increased significantly as plainclothes police officers or officers dressed in black fatigues with bullet-proof vests began regularly stopping black and Latino youth and inquiring about gang membership. Such tactics selectively overrepresented those who were predefined as gang members. White Gang Unit officers patrolled inner-city neighborhoods and perceived certain clothing worn by youth of color as denoting gang membership. Gang Unit officers began telling youth uninvolved with gangs that they were gang members.[18]

While people think of gangs as having a formal status of membership, they operate more as a loose grouping of adherents, hangers on, and others who simply claim to be from an area where gangs are active.[19] They resemble the fans of a sports team more than members of an organization. Ogden's gang database combined many people—some closely affiliated, some loosely, and some who are not affiliated at all—under the umbrella of gang members, legally solidifying a deviant status.

This crusade against gangs, on its face about fighting crime, ended up subjecting Ogden's Latino populations to intense police scrutiny, while paying little attention to white gang members.[20] This boundary maintenance was not only demographic but also spatial. While authorities carefully watched young Latinos, who tend to live in the center of the city, they were less likely to treat those who tend to live outside of these neighborhoods as problems. Unsurprisingly, Latinos are overrepresented on the Ogden gang list (52 percent of the database, compared to 30 percent of the population), while whites are underrepresented (37 percent, compared to 64 percent).[21] This can lead them to be disproportionately exposed to further stigma and involvement in the criminal justice system. It also reinforces public perceptions that Latinos are prone to criminality.

This is because moral panics are less about public safety than the repression of a population that authorities see as dangerous.[22] Under the banner of fighting crime, police launched a crusade against a city defined by difference, and it targeted arguably the most different people within the city. Tellingly, a threat facing Ogden's citizens is large amounts of sexual assault (see Appendix). Many years, the rate of rape is more than three times the national average. Yet, authorities have not focused their energies, as they have with gangs, on reducing this crime. Such a campaign would negatively impact men, who hold an especially privileged position in Utah's culture.[23] Instead, they disproportionately target Latinos—a disreputable population—as a threat to people's safety.

While the residents of disreputable places generally are aware of their stigma and unequal treatment, many higher-status people also know this, and they appreciate the benefits of being virtually ignored by the police. For example, when leaving a residence on the eastern edge of Ogden for my home in this same neighborhood, where I lived at the time, a partygoer reassured me that police rarely patrol this area, much less stop cars. This implied that it was safe to drive intoxicated (that is, commit a crime) there with impunity from law enforcement. Such unequal interventions help to maintain boundaries between higher-status residents and a community, the city's lower-class and minority residents, that they found threatening.

## BOUNDARY BLURRING

Ogden's attempts to curtail disorder are examples of boundary maintenance, which sustains social and spatial divisions. Yet, these boundaries also are constantly breached, challenged, and transformed. Such defiance is found in interviews with Ogden residents, who overwhelmingly disputed perceptions that divided their city from the region. "Boundary blurring" involves acts—everything from friendly conversations to marriages—that bring people from differing social groups together.[24] Examples of boundary blurring, as found throughout the history of Utah, humanize the dominant, making their actions understandable—although certainly not acceptable!—given their social positions. They also reveal the humanity of the dominated by showing how they have their own stories—where dominant populations are only minor characters.

### BLURRING CONTEMPT AND RESPECT IN UTAH

Outsiders, the dominant whites and Mormons of the region, have not been simply separate from, and disdainful of, the people of Ogden. Throughout the city's notorious heyday in the late 1800s and early 1900s, many of Ogden's bars were Mormon-owned and -operated.[25] Today, a Mormon temple sits just blocks from 25th Street. Members of the church are intimately intertwined with Ogden, just as both whites and Mormons in the region have been intertwined with immigrants and people of color. Dominant groups exploit and exclude marginalized populations, but they mix this exploitation with aspects of reverence, inclusion, and support that blur these lines.[26] Additionally, Mormons themselves have been marginalized, and this may shape their feelings about, and sensitivity for, similarly treated people.

As with most U.S. institutions, the Mormon Church has a history filled with openly white supremacist ideas and practices. Most notoriously, church officials followed blatantly racist policies of not allowing black men as priests well into the 1970s (and black women, along with all women, are still restricted from this position).[27] Modern supporters of the policy banning black priests cited Brigham Young's words on the subject to justify the exclusion on religious grounds:

> Why are so many of the inhabitants of the earth cursed with a skin of blackness? It comes in consequence of their fathers rejecting the power of the Holy Priesthood and law of God. They will go down in death. And when all the rest of the children have received their blessings in the Holy Priesthood, then that curse will be removed from the seed of Cain, and they will then come up and possess the Priesthood, and receive all the blessings which we now are entitled to.[28]

Defenders of this policy invoked the "mark of Ham." As the biblical story goes, descendants of Cain—the son of Adam, the very first human—were cursed with a mark of dark skin that continued through the marriage of Ham, a son of Noah, to an Egyptian woman.[29]

This legacy of open racism and cultural insensitivity still haunts the church. The Mormon Church continues to draw controversy for its members posthumously baptizing Jews, especially victims and survivors of the holocaust, as Mormons.[30] This is despite the church publicly disavowing the practice. In 2013, thirty-five years after they lifted the ban on black priests, they released a statement on "Race and the Priesthood" that repudiated the practice.[31] Again in 2017, the church released another statement stating, in part, "No man who makes disparaging remarks concerning those of another race can consider himself a true disciple of Christ. Nor can he consider himself to be in harmony with the teachings of the Church of Christ."[32]

The racist attitudes of Utahans mirrored conditions in the rest of the United States, where minority populations regularly met with exclusion, discrimination, and violence. Yet, religious beliefs added further justification for the stigmatization and oppression of marginalized communities. "The nationwide view that Balkan and Mediterranean immigrants were of inferior heredity was deepened in Utah by the Mormon notion that the invaders had 'tainted blood.'"[33] The histories of people of color in Utah detail how most ethnic groups faced some measure of prejudice, hostility, and exclusion from the majority white and Mormon population.

At the same time, the relationship between Utah's dominant population of Mormons, who are mostly white, and others in the region has been a complicated mixture of exclusion and inclusion, rejection and acceptance, and attitudes that fall everywhere between hostility, isolation, respect, and even reverence. The history of Utah is filled with complex and seemingly contradictory attitudes toward marginalized populations. For example, Native Americans in the 1800s, following the theft of their land, received support from Mormons.

> Mormon communities actually made conscious efforts to help the Indian people in a paternalistic manner, and in some cases Mormons took destitute Indian children into their homes and raised them as part of their family. Despite this, Mormons effectively displaced the

Indians from their land, thus causing the predicament of the Native Americans.[34]

Indeed, Mormon theology simultaneously understood Native Americans as a venerated lost tribe of Israel and cursed with dark skin.

Along with clearly racist and exclusionary practices, a thread of respect and support for marginalized communities runs throughout Mormon history. Some of the first black people in Utah were pioneer slaves, including Green Flake—rumored to have driven Brigham Young's wagon upon his first arrival into Salt Lake City.[35] Flake—who joined the Mormon Church—and several other pioneer slaves are memorialized alongside whites on Salt Lake City monuments. Elijah Abel, a black man and Mormon who was born in the early 1800s and lived in Ogden for a time, also illustrates the complicated story of race in the region.[36] He, as well as two of his descendants, became Mormon priests in the early church, before its ban on black men. These patterns continue today. While Mormons tend to be white, a substantial number of them are people of color.

You may imagine that these nonwhites have been heavily swayed to join this dominant religion in order to gain its social rewards, or the Mormon Church heavily assimilated and acculturated these populations—colonizing, indoctrinating, and alienating them from their ethnic identities. While this may have been the experience of many, the historical record shows a more complicated relationship. Some black people, who the Mormon Church actively excluded and boldly pronounced as inferior, eagerly embrace the religion.

> It has been suggested that [black people's] roots in fundamentalism made them amenable to accepting the doctrines of LDS theology and that the self-sufficiency, unity, and independence from outside institutions, advocated by fundamentalist religions and mirrored in the Mormon church, further increase its appeal for Black converts.[37]

Many of the first people of color who entered the area, including black people, Latinos, and Pacific Islanders, were already members of the Mormon Church.[38] These patterns continue today.

Additionally, the church often provided immigrants and people of color a space for preserving their cultural traditions, including their native language and ties with their home countries, that they enthusiastically used.

The LDS Perpetual Emigrating Fund, church teams, and detailed church supervision were all part of the early migration and settlement. After statehood the assistance offered new colonists came in the form of tax-supported irrigation projects, stays of foreclosure on lands taken up, and hired experts to instruct colonists in up-to-date agricultural and domestic methods.[39]

Many Pacific Islanders (or "Polynesians") eagerly immigrated to Utah, and the church funded a ranch for the community in 1889.[40] This also was a project in cultural conservation, as "the First Presidency of the LDS church resolved that a separate community would preserve the Polynesian culture, permit the immigrants to be self-sufficient by raising crops and livestock, and provide a permanent gathering place for future South Pacific emigrants."[41]

Historically and today, people of color encounter respect and support from Mormons. Mormons set up the first Latino church in Utah, la Rama Mexicana, in 1920.[42] This Mormon branch helped to preserve the Spanish language as well as Mexican songs and dances. Recently, there is a huge "Latinization" of Mormonism. If current trends continue, soon more than 50 percent of church members will be in Latin America, with some of these foreign members making their way to Utah.[43] Additionally, in the early 1900s the governor of Utah personally encouraged Jewish settlers in New York and Pennsylvania to move there.[44] Today, the state has an especially large population of foreign refugees, supported by a large network of nonprofit organizations and government agencies.

Mormons are often wary of social movements and social justice causes, a main channel by which marginalized people seek equality. Leaders openly spoke out against the Civil Rights Act in the 1960s, the Equal Rights Amendment of the 1970s, and more recently, gay marriage and transgender rights causes.[45] Facing new immigration, the state of Utah made English the official language in 2002. This may be the result of the Mormon religion and its followers becoming more and more aligned with conservatism and the political right wing, which can have open contempt for government interventions that benefit people of color, immigrants, and other disadvantaged people. It also may have to do with the hierarchical nature of the church organization and its corresponding culture. For a community that embraces the idea that change comes from the top down, through divinely inspired authorities, and then ostracizes open critics of this system, public challenges from bottom-up activism and protest can seem alarmingly antagonistic—if not heresy.

Yet, the church also swims against the stream of these politics by welcoming people of color and immigrants, including those who are undocumented. In 1965, the heavily Mormon state legislature passed civil rights laws "with the intention of advancing the economic and social well-being of Utah's minority populations."[46] Then, they appropriated funds to recruit and support minority college students in 1971. Today, equally progressive state laws, like guest-worker permits, driver privilege cards, and in-state college tuition for the undocumented, reflect these trends. The church also endorsed the "Utah Compact," a statement that reads in part:

> Immigrants are integrated into communities across Utah. We must adopt a humane approach to this reality, reflecting our unique culture, history and spirit of inclusion. The way we treat immigrants will say more about us as a free society and less about our immigrant neighbors. Utah should always be a place that welcomes people of goodwill.[47]

While containing language that calls politicians to "lead efforts to strengthen federal laws and protect our national borders," thinly veiled language against undocumented immigration, this document encourages people, and especially church members, to welcome these vilified populations.

The vulnerable populations of Latino immigrants, especially those who are undocumented, appreciate these policies and the values of inclusion and respect underlying them. As a 66-year-old Latino stated when discussing what he most liked about Ogden:

> Despite how, in this state, they are Republicans and they suppose that the Hispanics, like me, in this case, undocumented—we have problems in the areas that are controlled by Republicans. In this state and in this city, it is reversed. They give you—they give you a driver's license that doesn't say license—a privilege [card]. But in the end, it is a driver's license. They let you drive. There are no detentions of immigrants. There is no detention by police. So, I feel that it has a lot of very good things in comparison to the state, to the cities, where I have lived.

These policies shield undocumented people from the extreme repression that they receive in other places.[48]

## MORMONS AS RACIAL OUTSIDERS

Mormons may be sensitive to the plight of the marginalized because of their own former status as vilified outsiders. Early adherents found themselves on the nonwhite side of racial color line. When the Mormon church originated in the early 1800s, members openly welcomed people of color, including black people.

> During those early months in New York and Ohio no mention was even made of Church attitudes towards blacks. The Gospel was for "all nations, kindreds, tongues and peoples," and no exceptions were made. A Negro, "Black Pete," was among the first converts in Ohio, and his story was prominently reported in the local press. W. W. Phelps opened a mission to Missouri in July, 1831, and preached to "all the families of the earth," specifically mentioning Negroes among his first audience.[49]

Such openness, including their doctrinal reverence for Native Americans and connections with Middle Easterners, showed a tolerance and even embrace of diversity. Yet, it also clashed with the racial order of the United States. As W. Paul Reeve states, "From its beginning, Mormonism found itself on the wrong side of white, a racially suspect religion that outsiders feared not only for its new doctrines but also for its reported violation of racial boundaries."[50]

The white Protestant elite of the 1800s disparaged Mormons as impure, suspicious, and even dangerous foreigners who had to "Americanize" in order to join the United States.[51] This dominant group linked Mormons to other racial groups—Asians, blacks, Muslims, and Native Americans. Given that these past Mormons were just as blonde and blue-eyed as many are today, it may seem odd that they became racialized in this way. Yet, nineteenth century perspectives connected racial groups with cultural development.[52] Whites, supported by the academic experts of the time, saw their supremacy demonstrated in highly developed civilizations. In contrast, they saw "lesser" groups as having cultures that were more rudimentary. Thus, people at the time connected the "inferiority" of Mormon civilization—with their "barbarian" practices of polygamy and "authoritarian" leanings toward charismatic leaders instead of democracy—to an inferior racial status.

In order to escape this vilified status, Mormons adopted the image of an "ultracitizen." Almost a caricature of the quintessential all-American, this image is clean cut, friendly, upbeat, polite, outgoing, hardworking, business oriented, patriotic, educated (yet wary of intellectualism and radical perspectives), religious and principled (yet pragmatic—submitting to government authority when legitimate channels are exhausted), family centered, committed to moderation and self-restraint, and sexually modest. If it is conventional, conservative, prudent, wholesome, and "traditionally" American, Mormons tend to embrace it.

Undergoing this "Americanization," Mormons also embraced standards of whiteness. Just as they abandoned polygamy in order to join the majority sexually (a condition of Utah becoming a part of the United States), Mormons also shifted their tolerant racial views in order to jump to the other side of the color line.[53] While church founder Joseph Smith was sympathetic to black people and openly antislavery, his successor Brigham Young encouraged the church to adopt mainstream racial views.[54] Their tolerance of slavery showed political pragmatism when they lived in the slave states of Missouri and then Utah.[55] As early leader Orson Hyde stated in 1851, "The church, on this point, assumes not the responsibility to direct. The laws of the land recognize slavery,—and we do not wish to oppose the laws of the country. If there is sin in selling a slave, let the individual who sells him bear that sin, and not the church."[56] Mormons gradually evolved into whites through such shifts. They went from challenging the prevailing racial order, and facing its scorn, to upholding it.

Unfortunately, the embrace of conventionalism that made Mormons exemplary Americans also made them very slow to bend to the winds of change. Their shift into whiteness and embrace of racial domination held fast, even through the civil rights era, when the country changed its collective views.[57] Other churches may collectively discuss, debate, and agree upon doctrine. For the Mormon believer, it is divinely inspired and not to be doubted. A favorite saying is "I know the Church is true." Thus, they saw the black priesthood ban as undisputable, just as they accepted changes to it that finally came in 1978.[58] Consequently, the open racism that made them quintessentially American in the Jim Crow era began to turn them un-American again in the post–civil rights era. As W. Paul Reeve puts it, Mormons moved "from not securely white in the nineteenth century to too white by the twenty-first century."[59]

Mormons' current blurring of contempt and respect for people of color and immigrants makes sense given how Mormons themselves faced past marginalization, and they escaped this vilified status by embracing mainstream American values. One of the ways that they overcame being dominated was to become dominators. At the same time, echoes of Mormons' past otherness still seem to influence them.

## RESHAPING THE EUROCENTRIC NARRATIVE

Another way that boundaries in the region have and will continue to blur is through its views about, and treatment of, people of color and immigrants. Comprehensive histories of Ogden and Utah are largely Eurocentric in timeline and focus. They consider the era that began when Mormon pioneers first arrived in 1847. A picture of Utah that emerges from both historical accounts and the popular local imagination is that, before the arrival of Mormon settlers, the region had little civilization. Yet, Mormons did not establish Utah. It already was home to the Ute and Paiute people that give the state its name as well as other indigenous and Mexican residents. There also were black and Latino explorers and fur traders in the area. In fact, Utah was officially a part of Mexico from when Mormons arrived until this land became a territory of the United States in 1848.

Additionally, combing through these histories and their parades of business leaders, politicians, and other elite white men, one could get the impression that there was no one else living in Utah. They only mention others occasionally, almost begrudgingly. While some histories do help to fill these gaps by capturing the experience and influence of women, people of color, and immigrants,[60] many accounts of Utah help to maintain the misconception that white and Mormon elites are the sole coordinators and caretakers of life there.

Such understandings of local dominant communities, as the hub of a wheel that shapes the experiences of marginalized populations, are not only Eurocentric but also geographically narrow. Recent international shifts to the economy and labor force are bringing about immigration and other transformations that more and more intimately link local experiences with global events. This further emphasizes the need to look beyond dominant groups in order to understand this region. Latino newcomers to Ogden are part of a much wider world, connected to long-standing and distinguished cultures and traditions. On this international stage, Utah's dominant groups are only bit players.

Although current dominant groups may see themselves as the undeniable and rightful ancestors of this place, Latinos can easily dispute this claim. These settlers on former Mexican lands, most with indigenous bloodlines, can assert much more of a historical legacy and inheritance than those who only entered the region in 1847 ever could. They are now reestablishing this heritage, which foreign invaders interrupted.

Given this broad historical view, the boundaries between the established and newcomers, the respectable and legitimate versus the disreputable intruders, become blurred and even inverted. Ogden's Latino immigrants may be reclaiming their futures, often after economic and political circumstances in their home countries compelled their exit. Yet, they also are reclaiming their past—even if they are not aware of this heritage.

# 10

# INTERVENTIONS

While many metropolitan neighborhoods continue to display the traditional pattern of "invasion and succession"—whereby the entrance of minority members results in "white flight"—there are a growing number of stable diverse communities. That is not to say that diversity necessarily translates into harmony. Ethnic conflict is common in diverse areas, and conflict is often exacerbated by class differences between groups. Despite this, ethnic groups that share residential space also at times work together because they share common goals associated with neighborhood improvement.

—*John Iceland*

I am Hispanic. And on one side, Hispanics still need to integrate into the community, in the everyday life of this city. On the other side, there are some American people, or whites as they say. The community is divided. That's what I feel. The community has groups. For example, Anglos are one part, Latinos—Hispanics—another part, African Americans also separate, and Asians. These would be the four big groups that exist in the city, I think. A union between those four groups does not exist.

—*Ogden resident, 47-year-old Latino immigrant*

Understanding urban reputations as moral frontiers, boundaries between higher- and lower-status groups of people, involves seeing them as grounded in the realm of meanings. These perceptions of place can shift when we collectively reevaluate our perspectives about them. Although such change can be accomplished by transforming conditions within areas, this is only one tool out of many, and it is a blunt and destructive one at that. Campaigns to reduce disorder can act as a "scorched earth policy" that improves a place, but they do this by eradicating its current residents as well as the cultures and histories that they have established. Finding alternative ways to dismantle negative assessments of place requires being thoughtful about how they are built—carefully evaluating the depictions, assumptions, and biases underlying these meanings.

Balancing negative representations with positive ones can be a first step to change. On its face, the industry that has emerged to help outsiders understand disreputable places zealously advocates for the disadvantaged. Exposés of the horrors found in disreputable places, including research publications, fit a long tradition of progressive struggles for reform. Yet, such portrayals of disreputable places overwhelmingly focus on the deficits of these communities, inadvertently solidifying their residents' stigma, isolation, and negative identities. Victor Rios warns that research in this vein reinforces colonized thinking by fortifying "white spaces" that exclude people of color:

> It is the white space that allows even the most well-meaning sociologists to create a logic trap for themselves by making the essence of their work a project of normalizing and humanizing the other. At best, the end result is sometimes a pandering to mass (white) audiences in an attempt to normalize foreign worlds (people of color).[1]

Such studies attempt to make the people in these settings relatable and explain how their attitudes and behaviors make sense given their environment. Yet, these depictions rarely leave outsider audiences with the impression that these are places where they would like to be, and their residents are people who they should befriend, hire, or even encounter on the street.

Situating the dysfunctions of disadvantaged groups and their neighborhoods at the center of studies, although a tradition deeply rooted in social science research, deflects accountability from oppressors, consigning it to the oppressed.[2] The efficiently simple and dispassionate logic linking disorder with a place's reputation, exemplified by the "broken windows theory" and interventions based on its logic, hides a subtle form of victim blaming. In 1903, W. E. B. DuBois argued that black people in the United States frequently face a question—"How does it feel to be a problem?"—that positions the sufferers of racial oppression as those who should account for it.[3] Past "culture of poverty" ideas explicitly blamed the marginalized for their own positions,[4] but urban researchers still focus on the victims of inequality more than their perpetrators, implicitly treating minority and lower-class populations as a problem. Researchers of disreputable places often fail to consider who is constructing these areas as disreputable, disordered, and dangerous, and why they are doing so.[5]

When viewing urban reputations through the lens of moral frontiers, it is little surprise that interventions based on disordered conditions have disastrous effects. If the roots of reputations lie outside of disreputable areas, then focusing on internal conditions to explain and improve the images of these places is misguided. Although unintentional, academic approaches and practical interventions alike treat the victims of urban reputations as their perpetrators, reinforcing inequality and marginality under the guise of assistance.[6]

Just as the bad reputation of Ogden's residents does not come from their bad acts and moral wickedness, the dominance of outsiders emerges less from their good acts and righteousness than their position on the other side of this boundary. In fact, the history of Mormon persecution shows how people have labeled Mormons as both disreputable and upstanding. The people who promote the bad reputations of places may be concerned, even deeply, with problems of poverty and racism. Still, dominant groups have large benefits that they do not want to give up, and they hold corresponding ideas that justify those benefits. Their isolation from disreputable populations has devastating effects on these vilified places. Ogden's bad reputation, even if spoken about innocently in jokes or offhand comments, is still a weapon wielded against its residents.

Yet, the socially constructed nature of bad reputations also means that these meanings can—and they even *will*—change, and their transformation can help undo the inequalities underlying such divisions and sow the seeds of unity. While negative perceptions further entrench, and even create, problems in communities, they also create possibilities. As Birgitte Mazanti and John Pløger put it:

> It may seem quite elementary, but what we need to do is build a bridge in the dialogue between an inside and outside understanding of the deprived neighbourhoods. When the political goal is to shape a positive place identity, the point of departure must be an understanding

of how place identity is formed and how the residents relate to their place of residence on an everyday basis. This understanding can only be fulfilled by investigating how everyday life is perceived and enacted by the people who live in the neighbourhoods. So far, this aspect has been virtually ignored.[7]

Feelings of attachment to a place contain the seeds of community—opportunities to bring people together.[8] Ogden residents felt a strong connection with their city that runs counter to others' negative perceptions. Additionally, historical circumstances of inequality and segregation, forcing black and Latinos into segregated neighborhoods with inequitable conditions and opportunities, also helped to make these areas centers of community for minorities and new immigrants. While these circumstances are problems, they also have the making of solutions for Ogden's reputation. The city's difference from the region unites its residents through shared characteristics and, although often uneven and hesitant, an embrace of their community.

The tremendous divisions underlying Ogden's reputation ultimately require interventions to our social world—and our moral order—that are fundamental and daunting. Here I offer two modest suggestions for transforming Ogden. First, residents can sow the seeds of unity by "boundary blurring," promoting structured settings that bring divided groups together. Secondly, they can create a "moral inversion" that upturns the problem of Ogden's bad reputation, reshaping it into a solution. This would involve addressing and even promoting the dangerous image of Ogden in the city's marketing. Yet, I also question whether Ogden should be transformed at all. Unless instituted very carefully, changes to Ogden's reputation could have negative effects for much of the population, including the loss of resident's current feelings of connection to the city.

## CONTINUED BOUNDARY BLURRING

One solution for Ogden's residents to undo these entrenched divisions is by consciously creating opportunities to break down boundaries. This "boundary blurring"[9] through daily contact, joint political, civic, and leisurely pursuits, friendship, and even intermarriage can happen by fostering events and other spaces where higher-class residents interact with the lower class, whites interact with minorities, and native residents interact with immigrants. This can have lasting effects on Ogden's reputation. Residents who feel more connected to each other see their communities as less disordered.¹⁰ Such boundary blurring could unite insiders and outsiders, as well as native residents and Latino immigrants, in shared positive understandings of the city.

There are few places in Ogden where people from different social groups collectively gather, sharing space and interactions. Most neighborhoods, schools, and businesses reflect racial and class segregation. The responses of interviewees reflect this division. Given the greatly differing ways that residents spoke about Ogden, at times it seemed as though they could not possibly be discussing the same place. While native residents greatly admired the east side of the city, Latino immigrants tended to find it alienating.

Yet, there were activities that cut across these lines. For example, residents of all kinds praised the Ogden Christmas Village—where the city decorates a downtown area on 25th Street with colored lights and tiny, elaborately ornamented cottages between Thanksgiving and New Year's—as one of the prized features of Ogden. White and minority, native and immigrant residents alike applauded this event. This resident thought it was their favorite thing about the city:

*Respondent (24-year-old white male):* Oooh! I wanna change my answer! My favorite part of Ogden is during wintertime, when they put up all their lights.

*Interviewer:* Oh, you like the Christmas Village?

*Respondent:* Mm hm. It gets all snowy, you go get some coffee and then walk around to look at all the lights. It's so nice!

Similarly, several Latino immigrants positively mentioned the lights and other decorations of Christmas Village:

*Respondent (38-year-old Latino):* It looks really nice here sometimes when they put all the lights up on the trees and all the stuff here in this park. Have you ever been here for that?

*Interviewer:* I don't think so. Is it for Christmas?

*Respondent:* Yes, for Christmas, and other things that they do down here.

This free, outdoor event cuts across class, racial, and immigrant divisions to unify residents.

Another example of such a shared space where boundaries blur is Ogden's taco trucks and food carts. Located downtown, many where the Christmas Village event is held, they attract a diverse variety of customers—white and Latino, Mormon and non-Mormon, immigrant and native. As with the Christmas Village, customers enjoy this shared space together. Long lines of people who are representative of Ogden's diversity regularly stand outside in the coldest of winter and burning summer, all waiting to be served. Office workers in professional dress assemble with construction workers in dirty coveralls. Defendants, heading to the downtown courts for their trials, stand with lawyers and police.

Unfortunately, city leaders have unevenly encouraged such shared public spaces. While the Christmas Village remains a celebrated feature of the holiday season, the food carts and trucks are more controversial. In 2014, the city council voted to heavily restrict their business. The stipulations included the following:

> Food trucks must not be parked within 200 feet of an existing restaurant, food cart or church; food trucks are not allowed in The Junction or Historic 25th Street District; food trucks can operate only between 7 a.m. and 6 p.m.; and access is required to a permanent bathroom facility when a food cart is parked on private property.[11]

Beyond stifling a more active downtown nightlife, these regulations were boundary work to protect brick and mortar restaurants in the area from threats by these new businesses, many if not most of them run by immigrants. Yet, a consequence of this policy was restricting a setting where immigrant and native born regularly interact.

Instead of limiting them, Ogden's city leaders can strategize to recognize, preserve, and create such unifying spaces, actively engineering interactions that bring different residents together as well as bring visitors from the surrounding region. Although far from a comprehensive solution, changes from new or existing businesses, housing options, schools, development programs, and events that cut across race, class, and cultural lines can reverberate throughout a community, helping to transform the reputations of places and lessen the racial divisions and structural inequality underlying them. In these shared places, people of different groups come together, if only superficially. These fleeting connections have the potential to develop into deeper associations. As Eric Oliver notes, "interracial friendships usually only emerge from structured social situations."[12] If inequality is partly built on the spatial separation of people, such shared spaces and the interactions that they encourage can help to ease divisions.

Higher-status people are likely to furiously oppose many of these interventions. After all, these populations ground their identities as good people on a separation from disreputable populations. They uphold unequal relations through fears of crime as well as economic, cultural, and moral decline. These collective groups bristle at such contamination to their status. They oppose interventions to undo or restructure government policies and other formal and informal mechanisms—such as segregated schools and preferences in hiring and housing—that have benefited them for generations. They even misrecognize these attempts at equal opportunity to the point of seeing them as unfair, giving marginalized people unearned benefits.

Yet, changes that blur boundaries can lead to familiarity and the lessening of fear and distrust between communities, as well as the widening of social worlds for everyone—whites as well as people of color, native residents and new Latino immigrants, higher class and lower class, and Mormon and non-Mormon. Such contact is beneficial for those on the dominant side of these divisions, giving them richer perspectives and experiences through connections to a wider world. I have yet to speak to anyone—even lapsed and resentful Mormons—who regrets their experience as a missionary and its structured encounters with very diverse people, often in a different country. Such connections also can be life changing for marginalized groups, opening up a universe of new opportunities and possibilities. Ironically, their interactions with dominant populations can also give them the collective efficacy, through education and political action, to challenge and reject prevailing standards and their inequalities of power.

## MORAL INVERSIONS

As I explained in Chapter Five, the current strategy for promoting Ogden involves treating much of the city, its people, and its history as a public shame to be underemphasized and even covered up. Such a view unintentionally supports the very people who maintain Ogden's bad reputation. It reinforces the idea that outsiders' higher status, lifestyles, and very presence in the city are superior and desirable. An alternative strategy could involve undermining the power of the city's reputation by playfully publicizing it, embracing and promoting Ogden's past and present image as a notorious place. This marketing device could invert the moral standards that negatively define the city, turning deficits into advantages and shame into appreciation. It also could free residents to embrace and show pride for who they are—and who they were.

An entire industry, and corresponding academic study, of place marketing has emerged with the goal of turning around the reputations of areas.[13] Place management and nation branding are big business, as countries and other places are desperate to upturn their image in order to attract industry, residents, and tourism. Advisors, consultants, and marketers earn large fees by creating and enacting plans to change the reputations of places. Among other efforts, the city of Ogden paid a marketing firm $131,000 to help reinvent its image.[14]

Research on place management suggests that, as a reputation runs deeply, changes to it need to run deeply as well. Transformations do not happen through empty slogans, short-term campaigns, and limited buy in from the wider community. As Simon Anholt says of countries' marketing efforts:

> In truth, nation branding is the problem, not the solution. It is public opinion which brands countries—in other words, reduces them to the weak, simplistic, outdated, unfair stereotypes that so damage their prospects in a globalized world—and most countries need to *fight against* the tendency of international public opinion to brand them, not encourage it. Governments need to help the world understand the real, complex, rich, diverse nature of their people and landscapes, their history and heritage, their products and their resources: to *prevent* them from becoming mere brands.[15]

Given this, the marketing of place usually has the same negative qualities as the damaging reputations that it attempts to counteract. It turns multifaceted experiences, cultures, histories, and iconic and treasured locations into crude simplifications, dismissively flattening and even erasing them. This works against promoting an area more than it helps these efforts. Given how Ogden's reputation is so deeply embedded in regional historical, demographic, and cultural dynamics, it is little surprise that current promotions of the city have been unsuccessful at reversing its bad reputation.

Instead of celebrating the city for what it is, Ogden's marketing reveals ambiguity and even resentment toward it and its working-class, minority, and immigrant populations. The very people tasked with promoting the virtues of Ogden seem to wish it to be a different place. City leaders attempt to replace, symbolically as well as physically, residents who they feel are disreputable with those who they feel are acceptable. They engage in "collective forgetfulness" to cover up the city's unique past and present. In the idealized image of promotional materials, the gangbanger becomes a skier. The lower-class Latina in the center of the city becomes a middle-class white woman on the eastern trails. The stinky dog food factory downtown becomes a mountain field filled with flowers. These "magical" efforts to rewrite Ogden's characteristics in order to reimagine the city as a middle- and upper-class haven, coupled with interventions against the city's disreputable populations through police campaigns and redevelopment, target the most marginalized and vulnerable members of the community.

City authorities should not be uniquely singled out and blamed for their reluctance. Instead of being "moral entrepreneurs"[16] that wage pioneering crusades to restrict or reinforce the lines between deviance and respectability, their views reflect those of many citizens. Native residents were hesitant to fully embrace the city. They argued against claims that Ogden was a bad place filled with crime and disorder, while talking about areas of the city in those very terms. These residents also expressed confusion, as the city's disreputable reputation did not fit their experiences. While studies often focus on how authorities impose a brand and other marketing on cities, the elites of Ogden seemed to be closely aligned with the feelings of most residents.

While city leaders and native residents alike tout the mountains to the east over the Mexican markets to the west, these "magical solutions," "collective forgetfulness," and other concealment of disreputable features also conceals aspects that residents could embrace. When residents ignore the "notorious" history of the area, they also miss learning about positive characteristics that they should feel proud about and celebrate. Along with the notoriety of 25th Street came a booming, influential, and world-famous destination. The town has historically embraced international and multicultural diversity in ways that rival most U.S. cities, many of which are still far behind this curve or only now catching up. Indeed, Ogden is ahead of most of Utah in this aspect—a model of international connections and the incorporation of numerous cultures. Furthermore, the madams and minority-owned establishments that filled the vibrant past of Junction City, in an era when women and people of color had very limited opportunities for success, are truly exceptional examples of shrewd business owners overcoming adversity. Tossing out the bathwater of Ogden's notorious past also removes the baby of this important heritage.

Instead of struggling against the past of Ogden, city leaders and residents could embrace and celebrate the intertwined histories of Ogden's notorious past and its diverse communities. The perceptions of Latino immigrants were a model of appreciation and embrace of the city. Such views could be a valuable resource of positivity and support, harnessed to transform negative images of the city. Ironically, this population that so unconditionally accepts the city is the same population that it largely shuns. Instead of ignoring them, city leaders would be wise to listen to their views. The features that Latino immigrants embrace could attract new residents and visitors as well.

Disreputable populations turning negative representations of themselves into points of pride and celebration are what I call a "moral inversion" of power dynamics. It is a popular strategy for reshaping reputations. Marginalized communities have distinctive characteristics that outsiders and even themselves often interpret as deficits. As a way to invert systems of power, many have recast the language of their oppression into positive traits.[17] They refashion derogatory words from the powerful's language of insult to fit the powerless' language of strength and defiance. For example, the LGBT community transformed the word "queer" from an ugly slur into a mark of identity, a point of pride, and even a professional academic designation through queer studies. This happens with cities as well, as many places have turned demeaning slurs into unifying slogans (for example, "Keep Austin Weird" and "Zoo York"). Such inversions of power dynamics question and even mock moral standards—transforming the inappropriate and disreputable into the embraced and celebrated.[18]

Ogden could similarly invert negative perceptions into positive features. The traits from which Ogden's residents and city leaders are quick to distance themselves and collectively disavow—urban diversity and even disorder—are aspects that some desire. People are reconsidering the safe, car-centered, and homogenous suburbs for culturally vibrant, aesthetically distinctive, and walkable neighborhoods.[19] The "creative class" and "new bohemians" seek out places with old architecture, diverse communities, and other authentically gritty urban experiences, even street crime.[20] We find these very characteristics in Ogden. Ironically, city leaders could draw the very residents that they wish to attract through their magical reimaginings of the city—middle- and upper-class residents—by advertising the discordant and multicultural aspects of their city. Instead, they hide these features as shameful deficits.

In other aspects of Utah life, similar moral inversions are extremely popular. People in the region especially love Halloween.[21] Come September, large haunted houses fill Northern Utah. "Zombie crawls"—where people dress as zombies and parade down city streets—are popular events. The city of Magna even holds a second Halloween festival during the summer.[22] Throughout the year, there are no shortages of audiences for screenings of horror films. This flirting with the "dark side" of life may have much to do with the conservative and religious nature of the area. It is an opportunity for those engulfed in boundaries of morality and status to temporarily reject these constraints and embrace the disreputable in a safe and socially acceptable manner.

Ogden's residents may be warming to a strategy of moral inversion. In 2016, the city adopted a tagline of "still untamed" that references its past and current image.[23] Instead of attempting to sweep the city's past under the rug, as previous campaigns have done, this is a subtle shift toward fully accepting the city. Although it took an out-of-state consultant and a small fortune, this change signals that city leaders are warming to an image of Ogden as it is, not as they wish it to be. Another example of moral inversion is the locally owned bar Alleged, which opened in 2013. The former 25th Street home of the infamous El Borracho Tavern, and earlier the Rose Rooms brothel run by Rose Davie, Alleged celebrates this history of vice through its name, proudly proclaiming how its setting used to be "Ogden's most notorious brothel," and naming their drinks (and bathroom stalls) after figures of vice.[24]

Widely instituted, this practice of playfully embracing disreputable elements of the city could come to redefine people's relationship with Ogden. Just as people seek out the grittiness of city life, or they flock to haunted houses for the simulation of a fearsome and dangerous environment, they also could come to Ogden for similar experiences. This does not mean that Ogden should bring back its brothels, gambling, or street violence. Just as haunted houses are safe places to experience violence and fear, residents need only the "light" stimulation of knowing that the building at 278 25th Street (standing just west of a former opium den—part of the city's Chinatown) was a brothel in the early 1900s.[25]

Instead of scaring residents and visitors away, these playful inversions of power could add to their experience with the city, attracting them to these spaces and deepening their connections to them. They also would redraw the line, currently blurred in the minds of people, between a dangerous past incarnation of Ogden city and its relatively sedate present. Residents and visitors could be educated about the fascinating history of Ogden, warts and all. They should be proud of the city, instead of collectively embarrassed, hesitant, or defensive. As Jonathan Foster states, "a city might remain exactly as it was yet become acceptable. Its residents could even benefit from doubling down on and exaggerating the event or characteristic for which they were once shamed.... This might be the most likely way for a city to escape the negative influences of stigmatization."[26] This tactic will not win over the majority of regional locals, initially if ever. Yet, such people are already repelled by the city, and current strategies to woo them have met little success.

## KEEP OGDEN BAD?

While places like Ogden can be branded and transformed, should they be? Such changes can be tricky, filled with difficulties and unintended consequences. While the dream of a diverse population of different races, class backgrounds, and cultures happily living together is appealing, the reality of such places is more complicated. While uniting different types of people can lead to greater understanding, connection, and friendship, those who live in such places tend to be less connected to their communities than those who live in more homogeneous places.[27] Diverse communities are often sites of conflict between groups, as recent studies of places where Latino immigrants have settled especially show.[28] The case of Ogden illustrates how people living in such places struggle with coming together, and many long to separate themselves from their lower-status neighbors.

Additionally, an effective city brand can bring many benefits to a city, but it also has drawbacks, especially to its most vulnerable communities. In 2000, small business leaders from Austin, Texas, instituted a "Keep Austin Weird" campaign (later adopted by Portland, then Louisville and Indianapolis) in order to promote the eclectic and diverse feel of the city. Ironically, such branding efforts may have been too successful to be able to keep these places "weird," as they have helped attract new residents, skyrocketing property values and diminishing the very cultural features that they claimed to be preserving and celebrating. These cities face concerns that gentrification is pushing out its lower-class and minority communities.[29]

The successful branding of Ogden ("Keep Ogden Bad"?) could have similar negative outcomes. Dismantling Ogden's negative reputation also could mean dismantling or fundamentally reorganizing the very fabric of this community, leading to outcomes that are arguably worse than the current problems facing residents. Changes that city leaders desire would greatly benefit higher-status residents, business leaders, and homeowners, who would profit from increased industry and rising property values. While Ogden's marginalized populations could benefit from lessening crime, as well as better jobs that raise them out of poverty, such advantages rarely reach the longtime residents of gentrifying areas.[30] Instead, these interventions probably would spell trouble for these people, initiating rising rents and eventually dislocating many or even most of them. Unless carefully instituted with an eye for avoiding negative outcomes, "urban renewal" and "revitalization" generally are not tools of social justice as much as they are tools of social inequality. They end up replacing disreputable populations with the reputable.

A further concern, for all residents, is how these transformations could change how they feel connected to the city. As Raymond Hester argues, beloved places

> exemplify, typify, reinforce, and perhaps even extol the everyday life patterns and special rituals of community life, places that have become so essential to the lives of the residents through use or symbolism that the community collectively identifies with these places. The places become synonymous with residents' concepts and use of their town. The loss of such places would reorder or destroy something or some social process familiar to the community's collective well-being.[31]

Tinkering with the formula of connections to place—slowly concocted through decades of day-to-day routine, familiarity, and deep and even multi-generational attachment—is a potentially explosive act that can easily alienate people from their own communities. The imbalances of power, repression of vulnerable communities, and feelings of stigma and inadequacy among residents that underlie Ogden's reputation are definitely social ills. Residents should attempt to remedy these problems. Yet, many of these very things also unify this community, and their cure is often worse than the original disease. Residents should carefully consider what type of community they want: one that they love but has the problem of a bad reputation, or one with a good reputation that could change, or even destroy, the unique features that they currently embrace.

# 11

# CONCLUSION

Urban researchers often ignore the fact that conceptions of pathological and mainstream behaviour are ideological constructs produced through an on-going public and academic discourse of inner-city culture. . . . Social marginality is not a product of cultural inferiority but rather the result of denied opportunities to people who are labelled culturally different. The very concept of social dysfunction and dislocation rests on the false assumption that social behavior and negative consequences are directly and causally linked, and detached from their wider socio-political context.

—Harald Bauder

Until 1965 when you walked down 25th Street, the black folks had to stay on the south side of the street and the white folks had to stay on the other side. . . . The sad thing about it all was that some of the best food in town and for the best price could be found on the black's side of the street.

—Joe Ritchie

This study considers the problem of urban reputations, how we understand them, and how we try to fix them. I have explored this problem through the example of Ogden, Utah, which offers an especially rich case for understanding the phenomenon. This is, in part, because perceptions of this place are so divergent. In contrast to urban ghettos that have "obvious" notoriety, Ogden was terrible or wonderful, dangerous or safe, frightening or comforting as seen through different people's eyes. I wanted to more closely examine these views and make sense of them, understanding how people can look at the same place and see such dramatically different things. To study Ogden's reputation, I had residents relate their perceptions of the city while they traveled through its neighborhoods.

On their face, differing responses to Ogden were chaotic, confused, and contradictory. They seemed to be idiosyncratic preferences based on individual opinions and personal tastes. A closer look at these views revealed two distinct layers of patterns. A first was between "insiders," Ogden's residents, and "outsiders" who lived beyond the boundaries of the city. Ogden's bad reputation negatively impacted the city's residents, who did not subscribe to it, nor did they promote it. Likewise, national news stories and other extra-local reports about Ogden did not portray it negatively. Instead, the city's reputation was a product of regional outsiders. They were the custodians of Ogden's bad reputation—creating, sustaining, and disseminating it.

While Ogden's residents overwhelmingly thought positively about the city as a whole, I noticed an additional layer of patterns in their responses. Native residents, those who had been raised in the United States, complained about the inaccuracy and unfairness of Ogden's bad reputation, which divided the city from the surrounding region, only to similarly split the city into reputable and disreputable parts. In contrast, Ogden's Latino immigrants were the most appreciative of the city. They did not accept—and rarely even mentioned—Ogden's bad reputation. Nor did they divide the city into good and bad areas, as native residents did.

Generally, we explain the reputation of a place as the result of conditions found there. Disorder and deprivation are important problems facing Ogden. There certainly is poverty, crime, and rundown conditions, and these things certainly inform some people's views of the city. Yet, perceptions of Ogden do not closely reflect its internal disorder. After all, those who most celebrated Ogden—Latino immigrants—probably had the most experience with the conditions that supposedly give the city its bad reputation. Conversely, those who most condemned Ogden had little experience with this place. Ogden's reputation makes little sense when seeing urban reputations as reflections of this place's internal disorder.

To explain these patterns, I argue that urban reputations are "moral frontiers." They are influential, yet contested and shifting, meanings that reflect attempts by collective groups to define what is upstanding or dishonorable.

This argument builds from constructionist understandings of deviance as well as perspectives of racial inequality. These theories emphasize how definitions of what is deviant do not emerge from characteristics of the deviant. Instead, they are the result of a process of meaning-making by the nondeviant, dominant people of a community. Their definitions of the bad—bad people, things, activities, ideas, and places—demarcate and uphold definitions of the good. This helps to preserve their power, including a respectable social standing and its corresponding benefits.

Given these understandings, urban reputations act as symbolic weapons on a field of competition between collective groups, each of them seeking to maintain or raise their status and define their own community as good. Studies of a place's image often focus on elites' branding and other top-down impositions, but I argue that entire communities are primarily responsible for generating and defending these understandings. Those of higher status— by characteristics such as social class, race, and culture (religion is especially important in Utah)—do symbolic work to isolate themselves from those below them. This includes the drawing of spatial lines. After all, challenges to their community boundaries threaten long-standing resources, opportunities, as well as their identities. At the same time, those with little status feel less need to make such distinctions. On the contrary, it advantages them to dismantle these barriers, as this improves their social position. They challenge, in attempts to lessen their marginalization and disadvantage, the partitions that higher-status people establish.

Understandings of Ogden corresponded with efforts of division and unification among dominant and marginalized groups. These collective patterns were often ironic and even paradoxical. Some people came together in order to separate themselves from others, while others united with people because they were separated. Some, such as Ogden's native residents and Mormons historically, fell on both sides of this divide. At times, they faced a disreputable status and sought integration. At other times, they claimed respectability and sought separation from the disreputable.

These patterns of unity and division were intertwined with various cultural, economic, historic, and political contexts. Ogden residents' positive views of the city, but also their demographic difference from the surrounding region, unified them. The city was a regional outlier, with diversity that varied from surrounding areas. It was a decidedly working-class place. It was a "new immigrant destination" with much racial and cultural diversity, especially from a large number of native and foreign-born Latinos. These unifying features contrasted with the predominantly higher-class, white, and Mormon residents living beyond Ogden's borders, making the city morally suspect to those people. The seeds of this difference originated more than a century ago with the coming of the railroad. The effects of the city's Wild West past still influence perceptions of Ogden, or perceptions of areas within the city.

While seeing Ogden positively overall, native residents also divided themselves from western areas of Ogden and their residents, many viewing such places as disreputable and dangerous "ghettos." While these respondents—through this process of spatial separation—promoted ideas that reinforced people of color's isolation and inequality, their perceptions of Ogden as divided were an ironic source of unity. I had expected to see large differences among native's views, as they had great variations in race, gender, age, occupation, and religion, but this diverse array of people came together to divide the city into respectable and disreputable areas. Their unity of views suggests that the spatial boundaries underlying segregation are not only racial, as researchers generally treat them. They can be intertwined into a complex, shifting, and even contradictory collection of identities and interests that include race as well as social class, national origin, and culture.

The perceptions of Latino immigrants were particularly disconnected from those of other residents. Ironically, their views of Ogden—how they praised the city and unified with others—revealed their great difference, even within Ogden's community of difference. Latino immigrants' understandings were more positive—and also more evenhanded, nuanced, and accurate—than those of native residents. This may reflect their seclusion from other residents or their socialization into foreign cultures with different understandings of racial dynamics and urban structures. Latino immigrants' greatly differing views did not happen *despite* their lack of knowledge or acceptance of others' understandings but *because of it*. The idea of Ogden's bad reputation did not taint their perceptions, as it did with native residents. Some native residents expressed confusion, having difficulty reconciling the city's image with what they saw with their own eyes.

People's attempts to raise or maintain their status through designations of good and bad are a much better explanation of Ogden's reputation than internal disorder. As lower-status residents, Latino immigrants' evenhanded views of the city reflected attempts to unify with others. This unification acted to improve their status, merging themselves with other places and people. Native residents, caught between higher-status outsiders and lower-status insiders, challenged perceptions of their community that lessened their status. At the same time, they upheld perceptions that distanced them from more disreputable populations. These were moral frontiers. Native residents' dual strategies of unity and division were both attempts to position them on the side of the good and away from the bad.

## REIMAGINING URBAN SPACE

Treating urban reputations as moral frontiers adds multiple insights and innovations for understanding disreputable places as well as the symbolic processes underlying how we perceive urban areas as a whole. Here I outline four main contributions of this study: (1) it moves analyses of spatial perceptions from the individual to collective level; (2) it emphasizes the moral dimension of these understandings, resurrecting cultural explanations of disreputable communities; (3) it shifts the analysis of disreputable places away from a focus on internal influences, especially by considering the local region; and (4) it encourages solutions that work to unify divided communities.

First, this study moves beyond individual-level understandings of reputations—how you or I think that we evaluate places—to how collective influences inform our perceptions. While people see their views as based on evaluations of objective conditions, these perceptions are intricately woven into the very mechanics of our communities, the collective interests of their residents, and perceptions of space that reflect these interests. People hold differing spatial understandings that fit their position in an unequal system. One way that this inequality manifests itself is through physical division and isolation, which urban reputations reinforce. Capturing a wide array of the community's voices, and understanding their views as grounded in collective interests, were central to this discovery.

The idea that very knowledgeable people hold such distorted understandings of urban space may seem counterintuitive. We tend to think of those who intimately know a place's good and bad areas as informed and shrewd (that is, "good") city dwellers. They are skilled at carefully negotiating urban space. Conversely, we may see the views of Ogden's Latino immigrants, blissfully wandering through inner city neighborhoods, as hopelessly naïve and even foolhardy. Yet, such a view mistakes perceptions of places for the undisputed reality of these areas, and it uncritically takes the side of the higher status and offhandedly dismisses the views of those with a lower status. Indeed, Ogden's

Latino immigrants tended to have much more impartial and nuanced understandings of the city than outsiders and native residents, both of whom relied on crude divisions between good and bad areas. The image of the "good" city negotiator actually encourages unfamiliarity and ignorance. Such people learn, and teach others, to avoid large sections of cities.

Readers also may conclude that negative assessments of Ogden by regional white and Mormon outsiders, or native resident insiders, make them "racists." Yet, such individual level assessments of people's personalities are irrelevant to this collective-level analysis.[1] Just as our personal opinions of poor and rich people do little to maintain or upend systems of social class, this system of social and spatial division has little to do with any individual's feelings about various racial groups. As Nicholas Christakis and James Fowler state, "You cannot understand a traffic jam by interrogating one person fuming at the wheel of the car, even though his immobile automobile contributes to the problem."[2]

Discovering the collective patterns and processes underlying Ogden's reputation was an eclectic and interdisciplinary pursuit, synthesizing research on deviance, historical continuity, immigration, place marketing, race and ethnicity, reputations, and urban studies, along with a unique immersive method for capturing the voices of residents. This more extensive theoretical and methodological approach suggests that researchers should keep their eyes open to the idiosyncratic forces shaping a phenomenon. Instead of framing the study under a single topic—such as "social class," "race," or "immigration"—and treating other factors as secondary, I integrated these issues under an umbrella term that I simply called "status." Had I followed the thread of existing research on disreputable places, only considering the economic and political forces shaping Ogden, or how residents adjusted their attitudes and behaviors based on these influences, I would have missed the multiple dynamics underlying Ogden's reputation.

Second, when viewed through a cultural lens that focuses on meanings, symbols, and perceptions, there is a moral dimension to urban reputations. These perceptions rest on designations of "good" and "bad" places, and they are intimately tied to designations of "good" and "bad" people. Efforts by the higher status to distance themselves from disreputable *places* are intertwined with efforts to distance themselves from disreputable *populations*, who they often see as immoral and incompetent. Thus, definitions of places, characteristics of people, and inequality are all intertwined.

At a deeper level, urban reputations reflect and influence how we perceive and negotiate reality, shaping engrained aspects of our collective consciousness. These cultural ideas help to mold the very boundaries of our moral order, affecting where we live, work, and play, with whom we interact, what we see as keys to success or threats to our safety, as well as the very construction of ourselves as upstanding or stigmatized. They are much more than simply the result of assessments of conditions, inequalities emerging from large-scale institutions, or top-down directives by elites and other authorities.

This approach to urban reputations, grounded in moral assessments, is a step toward reintroducing cultural explanations into the study of marginalized people and their communities. The focus on structural forces shaping disreputable places, and a neglect of cultural factors, is rooted in the history of urban studies. Following critiques of "culture of poverty" arguments from the 1950s and 1960s,[3] which understood people's marginalized status as partially the product of their own ideas and behaviors, urban researchers largely abandoned cultural explanations for fear of "victim blaming."[4] Yet, this evasion has not eliminated either culture or victim blaming. Current explanations of disreputable places tend to invoke culture in indirect ways, especially when understanding the (cultural) stigma of people as a reaction to (structural) conditions in their communities. Ultimately, these approaches view the residents of disreputable places, although forcefully pushed by institutions that impose isolation and deprivation, as generating the bulk of the internal disorder that stigmatizes them.

While the subsequent turn away from culture, and toward structural arguments, shied away from researching the cultures *of the insider residents* of disreputable places, this study brings back a cultural explanation by focusing on the cultures *of outsiders*. Instead of looking internally at a connection between deprivation, disorder, and disrepute within a place, I consider the external mechanisms that shape a community's bad reputation. This is not a culture of poverty argument about how insiders maintain their lowly status. Instead, outsider populations, who already have great privilege and benefits, uphold a "culture of abundance," self-serving understandings that further distance themselves from lower-status people. A place's bad reputation is one such understanding. Even as outsiders maintain these divisions through constant and aggressive vigilance, they tend to see such boundaries as spontaneous and even natural.

Third, this view of urban reputations shifts the focus of research on disreputable places away from analyses of internal environments. Urban studies have long focused on the problems found within ghettos, cataloguing their deficits in intimate detail. When explaining how these places become disreputable, they switch this lens to broad economic and political institutions such as governments, corporations, and the mass media. Such forces are important, but a focus on local contexts reveals how the bad reputations of places are not just the passive result of large-scale influences that help generate disordered conditions and then negative evaluations. Ogden's reputation developed and continued through regional patterns of culture, demographics, history, and other influences. It was interwoven into the commonsense understandings, moral standards, and everyday routines of residents and regional locals. Researchers virtually ignore the regional communities surrounding disreputable places, despite how they are so crucial to explaining urban reputations.

More specifically, this study challenges assumptions that urban reputations and feelings of "territorial stigmatization"[5] are more-or-less automatic outcomes of a community's internal disorder. As Ogden's Latino immigrants' wholesale rejection of a stigmatized status and the negative reputation of their neighborhoods especially reveals, these meanings can greatly shift between people while conditions remain the same. Not only were perceptions of place disconnected from the disorder found there, those who had the least experience with a place's conditions were the most likely to promote its bad reputation.

This focus on local influence led to an expanded analysis that produced new conceptual tools. Along with incorporating ideas from existing research, such as micro-differentiations, moral panics, and boundary blurring, I have developed multiple concepts—*culture of abundance, collective forgetfulness, historical echoes, moral inversions,* and of course, *moral frontiers.* These ideas helped to explain Ogden's reputation, but they also should be useful for others seeking to understand how definitions of places, like definitions of anything else, are collective and shifting constructions grounded in collective interests (moral frontiers); how higher-status people have more power to shape these ideas by producing or amplifying certain aspects of reality (culture of abundance) and obscuring others (collective forgetfulness); how historical circumstances of continuity and change also shape these ideas (historical echoes); and how people can challenge these prevailing views (moral inversions).

Finally, the perspective of moral frontiers suggests very different solutions for disreputable reputations. Understandings that link disrepute with disorder, while well intentioned, have encouraged policies that further criminalize, demean, and even erase the already marginalized populations living in disreputable places. By shifting the focus of these interventions—and research that legitimates them—away from the victims of oppression to those who are responsible for it, this study suggests less vindictive ways to understand and confront the problem of urban reputations. Given these insights, I suggested two modest ways that the city of Ogden could change its regional reputation, while noting the potential drawbacks of doing so.

I have a feeling that this book will make few local readers happy, as it incriminates most everyone—and especially those who see themselves as "good people"—as participants in a hostile and oppressive system. While Latino immigrants are largely spared from this criticism, this is only because just about everyone else vilifies them! Yet, my hope is that these harsh words contain the beginnings of a more just, equal, and unified world. This study speaks to the promise and possibilities of a different way of doing things, which begins with a different way of *seeing* things—a shift in perspective from disorder to boundaries.

## FROM DISORDER TO BOUNDARIES

In closing, recognizing urban reputations as moral frontiers necessitates widening our focus beyond analyzing the internal deprivation and disorder within disreputable places, the large-scale forces that generate these conditions, or how residents adjust to this reality. This means exploring reputations as cultural ideas, shaped by regional contexts that help to reproduce a place's reputation day after day. Such a focus underscores how understandings of place can change, even without any shifts in conditions or residents. If urban reputations are built on ideas that powerful outsiders shape in order to reinforce their status, people can transform these symbols in ways that lessen these divisions and unify people.

Maybe most significantly, this change in perspective from disorder to boundaries involves a move away from ideas that draw from—and benefit—dominant populations. Despite the fundamental ambiguity underlying perceptions of place, we tend to accept outsiders' negative understandings of disreputable areas, as well as the assumption that these places are bad based on the conditions found there, and disregard insiders' positive assessments. Regional locals and other outsiders adopt this collective consensus to actively maintain the boundaries separating themselves from disreputable places and their residents. Urban researchers also adopt these views, assuming them as fact, even as the outsider populations most responsible for them are largely absent from studies.

This analytical blind spot further benefits outsiders and hurts the residents of disreputable places. When removed from its perpetrators, the responsibility of a place's bad reputation falls onto the backs of its victims. Not only do current understandings remove outsiders from any accountability for constructing these harmful perceptions of place, they also direct us away from workable solutions to the problem. Stemming from this thinking are attempts to better the image of disreputable places through interventions that target conditions, but these are destructive, "scorched earth"-style solutions. While campaigns against disorder do improve perceptions of places, they tend to do this through invasive actions such as aggressive policing, mass incarceration, redevelopment, and gentrification. We all pay for these expensive and misguided interventions—which amplify racial and class inequality, deplete public funds, swell our prisons, displace long-established residents, and destroy the unique heritage of these places—based on our misunderstandings of the phenomenon.

Researchers and other authorities should stop being fooled by this symbolic sleight of hand, as it is extremely costly in human lives and resources. To change their collective ways, they would do well to listen to the voices of insiders and fully capture their humanity. When considering the residents of disreputable areas, studies often focus on the drug dealer, gang member, homeless person, thief, and other rare outliers, with few representations of these communities offering rich pictures of their residents.[6] As Mario Luis Small asks: "Low-income minorities have no monopoly on social difficulties. Middle-class whites are routinely represented as more than the sum of their problems. Why not they?"[7] Researchers' depictions reinforce beliefs that these communities, through their residents' antisocial and unlawful actions, are fundamentally broken and tragic. Outsider populations, with limited experience of disreputable places, have little ability to evaluate how these images of reality—backed by scientific authority—are extremely narrow and overwhelmingly negative.

Adopting the perspective of moral frontiers involves rethinking, and even inverting, many of our current understandings about urban areas in general and their reputations in particular. It involves viewing disreputable areas and their reputations as a problem of outsiders, not their residents. It also suggests interventions that focus on transforming dominant groups, not marginalized communities. Instead of portraying the marginalized as isolated, oppositional, and hostile, this thinking should be inverted. It is dominant populations that separate themselves from others, oppose sharing their spoils, and enforce these positions through harsh measures. One way that they accomplish this is through symbolic boundaries—including negative and self-serving views of the places where people who are lower status than them live.

Backed by powerful interests, exhibiting a reflexivity that tends to swallow any challenges, and currently resolved with aggressive solutions that are arguably worse for their residents than the original problems, urban reputations are certainly stubborn ideas. Yet, there are strategies for overcoming them, and these solutions begin with understanding what urban reputations are and how they work. After recognizing the roots of these spatial divisions, we then can do symbolic work to unify the boundaries between communities. Instead of encouraging punitive interventions against conditions, further harming the residents of disparaged places, a focus on boundaries suggests solutions that foster connections and unification, counteracting the collective interests and benefits that people gain from separation. While this path forward is daunting, filled with its own setbacks and unintended consequences, such new directions have the potential to crack through these seemingly permanent partitions between people.

# EPILOGUE

## Exploring Ogden

Ogden is a fascinating place to consider urban reputations. Indeed, the city has characteristics that mirror trends in the rest of the United States. By being a new immigrant destination, it is experiencing the effect of global shifts in economics and work, as well as people blown by those worldwide winds. At the same time, these shifts in the demographic landscape of the city are happening to a place with a distinct history. Ogden is certainly not representative of the rest of the country. It is far from a typical all-American city—or even a typical disreputable place.

Yet, the very idea of studying a representative city—or a representative ghetto—rests on conceptual error. Clifford Geertz calls the idea of a homogenous, mainstream America and a town that encapsulates that mainstream—often the explicit or implicit lesson of urban studies—the "Jonesville-is-the-U.S.A." fallacy. "The notion that one can find the essence of national societies, civilizations, great religions, or whatever summed up and simplified in so-called 'typical' small towns and villages is palpable nonsense."[1] Conceptualizing cities as ahistorical, homogenous, and single-minded entities is a hindrance, not a benefit, to understanding urban areas.

Indeed, Ogden is a unique place, and its distinct past and present are crucial to explaining its reputation. I began this research with an appreciation of this uniqueness, starting with the twin observations that Ogden has a bad reputation among many people, seemingly far beyond—and even contradicting—any measurements of crime and other problems, and the city has recently undergone a huge shift in its demographics from Latino immigrants. I had a hunch that recent Latino immigrants were leading to a decline in Ogden's image. Yet, I discovered a much more complicated dynamic that encompassed the entire region and more than a century of its history.

Studying Ogden involved a number of methods. In order to capture urban perceptions among residents of Ogden, I employed a modified version of a technique called a "go-along." Margarethe Kusenbach introduced the method as "an ethnographic research tool that brings to the foreground some of the transcendent and reflexive aspects of lived experience as grounded in place."[2] Go-alongs involve interviewing a person as they move around an area.

> When conducting go-alongs, fieldworkers accompany individual informants on their "natural" outings, and—through asking questions, listening and observing—actively explore their subjects' stream of experiences and practices as they move through, and interact with, their physical and social environment.[3]

My version of the go-along was a bit more formal than this, as I structured it around interviewees encountering much of the city of Ogden.

The go-along method fits the informal and emergent model of qualitative studies, in that data collection builds inductively from a social phenomenon rather than imposing a framework onto it.[4] As Kusenbach explains, the technique draws equally from ethnographic and qualitative interviewing practices. Like an interview, it involves a one-on-one discussion between investigator and respondent. Like ethnography, researchers immerse themselves into an environment, and they capture the meanings of subjects while in that context. This method allows respondents to witness and describe place while in that environment, as opposed to being asked to artificially invoke it (as with traditional interviews or surveys) or address only a narrow slice of it (as with the conventional ethnographic field site).

Additionally, this project—utilizing the efforts of local respondents, interviewers, historians, and other experts—was completed with the help of the community. Among other local support, I accomplished some of this research, buying supplies and hiring assistants to interview, transcribe, and translate, with the help of funds from an internal university grant financed by a local donor. While of course the residents being interviewed were part of the community, often the interviewers were as well. These people especially acted as bridges between myself and this world. I am especially grateful for their help in accessing Ogden's Latino immigrant community and recruiting subjects from this population.

I had research assistants recruit residents of Ogden for these interviews, where they asked the respondents to talk about areas of the city while they traveled through them. In order to make the interview approximate an informal conversation, as well as out of concerns of safety, interviewers chose respondents for this study by snowball method, generally drawing from friends and acquaintances, or friends of friends and acquaintances. Although this is not a representative sample, the research assistants—supervised by myself—strategically chose respondents to reflect the diversity of age, gender, race, religion, and social class in the city.

Along with these characteristics, interviewers recruited people purposefully from two main categories: native residents and Latino immigrants. Native residents were whites, Latinos, and those of other races who have mostly grown up in the city, region, or elsewhere the United States. The immigrants were first-generation Latinos who were born abroad and came to the city after their childhood. I separated "1.5 generation" immigrants, those who came to the United States at an early age and were socialized and assimilated here, from this group. Indeed, these respondents matched native residents in their perceptions much more than they matched first-generation immigrants. In the end, I analyzed sixty-four interviews, twenty-nine with native whites, fifteen with native Latinos, thirteen with Latino immigrants, as well as four with black respondents and three with Asian respondents.

I required that the go-alongs travel through each of six main areas of the city. To help both interviewer and respondent navigate these neighborhoods, I provided them with a map, and I asked the research assistants to mark the course that they took on it. While not fitting official boundaries of census tracts or neighborhood designations, these areas—the East Bench, Shadow Valley, central city, the downtown Central Business District, West Ogden, and Northern Ogden—were informal divisions that residents instantly recognized. They fit the "natural" borders that people used in their understandings of the city, as well as when negotiating its spaces. This way of dividing the city was a mixture of objective and subjective definitions of this space.[5] The objective boundaries were the official city limits. The subjective boundaries were the six neighborhoods within the city.

This research design submerged respondents into the environment of the city, and as much as possible, I had the respondent set the agenda. Whenever feasible, they would drive and create the route. I trained interviewers to ask open-ended questions (specifically "How do you feel about this area?" and "What do you like/dislike?"), as well as ask probing questions when respondents gave brief responses. Additionally, they asked respondents what they liked and disliked most about Ogden as a whole. Research assistants also asked residents about basic demographic information, including race, gender, age, religion, occupation, and the length of time that they had lived in Ogden. I trained interviewers to remain as neutral as possible, not volunteering strong opinions or otherwise guiding the conversation. I did *not* initially inform interviewers about the wider aims of the study, as I quickly found that this led a few of them to steer the conversation and ask leading questions.

Despite a few missteps, this minimal prompting generated the respondents' accounts that were reproduced throughout the book but especially in Part Two of the study—Chapters Four through Six. I found the respondents surprisingly outspoken, suggesting that they were comfortable enough in this situation to openly state their feelings. Their candid mentions of race and the reputation of Ogden were largely "spontaneous"—not specifically provoked by anything more than the most basic and neutral of questions.

Research assistants recorded these interviews onto digital audio, and they transcribed them (and translated them from Spanish to English, if needed). I did periodic checks of the accuracy of these transcripts by comparing them to the audio recordings. I then began analysis by "open coding" the transcripts, looking for broad patterns in order to develop theory, as fitting the grounded theory method.[6] I formed various categories and placed mentions of those topics into each of the groupings, developing more and more specific analyses out of these general topics. In the segments of interviews quoted throughout the book, I used dashes ("—") to show pauses or ungrammatical phrases, while ellipses ("...") show where I had cut text.

Along with go-along interviews, I also drew upon secondary sources, primarily histories of Ogden and Utah, but also historical documents, newspaper articles, and a community survey. Additionally, I used data from the U.S. Census, FBI crime statistics, and other sources. This methodological elaboration and triangulation provided me with a deep and multidimensional picture of the city that both complemented and contested the findings of go-along interviews. Ethnographic and qualitative research is often narrow and ahistorical, as those using the method struggle to include wider contexts.[7] It also tends to be based solely in the present day, or it presents historical circumstances as a "background" onto which the authors paint their study.[8] In this research, I used the broader contexts and history of Ogden as a "foreground" player in the action, an analytic component that shapes current conditions in important ways.

## THE BENEFITS AND LIMITATIONS OF GO-ALONGS

The go-along method offers several benefits for studying Ogden. Most importantly, it captures the voices of residents while they are immersed in the contexts of a city. The open-ended style of go-alongs allows for capturing the perspectives of residents, and they document how those perspectives change between different people. These voices reveal multiple, varied, and even contradictory views of urban space, instead of imposing an overarching view of the city based on depictions from marketing and the mass media or a researcher's singular interpretation. Indeed, I quickly learned that representations such as Ogden's cheery promotions of itself, or conversely how I thought that the city's bad reputation was something that every resident knew, were not to be trusted as a complete and definitive image of Ogden.

Additionally, the method makes the setting an integral part of the research process. A basic finding of social science is that people think and act differently while in different environments. Despite this, many studies ask people to artificially invoke urban contexts while removed from these places. These techniques include surveys and interviews given off-site, as well as having subjects react to cards depicting various types of neighborhoods or watch videos of fictional residents. In these instances, researchers ask respondents to imagine a place, reacting to an artificial and often hypothetical scenario. While researchers often understand these methods, and their distance from the places being studied, as a more consistent and rigorous way of doing research, the setting where research is conducted shapes how people respond. The go-along method, while also artificial, comes closer to approximating the "natural" experiences that respondents would have in this place and their "normal" responses while interacting with those familiar to them.

The format of go-alongs is grounded in emergence and informality, allowing the flexibility to uncover perceptions while in urban settings. While there were set questions, interviews often took the form of conversations, with both interviewer and respondent relaxed and discussing the scenery as they might in their everyday travels with friends. Occasionally, this made for a kind of "double interview," where both respondent and interviewer were contributing data to the project.

This naturalistic method also may uncover understandings about cities that would be hidden in other methods. Feelings about urban space often happen at an unconscious level, with residents not knowing what places they value, or even that they value those places, until these are pointed out to them. To unearth submerged feelings of connection, studies evaluate how people "use" a city as well as how they feel about changes to urban space.[9] Documenting where residents go (but also where they do not go), what they do (and what they do not do), is important to understanding how they perceive that city. Methods where people are removed from these environments miss capturing this dimension of urban perceptions.

Furthermore, studying how a wide range of residents consider a number of neighborhoods provided clues to understanding the mechanisms behind inequality, especially racial divisions. As Camille Charles puts it:

> Qualitative analyses—whether from elaborations to closed-ended questions or in-depth interviews—represent another direction for future research. The next logical step in this case is to explore the attitudes, perceptions, and justifications of Hispanics and Asians for their neighborhood racial composition preferences; this is particularly important for capturing the importance of immigration-related characteristics.[10]

How people—white, minority, and immigrant—choose to live (or not live) in certain areas and how they frequent or avoid certain areas of cities over others for shopping, recreation, and other everyday activities are tied to patterns that privilege some groups of people while disadvantaging others. The go-alongs revealed how people formulated preferences that underlie such divisions and inequalities, a rare pursuit in urban studies.

At the same time, the informal nature of go-alongs, coupled with the "amateur" status of interviewers, also had limitations. A main limitation was that I did not capture the voices of nonresident outsiders. Although this is unfortunate, I feel that the responses of Ogden's residents, in addition to secondary sources, provided ample evidence of the overwhelmingly negative feelings about the city in the region. (At a talk that I gave in Ogden about this research, a man told me that, since moving there from out of state a few months before, people had warned him to move out of the city *seven different times*.) Future research on this key population can fill this gap. As research on disreputable places almost always focuses on their residents, when I first designed this study I never would have imagined that outsiders would end up being so important to my argument.

An additional limitation is that this is not a representative sample of Ogden residents. This has the danger of introducing sample bias, as I did not choose respondents at random. Indeed, the respondents were often friends, family, or acquaintances of the interviewers. Most of the interviewers were undergraduate college students. Yet, there were many interviewers (twenty-eight in total) of greatly varying backgrounds, and I carefully monitored their recruitment so that it captured a wide variety of people. In the end, the respondents largely mirrored the wider demographics of Ogden in terms of age, gender, educational attainment, occupation, race, and religion. Also, the findings of these interviews corresponded with other sources. For example, how insider residents of Ogden thought highly of their community in contrast to the views of outsiders, as well as how many practice "micro-differentiation" to further divide themselves, fit the findings of other research about disreputable places. Also, how Latino immigrants find the city safe and welcoming mirrored the results of a large community survey of Ogden.[11] This suggests that the patterns emerging from these interviews were not simply the quirks of a unique sample.

Furthermore, the informality of the go-along veers from models of social science research that privilege clearly defined research protocols and data-gathering techniques that distance researchers from researched. In such traditions, data is "biased" by the interjections and emotions of the interviewer. While I feel that the ethnographic style of these interviews—embracing informality and familiarity—added much to the richness of the data, this method also had drawbacks. As I mentioned above, a limitation of this method was that interviewers—despite their training—occasionally went "off script," asking leading questions or inserting topics that steered the conversation. I avoided including responses elicited through these techniques in my analysis, although some examples of this—such as an immigrant respondent insisting that Ogden was not dangerous despite the interviewer's continued prompting—were very informative.

Another issue was how the clear-cut and objective designations of official city limits butted against how residents imagined and constructed these borders. Such geographical messiness can generate problems. As Elizabeth Campbell, Julia Henly, Delbert Elliott, and Katherine Irwin state: "A researcher's characterization of the social, organizational, and cultural capacity of a neighborhood, its level of disorganization, or its cohesiveness, depends on where the neighborhood's boundaries are drawn a priori. If these initial boundaries miss the mark, the study findings may be misleading."[12]

Many interviewers and respondents were surprised at Ogden's objective borders, as their own understandings of city limits were fuzzy, at best. This is not surprising given their amoeba-like shape. Ogden's city boundaries wander along railroad lines and between various roads in seemingly random ways that do not fit the understandings of residents. According to maps, areas of Ogden city seem to surround places that are not Ogden city, creating an oasis of unincorporated land. Further complicating this is how two completely independent cities—North Ogden and South Ogden—adjoin and share the name "Ogden." Despite my attempts to avoid this by giving the interviewers maps, respondents and interviewers alike were unclear as to where Ogden proper ends and neighboring cities begin. As my research specifically considered Ogden's six main neighborhoods, I did exclude discussions about places that were clearly outside of these boundaries.

While many of these limitations are regrettable, I feel that the benefits of this innovative method of data collection far outweigh them. As I explained above, I designed the study, like the original method of the "go-along," to be a combination of interviews and ethnography that embraces, instead of attempting to artificially constrain, the informal, interactional, emergent, and just plain messy aspects of social life. While I agree that researchers should be careful about how they understand and circumscribe neighborhoods, I also feel that fuzzy and shifting meanings reflect the inherently social constructed nature of all spaces. Thus, for example, I understood how the go-along went a bit south of 36th Street into the city of South Ogden, as these boundaries were unclear in people's minds.

# APPENDIX

## Ogden's Crime Rates

In interviews, Ogden residents compared their city with nearby Salt Lake City, often understanding Salt Lake City as the less dangerous, or at least perceived to be less dangerous, of the two towns. They also compared the city with other places, often arguing that crime in Ogden was not as bad as its reputation suggests. Thus, this appendix compares Ogden's crime rates, based on the FBI Uniform Crime Reports, with those of Salt Lake City and nationally. The police departments of these cities report crimes to the FBI, and the FBI also makes a national estimate based on a combination of these local measures. These rates provide a way to evaluate claims about these places and their relative crime and disorder. For clarity while swimming through this sea of numbers, I have noted where Ogden's crime rates are higher than national and Salt Lake City rates.

Yet, I urge a strong word of caution when considering this data based on self-reports from law enforcement agencies. There are multiple problems with assessing these images of reality against any actuality of crime in an area.[1] Maybe the most basic issue is how those who report crimes—the police—usually do not witness them happening, leading to fundamental problems when determining what "really" occurred. Also, political mandates and funding concerns—such as differing budgets, local crackdowns, or resources for drug or gang interventions—shape crime numbers. Ogden's law enforcement includes special funding for gang units and SWAT teams, and the city even floated the idea of a crime-fighting blimp.[2] Additionally, what officials deem as deviant influences crime rates, tilting numbers in favor of stopping, questioning, searching, arresting, and sentencing minority and lower-class offenders.[3] These factors artificially skew rates upward for places like Ogden—where there is a relatively large proportion of poor and Latino residents, as well as tough and even repressive interventions against perceived problems of drugs and gangs.[4] A further problem may be the reports themselves, as they are only as good as the measurement and bookkeeping of these various agencies. Returning to Emile Durkheim's classic insights, mentioned in the introductory chapter, crime rates reflect patterns of definition and regulation as much as they reflect patterns of deviance.[5]

There also are issues with making comparisons between different places. Among other concerns, the population of Salt Lake City is about two and a half times that of Ogden, and larger cities generally have more crime than smaller ones. The FBI even posts a warning against making such comparisons on its website. Thus, evaluating crime in these two cities is not a good, or even fair, appraisal. Again, this comparison emerged from interviews, as Ogden's residents reported that they and others see their community as the most dangerous place in the region.

Even considering such issues, these crime rates do reveal several patterns. Ogden's law enforcement does not report an especially large amount of crime, especially when compared to Salt Lake City. In fact, Ogden's rates—violent as well as property—fall between 60 and 90 percent of those of Salt Lake. Also, reports of violent crime in Ogden have remained largely constant, while reports of property crime have fallen dramatically—from almost five times the national rate in the mid-1980s to lower than the national rate today. Today, Ogden may not be a safer place for its residents, but it seems to be safer for their possessions. Additionally, sexual assault seems to be a pressing problem facing Ogden's residents. Although rates of rape are especially high in the city, law enforcement seems to underemphasize this. Instead, they pursue and publicize campaigns against other issues, especially gangs.

Table A.1. Ogden Reported and United States Estimated Violent Crime Rate per 100,000 Residents, 1985–2014

| Year | Murder and non-negligent manslaughter | | Rape | | Robbery | | Aggravated assault | | Total | |
|---|---|---|---|---|---|---|---|---|---|---|
| | Ogden | U.S. | Ogden | U.S. | Ogden | U.S. | Ogden | U.S. | Ogden | U.S. |
| 1985 | **11.5** | 8 | **66** | 36.8 | 130.6 | 209.3 | 254 | 304 | 462 | 558.1 |
| 1986 | 4.4 | 8.6 | **71.3** | 38.1 | 168.8 | 226 | 224 | 347.4 | 468.5 | 620.1 |
| 1987 | **8.8** | 8.3 | 72 | 37.6 | 135.1 | 213.7 | 189.5 | 352.9 | 405.4 | 612.5 |
| 1988 | **11.7** | 8.5 | **59.8** | 37.8 | 132.7 | 222.1 | 172.1 | 372.2 | 376.3 | 640.6 |
| 1989 | 9 | 8.7 | **62.7** | 38.3 | 143.3 | 234.3 | 265.7 | 385.6 | 480.6 | 666.9 |
| 1990 | 1.6 | 9.4 | 72 | 41.1 | 103.3 | 256.3 | 333.3 | 422.9 | 510.1 | 729.6 |
| 1991 | 3 | 9.8 | **85.3** | 42.3 | 146.2 | 272.7 | 322.9 | 433.4 | 557.4 | 758.2 |
| 1992 | 8.9 | 9.3 | **66.9** | 42.8 | 145.7 | 263.7 | 319.7 | 441.9 | 541.2 | 757.7 |
| 1993 | 8.8 | 9.5 | **61.7** | 41.1 | 144.1 | 256 | 373.4 | 440.5 | 588 | 747.1 |
| 1994 | 4.3 | 9 | **60.2** | 39.3 | 159.1 | 237.8 | 331 | 427.6 | 554.6 | 713.6 |
| 1995 | 7.2 | 8.2 | **44.7** | 37.1 | 164.5 | 220.9 | 392.6 | 418.3 | 609 | 684.5 |
| 1996 | 7 | 7.4 | **80.2** | 36.3 | 143.6 | 201.9 | 306.9 | 391 | 537.8 | 636.6 |
| 1997 | 5.5 | 6.8 | **77.9** | 35.9 | 145 | 186.2 | 303.6 | 382.1 | 532 | 611 |
| 1998 | **10.3** | 6.3 | **101.3** | 34.5 | **183.5** | 165.5 | 339.2 | 361.4 | **634.3** | 567.6 |
| 1999 | **8.9** | 5.7 | 80 | 32.8 | **167.5** | 150.1 | **373.6** | 334.3 | 630 | 523 |
| 2000 | 7.8 | 5.5 | **102.3** | 32 | **178.7** | 145 | 284.9 | 324 | **573.6** | 506.5 |
| 2001 | **11.5** | 5.6 | **67.5** | 31.8 | 133.8 | 148.5 | 243.3 | 318.6 | 456.1 | 504.5 |
| 2002 | **6.2** | 5.6 | **111.1** | 33.1 | 116.1 | 146.1 | **357.1** | 309.5 | **590.5** | 494.4 |
| 2003 | 2.5 | 5.7 | **61.4** | 32.3 | 116.5 | 142.5 | **310.6** | 295.4 | **491** | 475.8 |
| 2004 | 5 | 5.5 | **42.7** | 32.4 | 134.5 | 136.7 | 256.5 | 288.6 | 438.8 | 463.2 |
| 2005 | **6.2** | 5.6 | **49.3** | 31.8 | **149.1** | 140.8 | 267.4 | 290.8 | **471.9** | 469 |
| 2006 | 2.5 | 5.8 | **45.8** | 31.6 | **152.1** | 150 | **312.9** | 292 | **513.2** | 479.3 |
| 2007 | 3.8 | 5.7 | **47.3** | 30.6 | **175.3** | 148.3 | **422.2** | 287.2 | **648.7** | 471.8 |
| 2008 | 4.8 | 5.4 | **51.6** | 29.8 | **153.6** | 145.9 | 255.5 | 277.5 | **465.5** | 458.6 |
| 2009 | 4.8 | 5 | **39.8** | 29.1 | 128.9 | 133.1 | **299.9** | 264.7 | **473.4** | 431.9 |
| 2010 | 1.2 | 4.8 | **30.2** | 27.7 | **134** | 119.3 | 233 | 252.8 | 398.4 | 404.5 |
| 2011 | 2.4 | 4.7 | 23.7 | 27 | 113.7 | 113.9 | **324.6** | 241.5 | **464.3** | 387.1 |
| 2012 | 2.4 | 4.7 | **29.4** | 27.1 | 112.8 | 113.1 | **270.3** | 242.8 | **414.9** | 387.8 |
| 2013 | 2.4 | 4.5 | **107.1** | 35.9 | **133.3** | 109 | **271.3** | 229.6 | **514** | 379.1 |
| 2014 | **4.7** | 4.5 | **105.3** | 36.6 | **133.6** | 102.2 | **294.5** | 232.5 | **538.1** | 375.7 |

(The numbers in bold are higher than the national rate.)
Source: FBI Uniform Crime Reports

Table A.2. Ogden and Salt Lake City Reported Violent Crime Rate per 100,000 Residents, 1985–2014

| Year | Murder and non-negligent manslaughter | | Rape | | Robbery | | Aggravated assault | | Total | |
|---|---|---|---|---|---|---|---|---|---|---|
| | Ogden | S.L.C. | Ogden | S.L.C. | Ogden | S.L.C. | Ogden | S.L.C. | Ogden | S.L.C. |
| 1985 | **11.5** | 8.5 | **66** | 60.3 | 130.6 | 271.6 | 254 | 319.1 | 462 | 659.5 |
| 1986 | 4.4 | 12 | **71.3** | 64.4 | 168.8 | 304.5 | 224 | 368.9 | 468.5 | 749.8 |
| 1987 | **8.8** | 8.1 | **72** | 58.8 | 135.1 | 301.6 | 189.5 | 313.4 | 405.4 | 681.9 |
| 1988 | **11.7** | 9.3 | **59.8** | 55.6 | 132.7 | 300.6 | 172.1 | 274.1 | 376.3 | 639.5 |
| 1989 | 9 | 11.7 | 62.7 | 88.1 | 143.3 | 313.7 | 265.7 | 362.3 | 480.6 | 775.7 |
| 1990 | 1.6 | 15.6 | 72 | 104.4 | 103.3 | 337 | 333.3 | 390.2 | 510.1 | 847.2 |
| 1991 | 3 | 8.5 | 85.3 | 110.8 | 146.2 | 288.5 | 322.9 | 395 | 557.4 | 802.7 |
| 1992 | **8.9** | 8.3 | 66.9 | 111.1 | 145.7 | 279.3 | 319.7 | 383.8 | 541.2 | 782.5 |
| 1993 | 8.8 | 11.2 | 61.7 | 119.7 | 144.1 | 292.3 | 373.4 | 399.7 | 588 | 822.9 |
| 1994 | 4.3 | 11.4 | 60.2 | 90.4 | 159.1 | 287.1 | 331 | 366.1 | 554.6 | 755 |
| 1995 | 7.2 | 15.4 | 44.7 | 84.2 | 164.5 | 320.9 | **392.6** | 361.8 | 609 | 782.3 |
| 1996 | 7 | 11.1 | 80.2 | 84.4 | 143.6 | 328 | 306.9 | 409.6 | 537.8 | 833.1 |
| 1997 | 5.5 | 11.3 | **77.9** | 76 | 145 | 334.1 | 303.6 | 369.2 | 532 | 790.6 |
| 1998 | **10.3** | 9 | **101.3** | 81.8 | 183.5 | 334.9 | 339.2 | 394.8 | 634.3 | 820.4 |
| 1999 | 8.9 | 9 | 80 | 83 | 167.5 | 274 | **373.6** | 344.6 | 630 | 710.7 |
| 2000 | **7.8** | 5.5 | **102.3** | 75.4 | 178.7 | 316.9 | 284.9 | 318 | 573.6 | 715.8 |
| 2001 | **11.5** | 9.7 | **67.5** | 65.5 | 133.8 | 260.4 | 243.3 | 295.6 | 456.1 | 631.2 |
| 2002 | **6.2** | 5.8 | **111.1** | 58.4 | 116.1 | 253.6 | **357.1** | 339 | 590.5 | 656.7 |
| 2003 | 2.5 | 8.2 | **61.4** | 43.5 | 116.5 | 273.9 | 310.6 | 378.8 | 491 | 704.3 |
| 2004 | 5 | 7.7 | 42.7 | 50.9 | 134.5 | 253.9 | 256.5 | 414.7 | 438.8 | 727.2 |
| 2005 | **6.2** | 4.9 | **49.3** | 41.2 | 149.1 | 225.9 | 267.4 | 431.1 | 471.9 | 703 |
| 2006 | 2.5 | 4.4 | 45.8 | 51.7 | 152.1 | 276.2 | 312.9 | 485.6 | 513.2 | 817.8 |
| 2007 | 3.8 | 9.5 | 47.3 | 64.4 | 175.3 | 282.4 | 422.2 | 486.4 | 648.7 | 842.8 |
| 2008 | 4.8 | 6.6 | **51.6** | 42.1 | 153.6 | 269.2 | 255.5 | 470.9 | 465.5 | 788.9 |
| 2009 | **4.8** | 1.7 | 39.8 | 57 | 128.9 | 227.4 | 299.9 | 424.4 | 473.4 | 710.5 |
| 2010 | 1.2 | 4.3 | 30.2 | 78.8 | 134 | 192.6 | 233 | 418.4 | 398.4 | 694.1 |
| 2011 | 2.4 | 3.2 | 23.7 | 62.6 | 113.7 | 178.9 | 324.6 | 393.6 | 464.3 | 638.3 |
| 2012 | 2.4 | 4.2 | 29.4 | 63.4 | 112.8 | 164.2 | 270.3 | 443.7 | 414.9 | 675.4 |
| 2013 | 2.4 | 3.7 | 107.1 | 112 | 133.3 | 221.3 | 271.3 | 444.7 | 514 | 781.6 |
| 2014 | **4.7** | 3.6 | 105.3 | 115.9 | 133.6 | 233.4 | 294.5 | 401.8 | 538.1 | 754.8 |

(The numbers in bold are higher than the rate in Salt Lake City.)
Source: FBI Uniform Crime Reports

Table A.3. Ogden Reported and United States Estimated Property Crime Rate per 100,000 Residents, 1985–2014

| Year | Burglary | | Larceny-theft | | Motor vehicle theft | | Total | |
|---|---|---|---|---|---|---|---|---|
| | Ogden | U.S. | Ogden | U.S. | Ogden | U.S. | Ogden | U.S. |
| 1985 | **1,615.6** | 508.6 | **6,641.6** | 1,034.7 | **351.5** | 183 | **8,608.7** | 1,726.3 |
| 1986 | **1,721.1** | 518.9 | **7,063.2** | 1,045.4 | **408.8** | 183.6 | **9,193** | 1,747.9 |
| 1987 | **1,545.1** | 535.2 | **7,421.5** | 1,124.8 | **393.6** | 197.4 | **9,360.2** | 1,857.5 |
| 1988 | **1,444.1** | 576.4 | **6,695.2** | 1,219.1 | **318** | 216.6 | **8,457.2** | 2,012.1 |
| 1989 | **1,534.4** | 634.7 | **6,788.2** | 1,315.5 | **401.5** | 247.4 | **8,724** | 2,197.5 |
| 1990 | **1,242.4** | 662.7 | **6,942.7** | 1,329.3 | **384.9** | 256.8 | **8,570** | 2,248.8 |
| 1991 | **1,192.5** | 721 | **6,441** | 1,442.9 | **365.5** | 286.9 | **7,999** | 2,450.9 |
| 1992 | **1,281.7** | 826.6 | **6,474.2** | 1,575.8 | **362.8** | 334.1 | **8,118.7** | 2,736.5 |
| 1993 | **1,308.3** | 932.3 | **6,109.2** | 1,746.6 | 373.4 | 393 | **7,790.9** | 3,071.8 |
| 1994 | **1,233.8** | 984.1 | **6,415.6** | 1,930.9 | **455.7** | 436.2 | **8,105.1** | 3,351.3 |
| 1995 | **1,238.3** | 1,084.9 | **6,491.6** | 2,079.3 | **600.4** | 456.8 | **8,330.2** | 3,621 |
| 1996 | **1,305.1** | 1,163.5 | **6,643.7** | 2,145.5 | **571.6** | 459.8 | **8,520.3** | 3,768.8 |
| 1997 | **1,470.1** | 1,140.8 | **6,505.3** | 1,993.6 | **500.5** | 426.1 | **8,475.9** | 3,560.4 |
| 1998 | **1,387.6** | 1,222.5 | **6,371.3** | 2,071.9 | **515.4** | 442.6 | **8,274.4** | 3,737 |
| 1999 | 1,231.8 | 1,437.7 | **5,714.5** | 2,489.5 | 413.6 | 462.2 | **7,359.9** | 4,389.3 |
| 2000 | 1,105.8 | 1,532.1 | **4,972.4** | 2,804.8 | **503.7** | 473.7 | **6,582** | 4,810.7 |
| 2001 | 982.3 | 1,448.2 | **4,790.3** | 2,921.3 | 449.7 | 450 | **6,222.3** | 4,819.5 |
| 2002 | 1,141.1 | 1,419.8 | **4,375.8** | 2,729.9 | 549.3 | 451.9 | **6,066.2** | 4,601.7 |
| 2003 | 1,146.1 | 1,434.6 | **4,350.2** | 2,747.4 | **501** | 460.5 | **5,997.3** | 4,642.5 |
| 2004 | 1,008.2 | 1,511.9 | **4,929.3** | 2,999.1 | **535.6** | 505.6 | **6,473.1** | 5,016.6 |
| 2005 | 981.9 | 1,684.1 | **4,586.9** | 3,167 | **506.4** | 502.2 | **6,075.2** | 5,353.3 |
| 2006 | 1,014.1 | 1,647.2 | **4,666** | 3,135.3 | **539.2** | 474.1 | **6,219.3** | 5,256.5 |
| 2007 | 1,186 | 1,488 | **4,471.6** | 3,083.1 | **680.7** | 458.6 | **6,338.3** | 5,029.7 |
| 2008 | 843.4 | 1,338.7 | **3,810.3** | 2,871.3 | 419.9 | 431.1 | **5,073.6** | 4,641.1 |
| 2009 | 932.4 | 1,265.5 | **3,568** | 2,795.2 | 380.6 | 437.7 | **4,881** | 4,498.5 |
| 2010 | 1,046.8 | 1,291.7 | **4,218.5** | 2,911.2 | 377.9 | 463.5 | **5,643.2** | 4,666.4 |
| 2011 | 1,016.3 | 1,349.8 | **3,884** | 3,022.1 | 345.9 | 509.8 | **5,246.2** | 4,881.8 |
| 2012 | 862.7 | 1,335.7 | **3,585.9** | 3,095.4 | 253.9 | 531.9 | 4,702.5 | 4,963 |
| 2013 | 703.2 | 1,316.2 | **3,818.2** | 3,151.7 | 334.3 | 586.1 | 4,855.7 | 5,054 |
| 2014 | 643.4 | 1,283.6 | **3,422.5** | 3,189.6 | 326.4 | 634 | 4,392.3 | 5,107.1 |

(The numbers in bold are higher than the national rate.)
Source: FBI Uniform Crime Reports

## Table A.4. Ogden and Salt Lake City Reported Property Crime Rate per 100,000 Residents, 1985-2014

| Year | Burglary | | Larceny-theft | | Motor vehicle theft | | Total | |
|---|---|---|---|---|---|---|---|---|
| | Ogden | S.L.C. | Ogden | S.L.C. | Ogden | S.L.C. | Ogden | S.L.C. |
| 1985 | 1,615.6 | 2,437 | 6,641.6 | 7,843.9 | 351.5 | 652.2 | 8,608.7 | 10,933.2 |
| 1986 | 1,721.1 | 2,234.9 | 7,063.2 | 8,617.1 | 408.8 | 603 | 9,193 | 11,454.9 |
| 1987 | 1,545.1 | 2,500.6 | 7,421.5 | 9,298.7 | 393.6 | 577.5 | 9,360.2 | 12,376.8 |
| 1988 | 1,444.1 | 2,218.5 | 6,695.2 | 10,000.9 | 318 | 575.3 | 8,457.2 | 12,794.7 |
| 1989 | 1,534.4 | 2,497.7 | 6,788.2 | 10,051.6 | 401.5 | 790.6 | 8,724 | 13,339.9 |
| 1990 | 1,242.4 | 2,189 | 6,942.7 | 8,721.6 | 384.9 | 748.4 | 8,570 | 11,659 |
| 1991 | 1,192.5 | 2,105.7 | 6,441 | 8,886.7 | 365.5 | 884.9 | 7,999 | 11,877.3 |
| 1992 | 1,281.7 | 2,016.6 | 6,474.2 | 8,476.3 | 362.8 | 812.8 | 8,118.7 | 11,305.7 |
| 1993 | 1,308.3 | 1,656.9 | 6,109.2 | 7,530.8 | 373.4 | 819.9 | 7,790.9 | 10,007.6 |
| 1994 | 1,233.8 | 1,730.3 | 6,415.6 | 7,396.5 | 455.7 | 981.5 | 8,105.1 | 10,108.3 |
| 1995 | 1,238.3 | 1,678.4 | 6,491.6 | 8,799.8 | 600.4 | 1,321.7 | 8,330.2 | 11,799.8 |
| 1996 | 1,305.1 | 1,673.3 | 6,643.7 | 8,268.4 | 571.6 | 1,592.3 | 8,520.3 | 11,534 |
| 1997 | 1,470.1 | 1,568.8 | 6,505.3 | 7,731.5 | 500.5 | 1,611.4 | 8,475.9 | 10,911.7 |
| 1998 | 1,387.6 | 1,585.3 | 6,371.3 | 7,278 | 515.4 | 1,144.6 | 8,274.4 | 10,007.9 |
| 1999 | 1,231.8 | 1,267.7 | 5,714.5 | 7,300.2 | 413.6 | 1,042.3 | 7,359.9 | 9,610.2 |
| 2000 | 1,105.8 | 1,193.4 | 4,972.4 | 6,508.1 | 503.7 | 843.5 | 6,582 | 8,545 |
| 2001 | 982.3 | 1,195.8 | 4,790.3 | 6,171.9 | 449.7 | 899.7 | 6,222.3 | 8,267.5 |
| 2002 | 1,141.1 | 1,335.3 | 4,375.8 | 7,098 | 549.3 | 1,052 | 6,066.2 | 9,485.2 |
| 2003 | 1,146.1 | 1,283.5 | 4,350.2 | 6,785.1 | 501 | 1,047.7 | 5,997.3 | 9,116.3 |
| 2004 | 1,008.2 | 1,290.7 | 4,929.3 | 6,641.2 | 535.6 | 1,030.3 | 6,473.1 | 8,962.2 |
| 2005 | 981.9 | 1,182.4 | 4,586.9 | 6,328.4 | 506.4 | 1,132.6 | 6,075.2 | 8,643.4 |
| 2006 | 1,014.1 | 1,225.1 | 4,666 | 6,070.1 | 539.2 | 1,111.5 | 6,219.3 | 8,406.7 |
| 2007 | **1,186** | 1,150.5 | 4,471.6 | 6,281.9 | 680.7 | 1,115.7 | 6,338.3 | 8,548.1 |
| 2008 | 843.4 | 1,132.9 | 3,810.3 | 6,816.6 | 419.9 | 1,023.2 | 5,073.6 | 8,972.7 |
| 2009 | 932.4 | 1,202.9 | 3,568 | 6,028 | 380.6 | 799 | 4,881 | 8,029.9 |
| 2010 | 1,046.8 | 1,170.3 | 4,218.5 | 5,460.7 | 377.9 | 800.8 | 5,643.2 | 7,431.9 |
| 2011 | **1,016.3** | 872.5 | 3,884 | 5,080 | 345.9 | 781.9 | 5,246.2 | 6,734.4 |
| 2012 | 862.7 | 947.7 | 3,585.9 | 5,625.4 | 253.9 | 886.4 | 4,702.5 | 7,459.5 |
| 2013 | 703.2 | 1,095.4 | 3,818.2 | 6,031.1 | 334.3 | 995 | 4,855.7 | 8,121.6 |
| 2014 | 643.4 | 898.8 | 3,422.5 | 6,631 | 326.4 | 931 | 4,392.3 | 8,460.9 |

(The numbers in bold are higher than the rate in Salt Lake City.)
Source: FBI Uniform Crime Reports

# NOTES

## CHAPTER 1

1. Anholt, *Competitive Identity*; Anholt, *Places*; Hester, "Subconscious Landscapes"; Molotch, Freudenberg, and Paulson "History Repeats Itself."
2. For example, Chicago's high-crime areas make it internationally notorious as "the murder capital of America," an epicenter of violence. A 2013 European newspaper headline about a Belgian city proclaimed, "Rumes Isn't Another Chicago!" (Loerzel, "How the World").
3. Anderson "Iconic Ghetto"; Anderson, "White Space"; Arthurson, "Social Mix"; Kearns, Kearns, and Lawson, "Notorious Places"; Permentier, Bolt, and Van Ham, "Determinants of Neighbourhood"; Wacquant, "Territorial Stigmatization"; Wacquant, *Urban Outcasts*.
4. Anderson "Iconic Ghetto"; Anderson, "White Space"; Rios, *Punished*; Wacquant, "Territorial Stigmatization"; Wacquant, *Urban Outcasts*.
5. Arthurson, Darcy, and Rogers, "Televised Territorial Stigma"; Gieryn, "Space for Place"; Jones and Jackson, "'You Just Don't'"; Lewicka, "Place Attachment"; Trentelman, "Place Attachment."
6. Berger and Luckmann, *Social Construction*.
7. "Mormons" are followers of the prophet Joseph Smith, especially through the Church of Jesus Christ of Latter-day Saints. Church authorities announced in August 2018 that members should stop using the terms "LDS" and "Mormon," despite the ubiquity of these nicknames (even the church's main websites were named "lds.org" and "mormon.org") (Walsh, "Church"). Despite this, I still use the name "Mormon" because this is the most recognizable term for the church and its members. I certainly do not invoke it as a disrespectful expression.
8. Fetzer, "Tolstoy and Mormonism." As this source explains, the origin of this popular quote is questionable. It is based on a third-party description, written years after the event, of a conversation held between Tolstoy and a Mormon convert.
9. The term "Latino," like the population that it describes, is a social construction that reflects political struggles (Mora, *Making Hispanics*). As different people strongly prefer different terms—Latino, Hispanic, or descriptors of various nationalities (especially Chicano or Mexican in the western United States), no one expression will make every

reader happy. People also have made efforts to promote gender-neutral versions of this term, such as "Latin@" and more recently "Latinx."
10. Knight, "Outdoors."
11. *Los Angeles Times* (Lee, "In Quiet Ogden") and *Newsweek* (McGrath Goodman, "As Wealth Inequality"). While these reports relay how the city of Ogden has little income inequality, they actually use data from the much wider Ogden-Clearfield, Utah, Metropolitan Statistical Area. This area includes four counties, including Ogden's Weber County. Still, such national media reports, even if their methodological prowess is lacking, tend to positively portray the city.
12. Van Riper, "Best Cities."
13. Anderson et al., "Best Places."
14. Vandenack, "Ogden."
15. If Ogden was indeed a ghetto (Vandenack, "Ogden's Household Income"), if the central city was in decline (Vandenack, "Ogden"), what was Ogden's most dangerous neighborhood (Shaw, "Real Ogden"), and how the city's reputation is rooted in its history (Koch, "Ogden's Rough").
16. Vandenack, "Ogden."
17. Halling, "Ogden."
18. See Cresswell, *In Place*.
19. See, for example, Massey and Denton, *American Apartheid*; Sampson, *Great American City*; Wacquant, *Urban Outcasts*; Wilson, *Truly Disadvantaged*.
20. Exceptions include Barber, *Reno's Big Gamble*; Foster, *Stigma Cities*; Franzini et al., "Perceptions of Disorder"; Gragg, *Bright Light City*; Greenberg, *Branding New York*; Jones and Jackson, "'You Just Don't'"; Kaufman and Kaliner, "The Re-accomplishment"; Krysan, "Community Undesirability"; Krysan and Bader, "Perceiving the Metropolis"; Krysan et al., "Does Race Matter"; Sampson, "Disparity and Diversity"; Sampson and Raudenbush, "Seeing Disorder"; Sampson and Raudenbush, "Neighborhood Stigma."
21. Arthurson, "Social Mix"; Arthurson, Darcy, and Rogers, "Televised Territorial Stigma"; Jensen and Christensen, "Territorial Stigmatization"; Kallin and Slater, "Activating Territorial Stigma"; Kearns, Kearns, and Lawson, "Notorious Places"; Kirkness, "Cités"; Kirkness and Tijé-Dra, *Negative Neighbourhood Reputation*; Mazanti and Pløger, "Community Planning"; Osborne, Ziersch, and Baum, "Perceptions of Neighbourhood"; Permentier, Van Ham, and Bolt, "Behavioural Responses"; Permentier, Van Ham, and Bolt, "Same Neighbourhood"; Permentier, Van Ham, and Bolt, "Neighbourhood Reputation."
22. Anholt, *Competitive Identity*; Anholt, *Places*; Aronczyk, *Branding the Nation*; Dinnie, *Nation Branding*; Kotler, Haider, and Rein, *Marketing Places*.
23. While studies of neighborhood effects focus on the various characteristics of communities that collectively add up to extreme deprivation and disadvantage (Sampson, *Great American City*; Sampson, Morenoff, and Gannon-Rowley, "Assessing 'Neighborhood Effects'"; Sharkey and Faber, "Where, When, Why"), studies of "territorial stigmatization" emphasize how these conditions result in stigmatized identities (Kirkness and Tijé-Dra, *Negative Neighbourhood Reputation*; Wacquant, "Urban Outcasts"; Wacquant, "Territorial Stigmatization"; Wacquant, *Urban Outcasts*). Although researchers have

framed these as competing perspectives (Slater, "Your Life Chances"; Slater, "Territorial Stigmatisation"), critiques of the "neighborhood effects" approach through a "territorial stigma" lens still uphold a structural approach that neglects the cultural processes underlying how people develop and continue perceptions of these places.

24. Wacquant, "Revisiting Territories," 1080.
25. Research on "territorial stigma" focuses on the forces that maintain deprivation, on the one hand, and how these forces negatively affect the identities of those who live in places with bad reputations, on the other (see, for example, Arthurson, "Social Mix"; Hastings and Dean, "Challenging Images"; Kallin and Slater, "Activating Territorial Stigma"; Kearns, Kearns, and Lawson, "Notorious Places"; Kirkness and Tijé-Dra, *Negative Neighbourhood Reputation*; Wacquant, "Territorial Stigmatization"; Wacquant, Slater, and Pereira, "Territorial Stigmatization"). Yet, empirical studies challenge these claims, as they find that the residents of disreputable places tend to see themselves and their communities positively (Jensen and Christensen, "Territorial Stigmatization"; Morris, "Public Housing"). Research on territorial stigmatization contains little discussion of the mechanisms linking an environment of turmoil and scarcity with definitions of self, making this jump between collective and individual levels of analysis a leap of faith that the structural variables shape the cultural ones (see Bauder, "Neighbourhood Effects"). Further innovations built on this foundation, such as pointing out how these places are "hyperghettos" with increasingly worse conditions that make the stigmatization of their residents especially pronounced (Wacquant, *Urban Outcasts*; Wacquant, "Revisiting Territories"), only compound this arguable supposition.
26. Anderson "Iconic Ghetto"; Anderson, "White Space"; Hastings and Dean, "Challenging Images"; Kearns, Kearns, and Lawson, "Notorious Places"; Wacquant, "Urban Outcasts"; Wacquant, "Territorial Stigmatization"; Wacquant, *Urban Outcasts*.
27. Massey and Denton, *American Apartheid*.
28. Feagin and McKinney, *Many Costs*; Lipsitz, *Possessive Investment*; Lipsitz, "Racialization"; Oliver and Shapiro, *Black Wealth*; Wilson, *Truly Disadvantaged*; Yinger, *Closed Doors*.
29. Kearns, Kearns, and Lawson, "Notorious Places"; Permentier, Van Ham, and Bolt, "Behavioural Responses"; Permentier, Van Ham, and Bolt, "Same Neighbourhood"; Permentier, Van Ham, and Bolt, "Neighbourhood Reputation."
30. Mazanti and Pløger, "Community Planning," 309.
31. Sampson and Raudenbush, "Seeing Disorder," 319.
32. See Dekker, "Testing"; Franzini et al., "Perceptions of Disorder"; Sampson, "Disparity and Diversity"; Sampson and Raudenbush, "Seeing Disorder," Sampson and Raudenbush, "Neighborhood Stigma"; Wickes et al., "'Seeing' Minorities"; Zahnow et al., "Change and Stability."
33. Kearns, Kearns, and Lawson, "Notorious Places," 584. See also Jean, "Neighbourhood Attachment Revisited."
34. Anderson, "Iconic Ghetto," 8.
35. Anderson, *Imagined Communities*.

36. Jones and Jackson, "'You Just Don't'"; Permentier, Van Ham, and Bolt, "Behavioural Responses."
37. Becker, *Outsiders*; Fine, "Reputational Entrepreneurs"; Fine, *Sticky Reputations*; Goffman, *Stigma*.
38. Anholt, *Competitive Identity*; Anholt, *Places*; Foster, *Stigma Cities*. For example, city leaders of Las Vegas made a failed attempt to rebrand the city as "family friendly" in the 1990s (Foster, *Stigma Cities*).
39. Anholt, *Competitive Identity*; Anholt, *Places*; Hester, "Subconscious Landscapes"; Kotler, Donald Haider, and Rein, *Marketing Places*; Manzo and Perkins, "Finding Common Ground."
40. Despite this, people tend to see studies of the ghettos of large and famous cities as more authentic, important, and even generalizable, instead of the great outliers that they are (Bell and Jayne, "Small Cities"). The reasons for this are more social than scientific. Such places are more popular (a book about New York City will make a much bigger splash than similar research of Ogden), and the leading producers of urban research tend to be based there.
41. Wacquant, Slater, and Pereira, "Territorial Stigmatization."
42. Sampson, Morenoff, and Gannon-Rowley, "Assessing 'Neighborhood Effects'"; Sampson and Raudenbush, "Systematic Social Observation."
43. August, "Challenging the Rhetoric"; Jensen and Christensen, "Territorial Stigmatization"; Kearns, Kearns, and Lawson, "Notorious Places"; Kirkness, "Cités"; Kullberg et al., "Does the Perceived"; Morris, "Public Housing"; Osborne, Ziersch, and Baum, "Perceptions of Neighbourhood"; Permentier, Van Ham, and Bolt, "Same Neighbourhood."
44. Kearns, Kearns, and Lawson, "Notorious Places"; Pinyol, Sabater-Mir, and Cuní, "How to Talk."
45. Lee, "In Quiet Ogden."
46. Looking for images for an upcoming presentation, I performed this search on August 7, 2017. Google no longer shows this result.
47. For recent examples of news reports about Ogden's negative image, see Carlson, "Ogden Is One"; Halling, "Ogden"; Koch, "Ogden's Rough"; Shenefelt, "Ogden Best"; Trotter, "North Ogden Residents." In Chapter Seven, I present examples that date back to the late 1800s.
48. Barnes, *Notorious Two-Bit Street*; Holley, *25th Street Confidential*; Koch, "Ogden's Rough"; Roberts and Sadler, *Ogden*; Sadler and Roberts, *Weber County's History*.
49. Permentier, Van Ham, and Bolt, "Behavioural Responses."
50. This unity between all native residents, and difference from Latino immigrants, fits the findings of Cassi Meyerhoffer ("'I Have More'"). She studied how white Ogden residents understood different races and nationalities in their community. These residents saw nationality as a bigger problem than racial difference, as they embraced black residents more than they embraced Latinos, who they saw as intrusive foreigners.
51. Anderson, "Iconic Ghetto"; Anderson, "White Space"; Wacquant, "Urban Outcasts"; Wacquant, "Territorial Stigmatization"; Wacquant, *Urban Outcasts*.

52. Fine, "Reputational Entrepreneurs"; Fine, *Sticky Reputations*.
53. See Bonilla-Silva, *Racism without Racists*.
54. Farley et al., "Stereotypes and Segregation."
55. Becker, *Outsiders*; Durkheim, *Rules*; Erikson, *Wayward Puritans*; Kitsuse, "Societal Reaction"; Lemert, "Beyond Mead"; Paternoster and Iovanni, "Labeling Perspective."
56. Durkheim, *Rules*.
57. Becker, *Outsiders*.
58. While Becker refers to deviant populations as "outsiders," I invert this language to refer to the residents of disputable places as insiders and those living beyond their boundaries as outsiders. While an accurate description of Ogden's residents and nonresidents, this language also is a purposeful attempt to undo portrayals of marginalized populations as abnormal, deficient, and even pathological.
59. Erikson, *Wayward Puritans*.
60. Bell Jr., "Brown v. Board"; Blumer, "Race Prejudice"; Bonilla-Silva, *Racism without Racists*; Bonilla-Silva, "More Than Prejudice"; Delgado and Stefancic, *Critical Race Theory*; Mills, *Racial Contract*; Sidanius and Pratto, *Social Dominance*; Sidanius et al., "Social Dominance Theory."
61. Bonilla-Silva, *Racism without Racists*; Bonilla-Silva and Embrick, "'Every Place'"; Bonilla-Silva, Goar, and Embrick, "When Whites"; DiAngelo, "White Fragility."
62. Box, *Power, Crime and Mystification*; Liazos, "Poverty"; Spitzer, "Toward a Marxian."
63. Liazos, "Poverty," 106.
64. Many social scientists see Durkheim's theories as leaning conservative and critical race theory as a decidedly, even radically, leftist perspective.
65. Durkheim (*Elementary Forms*) argues that societies develop a "collective consciousness," feelings of togetherness, by separating the sacred from the profane. Similarly, anthropologist Mary Douglas (*Purity and Danger*) contends that cultures define themselves by dividing what is pure from what is impure. See also Shah, *Contagious Divides*.
66. Berger and Luckmann, *Social Construction*; Garfinkel, *Studies in Ethnomethodology*; Gramsci, *Antonio Gramsci*.
67. Bonilla-Silva, *Racism without Racists*; DiAngelo, "White Fragility."
68. Lewis, *Five Families*.
69. Bonilla-Silva, "More Than Prejudice"; Cross and Hernández, "Place, Identity"; McKittrick, *Demonic Grounds*; McKittrick, "On Plantations."
70. Gieryn, "Space"; Harvey, *Condition of Postmodernity*; Tuan, *Space and Place*.
71. Charles, "Dynamics"; Massey, "Residential Segregation"; Massey and Denton, *American Apartheid*.
72. Anderson "Iconic Ghetto"; Anderson, "White Space."
73. Glass, "Dividing and Defending"; Lamont and Molnár, "Study."
74. Bauder, "Neighbourhood Effects"; Slater, "Your Life Chances."
75. Harcourt, *Illusion of Order*; Sampson and Raudenbush, "Seeing Disorder"; Wilson and Kelling, "Broken Windows."
76. Reeve, *Religion*.

## CHAPTER 2

1. Anderson, "Iconic Ghetto"; Bonilla-Silva and Embrick, "'Every Place'"; Bonilla-Silva, Goar, and Embrick, "When Whites"; Jones and Jackson, "'You Just Don't.'"
2. Anholt, *Places*; Hester, "Subconscious Landscapes"; Wacquant, *Urban Outcasts*; Wilson and Kelling, "Broken Windows."
3. Bonilla-Silva and Embrick, "'Every Place'"; Bonilla-Silva, Goar, and Embrick, "When Whites"; Massey and Denton, *American Apartheid*.
4. Erikson, *Wayward Puritans*.
5. Bullard, Johnson, and Torres, *Highway Robbery*; Yago, "Sociology."
6. Anderson, "White Space."
7. Bonilla-Silva, *Racism without Racists*.
8. See Massey and Denton, *American Apartheid*.
9. Anderson, "Iconic Ghetto"; Anderson, "White Space."
10. Lewis, *Five Families*.
11. Kraus et al., "Social Class"; Piff, "Wealth"; Piff et al., "Higher Social Class"; Sidanius and Pratto, *Social Dominance*; Sidanius et al., "Social Dominance Theory."
12. Anderson, "Iconic Ghetto."
13. Rumbaut and Ewing, *Myth*; Sohoni and Sohoni, "Perceptions of Immigrant"; Stupi, Chiricos, and Gertz, "Perceived Criminal Threat"; Wang, "Undocumented Immigrants."
14. Wacquant, "Three Pernicious Premises," 348.
15. Rios, *Punished*, 260.
16. Bauder, "Neighbourhood Effects"; Slater, "Your Life Chances."
17. Dekker, "Testing the Racial"; Franzini et al., "Perceptions of Disorder"; Hipp, "Resident Perceptions"; Quillian and Pager, "Black Neighbors"; Sampson and Raudenbush, "Seeing Disorder," Sampson and Raudenbush, "Neighborhood Stigma"; Wickes et al., "'Seeing' Minorities"; Zahnow et al., "Change and Stability."
18. Anderson, "Iconic Ghetto," 9.
19. August, "Challenging the Rhetoric"; Jensen and Christensen, "Territorial Stigmatization"; Kearns, Kearns, and Lawson, "Notorious Places"; Kirkness, "Cités"; Kullberg et al., "Does the Perceived"; Morris, "Public Housing"; Osborne, Ziersch, and Baum, "Perceptions of Neighbourhood"; Permentier, Van Ham, and Bolt, "Same Neighbourhood." Jensen and Christensen as well as Morris note how this finding challenges the particularly dreary view of life in disreputable places found in Wacquant's concept of "territorial stigmatization" (Wacquant, "Territorial Stigmatization"; Wacquant, *Urban Outcasts*; Wacquant, Slater, and Pereira, "Territorial Stigmatization").
20. Anderson, *Code of the Street*.
21. Anderson, *StreetWise*; Anderson, *Code*; Bourgois, *In Search*; Rios, *Punished*; Wacquant, *Urban Outcasts*.
22. Reiman, *Rich*.
23. Anderson, "Iconic Ghetto," 22.
24. Dekker, "Testing the Racial"; Franzini et al., "Perceptions of Disorder"; Havekes, Coenders, and Van der Lippe, "Positive or Negative"; Jones and Jackson, "'You Just Don't'"; Krysan, "Community Undesirability"; Krysan and Bader, "Perceiving the Metropolis"; Krysan et al., "Does Race Matter"; Sampson and Raudenbush, "Seeing

Disorder"; Wickes et al., "'Seeing' Minorities"; Zahnow et al., "Change and Stability." "Perceptions of Disorder" and "Change and Stability" show that social class, not racial composition, shaped perceptions, and "'Seeing' Minorities" argues that neighborhood cohesion mediates this relationship, as people living in places where residents feel more connected to each other literally perceive fewer racial minorities.
25. Permentier, Van Ham, and Bolt, "Behavioural Responses," 203–4.
26. Anderson, *Code*; Osborne, Ziersch, and Baum, "Perceptions of Neighbourhood"; Permentier, Van Ham, and Bolt, "Behavioural Responses."
27. Wacquant, "Urban Outcasts," 374–75.
28. Florida, *Rise*; Lloyd, "Neo-Bohemia"; Lloyd, *Neo-Bohemia*.
29. Florida, *Rise*; Lloyd, *Neo-Bohemia*; Zukin, *Naked City*.
30. Pattillo, *Black*.
31. Lees, Slater, and Wyly, *Gentrification*; Smith, *New Urban*; Zukin, "Gentrification."
32. Kennedy et al., *Reducing Gun Violence*; Braga et al., "Problem-Oriented Policing."
33. Sampson, *Great American City*.
34. Kearns, Kearns, and Lawson, "Notorious Places"; Pinyol, Sabater-Mir, and Cuní, "How to Talk."
35. Bonilla-Silva, *Racism without Racists*; DiAngelo, "White Fragility."
36. Durkheim, *Rules*; Erikson, *Wayward Puritans*.

## CHAPTER 3
1. American Community Survey Five-Year Estimates, 2013–2017.
2. Lee, "In Quiet Ogden."
3. Hoe, "Park Blooms."
4. Ogden City, *Five Year Consolidated*.
5. Bonilla-Silva, "From Bi-Racial"; Frank, Akresh, and Lu, "Latino Immigrants"; Gallagher, "Racial Redistricting"; Gans, "Possibility"; Lee and Bean, "Reinventing the Color"; Marrow, "New Immigrant Destinations."
6. Lichter and Johnson, "Immigrant Gateways"; Massey, *New Faces*; Zuniga and Hernandez-Leon, *New Destinations*.
7. In her study of Ogden, Meyerhoffer ("'I Have More'") found that white residents preferred black neighbors to Latinos, who they saw as a foreign threat.
8. Meinig, "Mormon Culture"; Phillips et al., *Mormons*; Toney, Keller, and Hunter, "Regional Cultures"; Yorgason, *Transformation*.
9. Sorensen, "Zion."
10. Canham, "Salt Lake County."
11. According to reports by the Association of Statisticians of American Religious Bodies (www.thearda.com), Weber County was just under 60 percent Mormon in 2010, compared to the state average of 69 percent. In that same year, the five counties that surround Weber had rates of Mormon adherents totaling 81 percent (Box Elder), 82 percent (Cache), 75 percent (Davis), 89 percent (Morgan), and 88 percent (Rich).
12. Barnes, *Notorious Two-Bit Street*; Holley, *25th Street Confidential*; Sadler and Roberts, *Weber County's History*.

## CHAPTER 4

1. Jacobs, *Death*.
2. Kearns, Kearns, and Lawson, "Notorious Places"; Pinyol, Sabater-Mir, and Cuní, "How to Talk."
3. Pinyol, Sabater-Mir, and Cuní, "How to Talk," 90. Emphasis in the original.
4. Andersen, "Why Do Residents"; Anholt, *Competitive Identity*; Anholt, *Places*; Aronczyk, *Branding the Nation*; Barber, *Reno's Big Gamble*; Dinnie, *Nation Branding*; Mazanti and Pløger, "Community Planning"; Permentier, Van Ham, and Bolt, "Same Neighbourhood."
5. See Carlson, "Ogden Is One"; Holley, *25th Street Confidential*; Lee, "In Quiet Ogden"; Shenefelt, "Ogden Best"; Vandenack, "Ogden"; Vandenack, "Ogden's Household."
6. Lewicka, "Place Attachment"; Trentelman, "Place Attachment."
7. Garfinkel, *Studies in Ethnomethodology*.
8. See also Glass, "Using History." In that article, I also outline how residents thought that things were *worse* today than they were in the past.
9. Trotter, "North Ogden Residents."
10. Quoted in Holley, *25th Street Confidential*, 1.
11. Barnes, *Notorious Two-Bit Street*, 25.
12. Krysan et al., "Does Race Matter." See also Havekes, Coenders, and Van der Lippe, "Positive or Negative."
13. Dekker, "Testing the Racial"; Franzini et al., "Perceptions of Disorder"; Krysan, "Community Undesirability"; Krysan and Bader, "Perceiving the Metropolis"; Krysan et al., "Does Race Matter"; Quillian and Pager, "Black Neighbors"; Sampson and Raudenbush, "Seeing Disorder"; Sampson, "Disparity and Diversity."

## CHAPTER 5

1. Fine, *Sticky Reputations*.
2. Barber, *Reno's Big Gamble*; Kullberg et al., "Does the Perceived"; Permentier, Van Ham, and Bolt, "Neighbourhood Reputation"; Permentier, Van Ham, and Bolt, "Same Neighbourhood."
3. Anholt, *Competitive Identity*; Anholt, *Places*; Aula and Harmaakorpi, "Innovative Milieu"; Glückler, "Geography of Reputation."
4. Anderson, "Iconic Ghetto"; Anderson, "White Space"; DiAngelo, "White Fragility"; Johnson, *Privilege*.
5. DiAngelo, "White Fragility," 58–59.
6. Goffman, *Stigma*.
7. Anderson, *Code of the Street*; Anderson, "Iconic Ghetto"; Arthurson, "Social Mix"; Blokland, "'You Got to Remember'"; Hastings and Dean, "Challenging Images"; Jones and Jackson, "'You Just Don't'"; Kearns, Kearns, and Lawson, "Notorious Places"; Wacquant, "Territorial Stigmatization"; Wacquant, *Urban Outcasts*.
8. Matsueda, "Reflected Appraisals"; Rios, *Punished*.
9. The idea of a street being a main racial and class "divide" between areas of a city seems to be a common phenomenon. The most famous of these spatial boundaries is probably Detroit's Eight Mile Road and corresponding Eight Mile Wall, a half-mile-long concrete barrier meant to separate black and white communities (Marklew, "A Brief History").

Being from Missouri, I know that the two major cities there also have these divisions. Saint Louis has a "Delmar divide" (Harlan, "In St. Louis"), while the residents of Kansas City speak of the "Troost wall" (O'Higgins, "How Troost Became"). Unlike in Detroit, this is not a literal wall.
10. Researchers call this acceptance by marginalized people of dominant groups' negative understandings of themselves or their communities "internalized racism" or "internalized oppression" (Padilla, "Social and Legal"; Padilla, "But You're Not").
11. Halbwachs, *On Collective Memory*; Olick, "Collective Memory"; Olick and Robbins, "Social Memory Studies"; Zerubavel, *Time Maps*.
12. Trentelman, "New Economy."
13. A haven for retirees (Arthur, "Profile: Ogden, Utah"), a "college town" for students (Jenkins, "Ogden to Become"), and a winter wonderland for sports enthusiasts (Knight, "Outdoors Is the Way").
14. As quoted in McKitrick, "Ogden's Warm."
15. McKitrick, "Union Station Director."
16. I borrow the terms "magical" and "magical solutions" from the work of the Birmingham School (Hall and Jefferson, *Resistance through Rituals*). They argue that the members of various youth cultures attempt to solve large social problems in instantaneous and superficial ways—like reversing divisions of social class by dressing in working-class and deliberately tattered clothing. Ogden's city leaders, in contrast, were attempting instant upward social mobility.
17. Holley, *25th Street Confidential*, 41.
18. Foster, *Stigma Cities*; Gragg, *Bright Light City*.
19. Permentier, Van Ham, and Bolt, "Behavioural Responses."

## CHAPTER 6
1. Anderson, "Iconic Ghetto"; Bonilla-Silva and Embrick, "'Every Place'"; Jones and Jackson, "'You Just Don't'"; Krysan, "Community Undesirability"; Krysan and Bader, "Perceiving the Metropolis"; Krysan et al., "Does Race Matter"; Lewicka, "Place Attachment"; Manzo, "For Better"; Manzo and Perkins, "Finding Common Ground"; Osborne, Ziersch, and Baum, "Perceptions of Neighbourhood."
2. Mesa-Bains, "Domesticana"; Ybarra-Frausto, "Rasquachismo."
3. Exceptions include Lacy ("Cultural Enclaves"), Marrow (*New Destination Dreaming*) and Schmalzbauer (*Last Best*).
4. Meyerhoffer, "'I Have More.'"
5. The census did not measure Latinos before 1970, when it bowed to political pressure and reported "persons of Spanish language."
6. In his study of Venice, California, Andrew Deener ("'Black Section'"; *Venice*) found that residents saw their neighborhood as black despite its large Latino population. Although this is difficult for me to definitively show, my feeling is that Ogden residents and regional locals also tend to see the city's diversity as primarily black. As I mention in this chapter, they are often surprised when learning about the large numbers of Latinos living there, and histories of the city—as well as current celebrations of diversity—often

highlight the black experience. This may reflect the relative invisibility and powerlessness of Ogden's Latino community. This also may be because native residents tend to see Ogden's Latino immigrants—especially those who are undocumented—as much more controversial than black residents (Meyerhoffer, "'I Have More'").

7. See Jameson, *How Many Undocumented*. In 2009, the Census Bureau held a Spirit of Community Celebration in Ogden, in order to "get the word out about the importance of the [2010] census—a possible fourth seat in the U.S. House of Representatives—and to remind people it's not a hunt for illegal immigrants" (Gurrister, "Officials").
8. Lichter and Johnson, "Immigrant Gateways"; Marrow, "New Immigrant Destinations"; Marrow, *New Destination Dreaming*; Massey, *New Faces*; Winders, "New Immigrant Destinations"; Zuniga and Hernandez-Leon, *New Destinations*.
9. Singer, *Rise*.
10. Jimenez, *Replenished Ethnicity*.
11. Iceland, *Where We Live*.
12. Donato, Stainback, and Bankston, "Economic Incorporation"; Hiemstra, "Spatial Disjunctures"; Sandoval and Maldonado, "Latino Urbanism Revisited"; Shutika, "Ambivalent Welcome"; Shutika, *Beyond the Borderlands*.
13. Donato, Stainback, and Bankston, "Economic Incorporation," 98.
14. Donato, Stainback, and Bankston, "Economic Incorporation"; Maldonado, "Latino Incorporation"; Marrow, *New Destination Dreaming*; Shutika, "Bridging the Community."
15. Adelman et al., "Urban Crime Rates"; Sampson, "Rethinking Crime."
16. Bacon, *Illegal People*; Gardner, Johnson, and Wiehe, *Undocumented Immigrants*; Gitis and Varas, *Labor*.
17. Sarlin, "How America's Harshest"; Serrano, "Why Undocumented Workers."
18. Ogden United Promise Neighborhoods, *Community Needs Assessment*.
19. Duneier, *Sidewalk*; Jacobs, *Death*; Lofland, *Public Realm*; Whyte, *City*.
20. See, for example, Arthurson, "Social Mix"; Blokland, "'You Got to Remember'"; Hastings and Dean, "Challenging Images"; Kirkness and Tijé-Dra, *Negative Neighbourhood Reputation*; Slater and Anderson, "Reputational Ghetto"; Wacquant, "Territorial Stigmatization"; Wacquant, *Urban Outcasts*.
21. Lofland, *Public Realm*; Whyte, *City*.
22. Wacquant, *Urban Outcasts*.
23. Charles, *Won't You Be*, 56–57; Marrow, "New Immigrant Destinations."
24. Barros, "Simulating Urban Dynamics"; Rogler, "Slum Neighborhoods."
25. Lyons, Vélez, and Santoro, "Neighborhood Immigration"; Nelson and Hiemstra, "Latino Immigrants"; Schmalzbauer, "Gender"; Schmalzbauer, *Last Best*.
26. Charles, "Comfort Zones"; Ono, "Assimilation."

**CHAPTER 7**

1. Cadge et al., "City"; Foster, *Stigma Cities*; Hester, "Subconscious Landscapes"; Kaufman and Kaliner, "Re-accomplishment"; Molotch, Freudenberg, and Paulson, "History Repeats Itself"; Patterson, "Culture and Continuity."
2. Patterson, "Culture and Continuity."

3. Holley, *25th Street Confidential*.
4. Peterson and Parson, *Ogden City*, 168.
5. Ibid., 175.
6. Sadler and Roberts, *Weber County's History*, 91.
7. Cannon, "Change Engulfs," 25.
8. Ulibarri, "Utah's Ethnic Minorities."
9. Conley, "Pioneer Chinese"; Ulibarri, "Utah's Ethnic Minorities."
10. Solórzano, *We Remember*, 71.
11. Conley, "Pioneer Chinese"; Ulibarri, "Utah's Ethnic Minorities."
12. Papanikolas, "Introduction."
13. Barnes, *Notorious Two-Bit Street*, 42.
14. Ibid., 45.
15. Perlich, *Utah Minorities*.
16. Peterson and Parson, *Ogden City*; Sadler and Roberts, *Weber County's History*.
17. Sadler and Roberts, *Weber County's History*, 339.
18. Peterson and Parson, *Ogden City*, 32.
19. Barnes, *Notorious Two-Bit Street*; Del Richards, *White's City*; Holley, *25th Street Confidential*; Peterson and Parson, *Ogden City*; Sadler and Roberts, *Weber County's History*; Trentelman, "Good Old."
20. Barnes, *Notorious Two-Bit Street*; Holley, *25th Street Confidential*.
21. Kelley, "Legal and Protective." Emphasis in the original.
22. The Salt Lake Herald, "Salt Lake Blushes."
23. Barnes, *Notorious Two-Bit Street*; Sadler and Roberts, *Weber County's History*, 298–99.
24. Holley, *25th Street Confidential*, 57.
25. As quoted in Barnes, *Notorious Two-Bit Street*, 191.
26. Barnes, *Notorious Two-Bit Street*, 187.
27. Holley, *25th Street Confidential*, 13.
28. Ulibarri, "Utah's Ethnic Minorities," 12.
29. Solórzano, *We Remember*, 96.
30. Sadler and Roberts, *Weber County's History*, 339.
31. As quoted in Sadler and Roberts, *Weber County's History*, 340.
32. Anderson, *StreetWise*; Carr, "Complexity"; Wilson, *Truly Disadvantaged*.
33. Carr, "Complexity," 141. See also Anderson, *StreetWise*; Wilson, *Truly Disadvantaged*.
34. As quoted in Barnes, *Notorious Two-Bit Street*, 90.
35. Berger and Luckmann, *Social Construction*; Meyer and Kimeldorf, "Eventful Subjectivity."
36. Patterson, "Culture and Continuity"; Mahoney and Thelen, "Theory"; Moore, "Eventfulness"; Streeck and Thelen, "Introduction."
37. Foster, *Stigma Cities*; Hester, "Subconscious Landscapes"; Kaufman and Kaliner, "Re-accomplishment"; Molotch, Freudenberg, and Paulson, "History Repeats Itself"; Patterson, "Culture and Continuity."
38. As quoted in Koch, "Ogden's Rough." Here I have changed the word "lily" to the correct spelling.
39. Corchado, "Immigration Proposals."

40. Corchado, "Illegal Migrants"; Corchado, "Immigration Proposals"; Corchado, "One Man's Lament."
41. Corchado, "Life of Migrant."
42. Weiler, *Utah's African American*.
43. Barnes, *Notorious Two-Bit Street*, 175. Similarly, Joe Ritchie colorfully described 25th Street in the 1960s: "If you stood on the corner of 25th and Lincoln Avenue long enough six or more of the FBI's ten most wanted would have passed you by. It was a street filled with cocaine, heroin and alcoholism. Crime ran rampant at times. Some people made their living off of stealing and selling stolen property. Folks that lived in the suburbs and on Ogden's east side of Washington Boulevard, at the top of the hill, called it gangster's village" (as quoted in Del Richards, *White's City*, 33).
44. Hoe, "Ogden's 25th Street." See also Koch, "Ogden's Rough."
45. Holley, *25th Street Confidential*.
46. Rivera, "Forty Years Later"; Saal, "Black Community Members."
47. Koch, "Ogden's Rough."
48. Rogers, "Ogden Mall."
49. Peterson and Parson, *Ogden City*. See also Langsdon and Johnson, *Legendary Locals*; Larsen and Wilkerson, *Ogden's Trolley District*; Sadler and Roberts, *Weber County's History*; Sillito and Langsdon, *Ogden*.
50. Barnes, *Notorious Two-Bit Street*; Holley, *25th Street Confidential*.
51. This rumor is popular, and many people see the existence of these tunnels as absolute fact, despite how there never seems to be a camera handy to document them, and decades of new construction have turned up no evidence. Still, Ogden historian Lyle Barnes (*Notorious Two-Bit Street*, 104) states that there are indeed tunnels under 25th Street, although he admits that he has never seen them. He further speculates that the primary evidence of tunnels, closed-up basement entryways, simply could be concealing old entrances for deliveries from the street. As this rumor is perennial red meat for the local media, dozens of news reports over the years point to walled-in basement doorways as "evidence" of tunnels.
52. Lui, *Neon Signs*; Pierson, "Urban Legend"; Teng, "Artifacts."
53. As evidence of this change, developers are building new townhouses downtown, near the Junction mall. Yet, this area still seems to carry much stigma, as a resident there told me that he and all of his neighbors are transplants from out of state, none from the region. Residents and other locals may be comfortable visiting downtown, but they are not comfortable with living there.
54. Studies of other U.S. cities that have undergone changes to their images over time include Las Vegas (Gragg, *Bright Light City*), New York City (Greenberg, *Branding New York*), and Reno (Barber, *Reno's Big Gamble*). See also Strauss, *Images*.
55. Hampshire, Bradley, and Roberts, *History*; Rugh, "Branding Utah."
56. Hampshire, Bradley, and Roberts, *History*, 313.
57. Spangler, "La Vida Utah." Researchers have long documented this connection between high-paid professionals and low-paid immigrant workers in cities (Nelson and Nelson,

"Global Rural"; Sassen, *Mobility*). As a place with few high-income residents, Ogden does not fit this pattern.

## CHAPTER 8

1. Fine, "Reputational Entrepreneurs"; Fine, "Thinking about Evil"; Fine, *Sticky Reputations*; Fine, *Difficult Reputations*.
2. Fine, "Reputational Entrepreneurs"; Fine, *Sticky Reputations*; Fine, *Difficult Reputations*. This is an elaboration of Becker's (*Outsiders*) concept "moral entrepreneurs."
3. For example, when politicians promote laws against illicit drugs, this has less to do with protecting people from a dangerous substance than the separation from, and repression of, threatening populations that are associated with the substance (Alexander, *New*; Becker, *Outsiders*; Reiman, *Rich*; Reinarman and Levine, *Crack in America*).
4. Becker, *Outsiders*; Durkheim, *Rules*; Erikson, *Wayward Puritans*.
5. Durkheim, *Rules*; Erikson, *Wayward Puritans*.
6. Erikson, *Wayward Puritans*, 21.
7. Pond, *Portrait*.
8. Bell Jr., "Brown v. Board"; Blumer, "Race Prejudice"; Mills, *Racial Contract*; Sidanius and Pratto, *Social Dominance*; Sidanius et al., "Social Dominance Theory." The idea that struggles for power between collective groups shape our perceptions is central to critical race theory, but it is also found in constructionist understandings of deviance. An early version of this idea comes from Karl Marx, who famously stated:

   > The ideas of the ruling class are in every epoch the ruling ideas, i.e. the class which is the ruling *material* force of society, is at the same time its ruling *intellectual* force. The class which has the means of material production at its disposal, has control at the same time over the means of mental production, so that thereby, generally speaking, the ideas of those who lack the means of mental production are subject to it (Tucker, *Marx-Engels*, 136, emphasis in the original).

   Researchers of race argue that these dynamics not only shape the perceptions of ruling and subordinate *classes*, but also dominant and marginalized *races*.
9. Bonilla-Silva, *Racism without Racists*, 9.
10. Blumer, "Race Prejudice."
11. Allen et al., *Without Sanctuary*.
12. Alexander, *New*; Reiman, *Rich*.
13. Bonilla-Silva, *Racism without Racists*; Mills, *Racial Contract*; Morris, *Scholar Denied*; Zuberi, *Thicker Than Blood*.
14. Bonilla-Silva, *Racism without Racists*; DiAngelo, "White Fragility."
15. Sidanius and Pratto, *Social Dominance*; Sidanius et al., "Social Dominance Theory."
16. Gramsci, *Antonio Gramsci*.
17. Padilla, "Social and Legal"; Padilla, "But You're Not."
18. See Vick, "Different State."
19. Roche, "Buttars Apologizes."
20. Means, "Utah Magazine."

21. A local minor league baseball team, the Orem Owlz, planned a Caucasian Heritage Night in 2015, where visitors would be treated to white bread, mayonnaise, and videos clips from "white" television programs (Peña, "Utah Baseball"). As with the "Women of Color" controversy, the promoters of this attempt at tongue-in-cheek racial humor seemed oblivious to its explosiveness. This was despite being warned by their freshly hired (and tellingly, from out of state) media director, who quit in protest before the franchise announced the event. As he explained:

> After learning of the promotion during my first week, I raised serious concerns about it with multiple members of the front office, both verbally and via email. I registered my disagreement with carrying out such a promotion. I also warned that this event—no matter the intention of it—would cause public backlash. My concerns were not taken seriously, and my advice went unheeded.

Following international negative publicity, the team cancelled the promotion.
22. Holley, *25th Street Confidential*, 8–9.
23. Erikson, *Wayward Puritans*.
24. Fine, "Reputational Entrepreneurs," 1160.
25. Meinig, "Mormon Culture"; Phillips et al., *Mormons*; Toney, Keller, and Hunter, "Regional Cultures"; Yorgason, *Transformation*.
26. Stevens, "Passive-Aggression."
27. https://www.lds.org/topics/home-teaching?lang=eng. As the church abandoned this program in April 2018, this webpage no longer exists. The practice that replaced it, called "ministering," also involves regular contact with members.
28. Phillips et al., *Mormons*, 3.
29. Riley, *'Til Faith*.
30. Campbell, Green, and Monson, *Seeking the Promised*.
31. Klay, "Mormons Love."
32. Davidson, "How Utah's Capitol."
33. Fletcher Stack, "Program Aims"; Winslow, "'Safe and Sound.'"
34. Phillips et al., *Mormons*.

## CHAPTER 9

1. Charles, "Dynamics"; Massey and Denton, *American Apartheid*; Pager and Shepherd, "Sociology."
2. Bourgois and Schonberg, *Righteous Dopefiend*; Shah, *Contagious Divides*.
3. Alexander, *New*; Reiman, *Rich*; Rios, *Punished*.
4. Wilson and Kelling, "Broken Windows."
5. Harcourt, *Illusion of Order*; Hastings and Dean, "Challenging Images"; Meares, "Law"; Rios, *Punished*; Rosenfeld and Fornango, "Impact"; Sampson and Raudenbush, "Systematic Social Observation"; Sampson and Raudenbush, "Seeing Disorder."
6. Alexander, *New*; Fellner, "Decades of Disparity"; Reinarman and Levine, *Crack in America*.
7. Mohamed and Fritsvold, *Dorm Room Dealers*.

8. Reiman, *Rich*; Rios, *Punished*.
9. Arthurson, "Social Mix"; Sampson, *Great American City*.
10. Anderson, "Iconic Ghetto"; Hastings and Dean, "Challenging Images"; Kearns, Kearns, and Lawson, "Notorious Places"; Wacquant, "Urban Outcasts"; Wacquant, *Urban Outcasts*.
11. Lees, "Gentrification"; Lees, Slater, and Wyly, *Gentrification*; Smith, *New Urban*; Zukin, "Gentrification."
12. Larsen, "Nearly 900."
13. Alberty, "Utah Supreme Court."
14. Miller, "Ogden Redevelopment Plans"; Ogden City, *Neighborhood Revitalization*.
15. Durán, "Legitimated Oppression"; Durán, "Over-Inclusive Gang"; Durán, *Gang Life*.
16. Cohen, *Folk Devils*.
17. Larsen, "Nearly 900."
18. Durán, *Gang Life*, 112.
19. Garot, *Who You Claim*.
20. Durán, *Gang Life*.
21. Larsen, "Nearly 900."
22. Becker, *Outsiders*; Cohen, *Folk Devils*; Reinarman and Levine, *Crack in America*.
23. Basquiat, "Reproducing Patriarchy"; Bullock, "Framing Domestic Violence."
24. Iceland, *Where We Live*.
25. Holley, *25th Street Confidential*, 7.
26. See Lott, *Love and Theft*.
27. Bringhurst, "The 'Missouri Thesis'"; Stewart, *Mormonism*; Taggart, *Mormonism's Negro Policy*.
28. As quoted in Stewart, *Mormonism*, 51.
29. Fredrickson, *Racism*. As a notorious passage from the Book of Mormon states, "And he had caused the cursing to come upon them, yea, even a sore cursing, because of their iniquity. For behold, they had hardened their hearts against him, that they had become like unto a flint; wherefore, as they were white, and exceedingly fair and delightsome, that they might not be enticing unto my people the Lord God did cause a skin of blackness to come upon them" (2 Nephi 5:21).
30. Oppenheimer, "Twist"; Walsh, "Recent Mormon Baptisms."
31. https://www.lds.org/topics/race-and-the-priesthood?lang=eng.
32. https://www.lds.org/church/news/church-statement-against-racism-encourages-tolerance-and-love-following-violence-in-virginia?lang=eng.
33. Papanikolas, "Introduction," 5.
34. Roberts and Sadler, *Ogden*, 83.
35. Coleman, "Blacks in Utah"; Lythgoe, "Negro Slavery"; Ulibarri, "Utah's Ethnic Minorities."
36. Coleman, "Blacks in Utah"; Jackson, *Elijah Abel*.
37. Coleman, "Blacks in Utah," 139.
38. Mayer, "Evolution"; Panek, "Life at Iosepa"; Ulibarri, "Utah's Ethnic Minorities."
39. Cooley, "Clarion, Utah," 101–103.
40. Panek, "Life at Iosepa."

41. Panek, "Life at Iosepa," 89.
42. Mayer, "Evolution," 185–86.
43. Solórzano, *We Remember*, 181.
44. Cooley, "Clarion, Utah."
45. Semerad, "Utahns"; Walsh, "Utah"; Young, "Equal Rights."
46. Solórzano, *We Remember*, 145.
47. utahcompact.com.
48. See Coleman, "Geopolitics"; Coleman, "From Border Policing"; Maldonado, "Latino Incorporation"; Winders, "Bringing Back."
49. Bush, "Mormonism's Negro Doctrine," 11–12.
50. Reeve, *Religion*, 138.
51. Reeve, *Religion*.
52. Fredrickson, *Racism*; Reeve, *Religion*.
53. Reeve, *Religion*.
54. Bush, "Mormonism's Negro Doctrine."
55. Ibid.; Lythgoe, "Negro Slavery."
56. As quoted in Lythgoe, "Negro Slavery," 50.
57. This can happen to cities as well, as the image of Birmingham, Alabama, failed to fit new racial understandings. "As the cultural context in which the city existed changed to such a great degree, the city's racist image became deeply entrenched and at odds with the nation's post–civil rights movement standard of acceptable racial beliefs and activities. Birmingham, although it made great strides regarding race relations, assumed the identity of the nation's racist pariah" (Foster, *Stigma Cities*, 183).
58. This shift in doctrine did inspire a small number of adherents to leave the Mormon Church and join its fundamentalist offshoots (Carlisle, "Right After"; Krakauer, *Under the Banner*). These defectors felt that the central church, by making this change, was straying from its divine path.
59. Reeve, *Religion*, 3.
60. See Layton, *Being Different*; Papanikolas, *Peoples*; Scott and Thatcher, *Women in Utah*; Solórzano, *We Remember*.

**CHAPTER 10**

1. Rios, *Punished*, 259. See also Small, "De-exoticizing."
2. Mills, *Racial Contract*; Morris, *Scholar Denied*; Steinberg, *Race Relations*.
3. DuBois, *Souls*.
4. Ryan, *Blaming the Victim*.
5. Exceptions include Bauder, "Neighbourhood Effects"; Sampson, *Great American City*; Sampson and Raudenbush, "Seeing Disorder"; Slater, "Your Life Chances."
6. Researchers also are participants in this social system, enveloped in these collective groups. The vast majority of them are either from higher-status backgrounds or they have moved into these social realms. In their acceptance of these prevailing understandings of disreputable places, they may be inadvertently supporting their own collective interests—while simultaneously retaining identities as good people who fight injustice.

7. Mazanti and Pløger, "Community Planning," 325.
8. Manzo and Perkins, "Finding Common Ground"; Mazanti and Pløger, "Community Planning."
9. Iceland, *Where We Live*.
10. Wickes et al., "'Seeing' Minorities."
11. Shaw, *Contagious Divides*.
12. Oliver, *The Paradoxes*, 20.
13. See, for example, Anholt, *Competitive Identity*; Aronczyk, *Branding the Nation*; Dinnie, *Nation Branding*. An international consulting firm—the Reputation Institute—ranks the reputation of one hundred cities for its City RepTrak (https://www.reputationinstitute.com). Using the indicators of Advanced Economy, Effective Government, and Appealing Environment (which measures beauty and safety), they argue that reputations contain both "rational" and "emotional" components, such as economic success and feelings of safety, that influence each other.
14. McKitrick, "Ogden's Warm."
15. Anholt, *Places*, 3. Emphasis in the original.
16. Becker, *Outsiders*.
17. David, "Deficit Model"; Harry and Klingner, "Discarding the Deficit."
18. Bakhtin, *Rabelais*; Scott, *Weapons*.
19. Lloyd, "Neo-Bohemia"; Lloyd, *Neo-Bohemia*; Speck, *Walkable City*.
20. "Creative class" (Florida, *Rise*) and "new bohemians" (Lloyd, *Neo-Bohemia*).
21. Cairns, "Why Are Utahns"; Curtis, "Utah Loves Halloween."
22. http://halloweeninsummerfestival.com.
23. McKitrick, "Ogden's Warm."
24. Brown, "Ogden Rooftop." While promising, Alleged's embrace of Ogden's seedy history is more the exception than the rule. The previous owner of the building engaged in a heated, decade-long battle with the city to restore a historic sign that read "Every hour upon the hour for about an hour Drink Becker's Beer—Ogden's Famous Beer" (Smart, "It Took"). Ironically, the city's own Landmark Commission challenged this effort at historical preservation. According to this owner, it was because the sign promoted a disreputable image of the city. He reported that one member of the commission said, "We can't have beer on that sign; we want 25th Street to be family oriented."
25. Barnes, *Notorious Two-Bit Street*, 230–33.
26. Foster, *Stigma Cities*, 15–16.
27. Lewicka, "Place Attachment."
28. Griffiths, "New Midwesterners"; Jones, "Cultural Retrenchment"; Marrow, *New Destination Dreaming*; Ochoa, "Mexican Americans' Attitudes"; Shutika, "Ambivalent Welcome"; Shutika, *Beyond the Borderlands*; Sohoni and Mendez, "Defining Immigrant Newcomers"; Wang, "Undocumented Immigrants."
29. Austin (McGlinchy, "Residents"), Indianapolis (Paschall II, "Gentrifying Indy"; Taylor, "Are Indy Neighborhoods"), Louisville (Stevens, "Change Is Coming"; Yoo, "Neighbors Express"), Portland (Parks, "Urban Renewal").
30. Holcomb and Beauregard, *Revitalizing Cities*; Lees, "Gentrification."

31. Hester, "Subconscious Landscapes," 15.

## CHAPTER 11

1. See Bonilla-Silva, "Rethinking Racism"; Bonilla-Silva, *Racism without Racists*.
2. Christakis and Fowler, *Connected*, 25.
3. Lewis, *Five Families*.
4. Kasinitz et al., *Inheriting the City*; Ryan, *Blaming the Victim*; Small, Harding, and Lamont, "Reconsidering Culture."
5. Wacquant, "Territorial Stigmatization"; Wacquant, Slater, and Pereira, "Territorial Stigmatization."
6. Exceptions include Anderson, *StreetWise*; Anderson, *Code*; Pattillo, *Black*; Pattillo-McCoy, *Black Picket Fences*; and Rios, *Punished*. It is probably no coincidence that these researchers are all people of color, the members of marginalized communities.
7. Small, "De-exoticizing," 356. See also Rios, "Decolonizing."

## EPILOGUE

1. Geertz, "Thick Description," 22.
2. Kusenbach, "Street Phenomenology," 474.
3. Ibid., 463.
4. Gubrium and Holstein, *New Language*; Lofland et al., *Analyzing Social Settings*.
5. Campbell et al., "Subjective Constructions"; Coulton et al., "Mapping Residents' Perceptions."
6. Charmaz, *Constructing Grounded Theory*; Glaser and Strauss, *Discovery*.
7. Burawoy, *Ethnography Unbound*; Burawoy, *Global Ethnography*; Katz, "Time for New."
8. Glass, "Using History."
9. Hester, "Subconscious Landscapes"; Molotch, Freudenberg, and Paulson, "History Repeats Itself"; Seamon, "Body-Subject"; Whyte, *City*.
10. Charles, "Dynamics," 200.
11. Ogden United Promise Neighborhoods, *Community Needs Assessment*.
12. Campbell et al., "Subjective Constructions," 462.

## APPENDIX

1. See Box, *Power*; Kitsuse and Cicourel, "Note on"; Skogan, "Validity."
2. Gurrister, "Ogden Blimp."
3. Box, *Power*; Reiman, *Rich*.
4. Durán, "Legitimated Oppression"; Durán, "Over-inclusive."
5. Durkheim, *Rules*.

# BIBLIOGRAPHY

Adelman, Robert, Lesley Williams Reid, Gail Markle, Saskia Weiss, and Charles Jaret. "Urban Crime Rates and the Changing Face of Immigration: Evidence across Four Decades." *Journal of Ethnicity in Criminal Justice* 15, no. 1 (2017): 52–77.

Alberty, Erin. "Utah Supreme Court Throws Out Ogden Gang Injunction." *Salt Lake Tribune*, October 19, 2013. http://archive.sltrib.com/story.php?ref=/sltrib/news/57016397-78/gang-county-injunction-court.html.

Alexander, Michelle. *The New Jim Crow: Mass Incarceration in the Age of Colorblindness*. New York: New Press, 2010.

Allen, James, Hilton Als, John Lewis, and Leon F. Litwack. *Without Sanctuary: Lynching Photography in America*. Santa Fe: Twin Palms, 2000.

Andersen, Hans Skifter. "Why Do Residents Want to Leave Deprived Neighbourhoods? The Importance of Residents' Subjective Evaluations of Their Neighbourhood and Its Reputation." *Journal of Housing and the Built Environment* 23, no. 2 (2008): 79–101.

Anderson, Benedict. *Imagined Communities: Reflections on the Origin and Spread of Nationalism*. London: Verso Books, 2006.

Anderson, Bruce, Peter Fish, Caroline Hetzel, Matthew Jaffe, Michelle Lau, Sarah Max, Ken McAlpine, Jessica Mordo, and Nora Burba Trulsson. "Best Places to Live at Any Age." *Sunset*, February 2016.

Anderson, Elijah. *Code of the Street: Decency, Violence, and the Moral Life of the Inner City*. New York: W. W. Norton, 2000.

———. "The Iconic Ghetto." *Annals of the American Academy of Political and Social Science* 642, no. 1 (2012): 8–24.

———. *StreetWise: Race, Class, and Change in an Urban Community*. Chicago: University of Chicago Press, 1990.

———. "The White Space." *Sociology of Race and Ethnicity* 1, no. 1 (2015): 10–21.

Anholt, Simon. *Competitive Identity: The New Brand Management for Nations, Cities and Regions*. New York: Palgrave Macmillan, 2007.

———. *Places: Identity, Image and Reputation*. New York: Palgrave Macmillan, 2010.

Aronczyk, Melissa. *Branding the Nation: The Global Business of National Identity*. Oxford: Oxford University Press, 2013.

Arthur, Jean. "Profile: Ogden, Utah." *Where to Retire* (2014): 66–74.

Arthurson, Kathy. "Social Mix, Reputation and Stigma: Exploring Residents' Perspectives of Neighbourhood Effects." In *Neighbourhood Effects Research: New Perspectives*, edited by Maarten van Ham, David Manley, Nick Bailey, Ludi Simpson, and Duncan Maclennan, 101–19. Dordrecht: Springer Netherlands, 2012.

Arthurson, Kathy, Michael Darcy, and Dallas Rogers. "Televised Territorial Stigma: How Social Housing Tenants Experience the Fictional Media Representation of Estates in Australia." *Environment and Planning A* 46, no. 6 (2014): 1334–50.

August, Martine. "Challenging the Rhetoric of Stigmatization: The Benefits of Concentrated Poverty in Toronto's Regent Park." *Environment and Planning A* 46, no. 6 (2014): 1317–33.

Aula, Pekka, and Vesa Harmaakorpi. "An Innovative Milieu—a View on Regional Reputation Building: Case Study of the Lahti Urban Region." *Regional Studies* 42, no. 4 (2008): 523–38.

Bacon, David. *Illegal People: How Globalization Creates Migration and Criminalizes Immigrants*. Boston: Beacon, 2008.

Bakhtin, Mikhail. *Rabelais and His World*. Bloomington: Indiana University Press, 1941.

Barber, Alicia. *Reno's Big Gamble: Image and Reputation in the Biggest Little City*. Lawrence: University Press of Kansas, 2008.

Barnes, Lyle J. *Notorious Two-Bit Street*. West Conshohocken: Infinity, 2009.

Barros, Joana. "Simulating Urban Dynamics in Latin American Cities." In *GeoDynamics*, edited by Peter M. Atkinson, Giles M. Foody, Steven E. Darby, and Fulong Wu, 313–28. Boca Raton: CRC Press, 2005.

Basquiat, Jennifer Huss. "Reproducing Patriarchy and Erasing Feminism: The Selective Construction of History within the Mormon Community." *Journal of Feminist Studies in Religion* 17 no. 2 (2001): 5–37.

Bauder, Harald. "Neighbourhood Effects and Cultural Exclusion." *Urban Studies* 39, no. 1 (2002): 85–93.

Becker, Howard S. *Outsiders*. New York: Free Press, 1963.

Bell, David, and Mark Jayne. "Small Cities? Towards a Research Agenda." *International Journal of Urban and Regional Research* 33, no. 3 (2009): 683–99.

Bell, Derrick A., Jr. "Brown v. Board of Education and the Interest-Convergence Dilemma." *Harvard Law Review* 93, no. 3 (1980): 518–33.

Berger, Peter L., and Thomas Luckmann. *The Social Construction of Reality: A Treatise in the Sociology of Knowledge*. Garden City: Doubleday, 1966.

Blokland, Talja. "'You Got to Remember You Live in Public Housing': Place-Making in an American Housing Project." *Housing, Theory and Society* 25, no. 1 (2008): 31–46.

Blumer, Herbert. "Race Prejudice as a Sense of Group Position." *Pacific Sociological Review* 1, no. 1 (1958): 3–7.

Bonilla-Silva, Eduardo. "From Bi-Racial to Tri-Racial: Towards a New System of Racial Stratification in the U.S.A." *Ethnic and Racial Studies* 27, no. 6 (2004): 931–50.

———. "More Than Prejudice: Restatement, Reflections, and New Directions in Critical Race Theory." *Sociology of Race and Ethnicity* 1, no. 1 (2015): 73–87.

———. *Racism without Racists: Color-Blind Racism and the Persistence of Racial Inequality in America*. Lanham: Rowman and Littlefield, 2009.

———. "Rethinking Racism: Toward a Structural Interpretation." *American Sociological Review* 62, no. 3 (1997): 465–80.

Bonilla-Silva, Eduardo, and David G. Embrick. "'Every Place Has a Ghetto...': The Significance of Whites' Social and Residential Segregation." *Symbolic Interaction* 30, no. 3 (2007): 323–45.

Bonilla-Silva, Eduardo, Carla Goar, and David G. Embrick. "When Whites Flock Together: The Social Psychology of White Habitus." *Critical Sociology* 32, no. 2–3 (2006): 229–53.

Bourgois, Philippe. *In Search of Respect: Selling Crack in El Barrio*. Cambridge: Cambridge University Press, 2003.

Bourgois, Philippe, and Jeffrey Schonberg. *Righteous Dopefiend*. Berkeley: University of California Press, 2009.

Box, Steven. *Power, Crime and Mystification*. London: Routledge, 2002.

Braga, Anthony A., David M. Kennedy, Elin J. Waring, and Anne Morrison Piehl. "Problem-Oriented Policing, Deterrence, and Youth Violence: An Evaluation of Boston's Operation Ceasefire." *Journal of Research in Crime and Delinquency* 38, no. 3 (2001): 195–225.

Bringhurst, Newell G. "The 'Missouri Thesis' Revisisted: Early Mormonism, Slavery, and the Status of Black People." In *Black and Mormon*, edited by Newell G. Bringhurst and Darron T. Smith, 13–33. Urbana: University of Illinois Press, 2006.

Brown, Bubba. "Ogden Rooftop Bar Wants to Attract Locals." *Standard-Examiner*, July 9, 2013. https://www.standard.net/news/business/ogden-rooftop-bar-wants-to-attract-locals.

Bullard, Robert Doyle, Glenn Steve Johnson, and Angel O. Torres. *Highway Robbery: Transportation Racism and New Routes to Equity*. Cambridge: South End Press, 2004.

Bullock, Cathy Ferrand. "Framing Domestic Violence Fatalities: Coverage by Utah Newspapers." *Women's Studies in Communication* 30, no. 1 (2007): 34–63.

Burawoy, Michael. *Ethnography Unbound: Power and Resistance in the Modern Metropolis*. Berkeley: University of California Press, 1991.

———. *Global Ethnography*. Berkeley: University of California Press, 2000.

Bush, Lester E. "Mormonism's Negro Doctrine: An Historical Overview." *Dialogue: A Journal of Mormon Thought* 8 (1973): 11–68.

Cadge, Wendy, Sara Curran, B. Nadya Jaworsky, and Peggy Levitt. "The City as Context: Culture and Scale in New Immigrant Destinations." *Amérique Latine Histoire et Mémoire: Les Cahiers ALHIM* 20 (2010): 109–36.

Cairns, Becky. "Why Are Utahns So Obsessed with Halloween?" *Standard-Examiner*, October 20, 2013. http://www.standard.net/Lifestyle/2013/10/20/Why-are-Utahns-so-obsessed-with-HalloweenIJ.

Campbell, David E., John C. Green, and J. Quin Monson. *Seeking the Promised Land: Mormons and American Politics*. Cambridge: Cambridge University Press, 2014.

Campbell, Elizabeth, Julia R. Henly, Delbert S. Elliott, and Katherine Irwin. "Subjective Constructions of Neighborhood Boundaries: Lessons from a Qualitative Study of Four Neighborhoods." *Journal of Urban Affairs* 31, no. 4 (2009): 461–90.

Canham, Matt. "Salt Lake County Is Becoming Less Mormon—Utah County Is Headed in the Other Direction." *Salt Lake Tribune*, July 16, 2017. http://archive.sltrib.com/article.php?id=5403049&itype=CMSID.

Cannon, Brian Q. "Change Engulfs a Frontier Settlement: Ogden and Its Residents Respond to the Railroad." *Journal of Mormon History* 12 (1985): 15–28.

Carlisle, Nate. "Right after the Mormon Church Gave Blacks the Priesthood, a Polygamous Offshoot Saw Its Ranks Grow." *Salt Lake Tribune*, May 25, 2018. https://www.sltrib.com/news/polygamy/2018/05/25/right-after-the-mormon-church-gave-blacks-the-priesthood-a-polygamous-offshoot-saw-its-ranks-grow.

Carlson, Sonja. "Ogden Is One of Utah's Worst Places? Whose Survey Is This?" *Standard-Examiner*, August 22, 2015. http://www.standard.net/Local/2015/08/21/Ogden-is-one-of-Utah-s-worst-places-Whose-survey-is-this.

Carr, James H. "The Complexity of Segregation: Why It Continues 30 Years after the Enactment of the Fair Housing Act." *Cityscape: A Journal of Policy Development and Research* 4, no. 3 (1999): 139–46.

Charles, Camille Zubrinsky. "Comfort Zones: Immigration, Acculturation, and the Neighborhood Racial-Composition Preferences of Latinos and Asians." *Du Bois Review: Social Science Research on Race* 4, no. 1 (2007): 41–77.

———. "The Dynamics of Racial Residential Segregation." *Annual Review of Sociology* 29 (2003): 167–207.

———. *Won't You Be My Neighbor?: Race, Class, and Residence in Los Angeles*. New York: Russell Sage Foundation, 2009.

Charmaz, Kathy. *Constructing Grounded Theory: A Practical Guide through Qualitative Analysis*. London: Sage, 2006.

Christakis, Nicholas A. and James H. Fowler. *Connected: The Surprising Power of Our Social Networks and How They Shape Our Lives*. New York: Little, Brown, 2009.

Cohen, Stanley. *Folk Devils and Moral Panics: The Creation of the Mods And Rockers*. London: MacGibbon and Kee, 1972.

Coleman, Mathew. "From Border Policing to Internal Immigration Control in the United States." In *A Companion to Border Studies*, edited by Thomas M. Wilson and Hastings Donnan, 419–37. Chichester: John Wiley and Sons, 2012.

———. "A Geopolitics of Engagement: Neoliberalism, the War on Terrorism, and the Reconfiguration of U.S. Immigration Enforcement." *Geopolitics* 12, no. 4 (2007): 607–34.

Coleman, Ronald G. "Blacks in Utah History: An Unknown Legacy." In *The Peoples of Utah*, edited by Helen Z. Papanikolas, 115–40. Salt Lake City: Utah State Historical Society, 1976.

Conley, Don C. "The Pioneer Chinese of Utah." In *The Peoples of Utah*, edited by Helen Z. Papanikolas, 251–77. Salt Lake City: Utah State Historical Society, 1976.

Cooley, Everett L. "Clarion, Utah, Jewish Colony in 'Zion.'" In *Being Different: Stories of Utah's Minorities*, edited by Stanford J. Layton, 101–19. Salt Lake City: Signature Books, 2001. Original edition, 1968.

Corchado, Alfredo. "Illegal Migrants Sometimes Exploited." *Standard-Examiner*, August 13, 1985.

———. "Immigration Proposals Draw Fire." *Standard-Examiner*, August 14, 1985.

———. "Life of Migrant Often Very Short." *Standard-Examiner*, August 12, 1985.

———. "One Man's Lament: No Respect." *Standard-Examiner*, August 11, 1985.

Coulton, Claudia J., Jill Korbin, Tsui Chan, and Marilyn Su. "Mapping Residents' Perceptions of Neighborhood Boundaries: A Methodological Note." *American Journal of Community Psychology* 29, no. 2 (2001): 371–83.

Cresswell, Tim. *In Place/Out of Place: Geography, Ideology, and Transgression*. Minneapolis: University of Minnesota Press, 1992.

Cross, John C., and Alfonso Hernández. "Place, Identity, and Deviance: A Community-Based Approach to Understanding the Relationship Between Deviance and Place." *Deviant Behavior* 32, no. 6 (2011):503–37.

Curtis, Larry D. "Utah Loves Halloween." KUTV, October 31, 2017. http://kutv.com/news/local/utah-loves-halloween.

David, Gary C. "Deficit Model of Ethnicity." In *Encyclopedia of Race, Ethnicity, and Society*, edited by Richard T. Schaefer, 379–80. Thousand Oaks: Sage, 2008.

Davidson, Lee. "How Utah's Capitol Marches to a Mormon Beat." *Salt Lake Tribune*, March 28, 2012. https://archive.sltrib.com/article.php?id=53709967&itype=cmsid.

Deener, Andrew. "The 'Black Section' of the Neighborhood: Collective Visibility and Collective Invisibility as Sources of Place Identity." *Ethnography* 11, no. 1 (2010): 45–67.

———. *Venice: Conflict and Community in Los Angeles*. Chicago: University of Chicago Press, 2012.

Dekker, Karien. "Testing the Racial Proxy Hypothesis: What Is It That Residents Don't Like about Their Neighbourhood?" In *Understanding Neighbourhood Dynamics: New Insights for Neighbourhood Effects Research*, edited by Maarten van Ham, David Manley, Nick Bailey, Ludi Simpson, and Duncan Maclennan, 225–54. Dordrecht: Springer Netherlands, 2012.

Del Richards, Allen. *White's City*. Bloomington: First Books, 2003.

Delgado, Richard, and Jean Stefancic. *Critical Race Theory: An Introduction*. New York: New York University Press, 2017.

DiAngelo, Robin. "White Fragility." *International Journal of Critical Pedagogy* 3, no. 3 (2011): 54–70.

Dinnie, Keith. *Nation Branding: Concepts, Issues, Practice*. London: Routledge, 2015.

Donato, Katharine M., Melissa Stainback, and Carl L. Bankston. "The Economic Incorporation of Mexican Immigrants in Southern Louisiana: A Tale of Two Cities." In *New Destinations: Mexican Immigration in the United States*, edited by Victor Zuniga and Ruben Hernandez-Leon, 76–100. New York: Russell Sage Foundation, 2005.

Douglas, Mary. *Purity and Danger: An Analysis of Concepts of Pollution and Taboo*. London: Routledge and Keegan Paul, 2003.

DuBois, W. E. B. *The Souls of Black Folks*. New York: Bantam Books, 1989. Original edition, 1903.

Duneier, Mitch. *Sidewalk*. New York: Farrar, Straus, and Giroux, 1999.

Durán, Robert J. *Gang Life in Two Cities: An Insider's Journey*. New York: Columbia University Press, 2013.

———. "Legitimated Oppression: Inner-City Mexican American Experiences with Police Gang Enforcement." *Journal of Contemporary Ethnography* 38, no. 2 (2009a): 143–68.

———. "Over-Inclusive Gang Enforcement and Urban Resistance: A Comparison between Two Cities." *Social Justice* 36, no. 1 (2009b): 82–101.

Durkheim, Emile. *The Elementary Forms of the Religious Life*. Mineola: Dover, 2008. Original edition, 1915.

———. *The Rules of Sociological Method: And Selected Texts on Sociology and Its Method*. New York: Free Press, 2014.

Erikson, Kai T. *Wayward Puritans: A Study in the Sociology of Deviance*. New York: Wiley, 1966.

Farley, Reynolds, Charlotte Steeh, Maria Krysan, Tara Jackson, and Keith Reeves. "Stereotypes and Segregation: Neighborhoods in the Detroit Area." *American Journal of Sociology* 100, no. 3 (1994): 750–80.

Feagin, Joe R., and Karyn D. McKinney. *The Many Costs of Racism*. Lanham: Rowman and Littlefield, 2003.

Fellner, Jamie. *Decades of Disparity: Drug Arrests and Race in the United States*. New York: Human Rights Watch, 2009.

Fetzer, Leland A. "Tolstoy and Mormonism." *Dialogue: A Journal of Mormon Thought* 6, no. 1 (1971): 13–29.

Fine, Gary Alan. *Difficult Reputations: Collective Memories of the Evil, Inept, and Controversial*. Chicago: University of Chicago Press, 2014.

———. "Reputational Entrepreneurs and the Memory of Incompetence: Melting Supporters, Partisan Warriors, and Images of President Harding." *American Journal of Sociology* 101, no. 5 (1996): 1159–93.

———. *Sticky Reputations: The Politics of Collective Memory in Midcentury America*. London: Routledge, 2012.

———. "Thinking about Evil: Adolf Hitler and the Dilemma of the Social Construction of Reputation." In *Culture in Mind: Toward a Sociology of Culture and Cognition*, edited by Karen Cerulo, 227–37. London: Routledge, 2002.

Fletcher Stack, Peggy. "Program Aims to Stop Suicide, Homelessness in LGBT Mormon Youth." *Salt Lake Tribune*, March 15, 2015. http://archive.sltrib.com/article.php?id=57682784&itype=CMSID.

Florida, Richard. *The Rise of the Creative Class: And How It's Transforming Work, Leisure, Community and Everyday Life*. New York: Basic Books, 2002.

Foster, Jonathan. *Stigma Cities: The Reputation and History of Birmingham, San Francisco, and Las Vegas*. Norman: University of Oklahoma Press, 2018.

Frank, Reanne, Ilana Redstone Akresh, and Bo Lu. "Latino Immigrants and the U.S. Racial Order: How and Where Do They Fit In?" *American Sociological Review* 75, no. 3 (2010): 378–401.

Franzini, Luisa, Margaret O'Brien Caughy, Saundra Murray Nettles, and Patricia O'Campo. "Perceptions of Disorder: Contributions of Neighborhood Characteristics to Subjective Perceptions of Disorder." *Journal of Environmental Psychology* 28, no. 1 (2008): 83–93.

Fredrickson, George M. *Racism: A Short History*. Princeton: Princeton University Press, 2002.

Gallagher, Charles A. "Racial Redistricting: Expanding the Boundaries of Whiteness." In *The Politics of Multiracialism*, edited by Heather M. Dalmage, 59–76. Albany: State University of New York Press, 2004.

Gans, Herbert J. "The Possibility of a New Racial Hierarchy in the Twenty-First Century United States." In *The Cultural Territories of Race*, edited by Michele Lamont, 371–90. Chicago: University of Chicago Press and Russell Sage Foundation, 1999.

Gardner, Matthew, Sebastian Johnson, and Meg Wiehe. *Undocumented Immigrants' State and Local Tax Contributions*. Washington, D.C.: Institute on Taxation and Economic Policy, 2015.

Garfinkel, Harold. *Studies in Ethnomethodology*. Englewood Cliffs: Prentice Hall, 1967.

Garot, Robert. *Who You Claim: Performing Gang Identity in School and on the Streets*. New York: New York University Press, 2010.

Geertz, Clifford. "Thick Description: Toward an Interpretive Theory of Culture." In *The Interpretation of Cultures*. New York: Basic Books, 1973.

Gieryn, Thomas F. "A Space for Place in Sociology." *Annual Review of Sociology* 26 (2000): 463–96.

Gitis, Ben, and Jacqueline Varas. *The Labor and Output Declines from Removing All Undocumented Immigrants*. Washington, D.C.: American Action Forum, 2016.

Glaser, Barney G., and Anselm L. Strauss. *The Discovery of Grounded Theory: Strategies for Qualitative Research*. Chicago: Aldine, 1967.

Glass, Pepper G. "Dividing and Defending Ogden: The Intersection of Race Making and Space Making in a Diverse Community." *Ethnic and Racial Studies* 40, no. 14 (2017): 2520–38.

———. "Using History to Explain the Present: The Past as Born and Performed." *Ethnography* 17, no. 1 (2016): 92–110.

Glückler, Johannes. "Geography of Reputation: The City as the Locus of Business Opportunity." *Regional Studies* 41, no. 7 (2007): 949–61.

Goffman, Erving. *Stigma: Notes on the Management of Spoiled Identity*. Eaglewood Cliffs: Prentice Hall, 2009. Original edition, 1963.

Gragg, Larry Dale. *Bright Light City: Las Vegas in Popular Culture*. Lawrence: University Press of Kansas, 2013.

Gramsci, Antonio. *Antonio Gramsci: Selections from the Prison Notebooks*. New York: International Publishers, 1971.

Greenberg, Miriam. *Branding New York: How a City in Crisis Was Sold to the World*. London: Routledge, 2009.

Griffiths, David. "New Midwesterners, New Southerners: Immigration Experiences in Four Rural American Settings." In *New Faces in New Places: The Changing Geography of American Immigration*, edited by Douglas S. Massey, 179–210. New York: Russell Sage Foundation, 2008.

Gubrium, Jaber F., and James A. Holstein. *The New Language of Qualitative Method*. Oxford: Oxford University Press, 1997.

Gurrister, Tim. "Officials: Census Not a Crackdown: Illegal Immigrants Need Not Fear Being Turned In." *Standard-Examiner*, December 10, 2009.

———. "Ogden Blimp May Be Patrolling by Christmas." *Standard-Examiner*, August 31, 2011.

Halbwachs, Maurice. *On Collective Memory*. Chicago: University of Chicago Press, 1992.

Hall, Stuart, and Tony Jefferson. *Resistance through Rituals: Youth Subcultures in Post-war Britain*. London: Hutchinson, 1976.

Halling, Greg. "Ogden—Boomtown or Ghetto? An S-E Reader Conversation." *Standard-Examiner*, April 8, 2017. https://www.standard.net/opinion/guest-commentary/ogden-boomtown-or-ghetto-an-s-e-reader-conversation/article_b86ea7a1-fbf8-55c8-9195-dab69080d626.html.

Hampshire, David, Martha Sonntag Bradley, and Allen D. Roberts. *A History of Summit County*. Salt Lake City: Utah State Historical Society, 1998.

Hannerz, Ulf. *Soulside: Inquiries into Ghetto Culture and Community*. New York: Columbia University Press, 1969.

Harcourt, Bernard E. *Illusion of Order: The False Promise of Broken Windows Policing*. Cambridge: Harvard University Press, 2009.

Harlan, Chico. "In St. Louis, Delmar Boulevard Is the Line That Divides a City by Race and Perspective." *Washington Post*, August 22, 2014. https://www.washingtonpost.com/national/in-st-louis-delmar-boulevard-is-the-line-that-divides-a-city-by-race-and-perspective/2014/08/22/de692962-a2ba-4f53-8bc3-54f88f848fdb_story.html.

Harry, Beth, and Janette Klingner. "Discarding the Deficit Model." *Educational Leadership* 64, no. 5 (2007): 16–21.

Harvey, David. *The Condition of Postmodernity: An Enquiry into the Origins of Cultural Change*. New York: Blackwell, 1989.

Hastings, Annette, and Jo Dean. "Challenging Images: Tackling Stigma through Estate Regeneration." *Policy and Politics* 31, no. 2 (2003): 171–84.

Havekes, Esther, Marcel Coenders, and Tanja van der Lippe. "Positive or Negative Ethnic Encounters in Urban Neighbourhoods? A Photo Experiment on the Net Impact of Ethnicity and Neighbourhood Context on Attitudes towards Minority and Majority Residents." *Social Science Research* 42, no. 4 (2013): 1077–91.

Hester, Raymond. "Subconscious Landscapes of the Heart." *Places* 2, no. 3 (1982): 10–22.

Hiemstra, Nancy. "Spatial Disjunctures and Division in the New West: Latino Immigration to Leadville, Colorado." In *Immigrants Outside Megalopolis: Ethnic Transformation in the Heartland*, edited by Richard C. Jones, 89–113. Lanham: Lexington Books, 2008.

Hipp, John R. "Resident Perceptions of Crime: How Much Is 'Bias' and How Much Is Microneighborhood Effects?" *Criminology* 48, no. 2 (2010): 475–508.

Hoe, Charlotte. "Ogden's 25th Street Jump Place for Tramps, Road's End for Alcoholics, but It's Home." *Salt Lake Tribune*, October 23, 1972.

———. "Park Blooms for West Ogden, Breaks Down Isolation of Sector." *Salt Lake Tribune*, October 10, 1971.

Holcomb, H. Briavel, and Robert A. Beauregard. *Revitalizing Cities*. Washington, D.C.: Association of American Geographers, 1981.

Holley, Val. *25th Street Confidential: Drama, Decadence, and Dissipation along Ogden's Rowdiest Road*. Salt Lake City: University of Utah Press, 2013.

Iceland, John. *Where We Live Now: Immigration and Race in the United States*. Berkeley: University of California Press, 2009.
Jackson, W. Kesler. *Elijah Abel: The Life and Times of a Black Priesthood Holder*. Springville: Cedar Fort, 2013.
Jacobs, Jane. *The Death and Life of Great American Cities*. New York: Vintage Books, 1961.
Jameson, Kenneth P. *How Many Undocumented Immigrants Live in Utah? A Direct Measure*. New York: Russel Sage Foundation, 2009.
Jean, Sandrine. "Neighbourhood Attachment Revisited: Middle-Class Families in the Montreal Metropolitan Region." *Urban Studies* 53, no. 12 (2016): 2567–83.
Jenkins, Cozette. "Ogden to Become a 'College Town.'" *The Signpost*, July 30, 2012. http://signpost.mywebermedia.com/2012/07/30/ogden-to-become-a-college-town/.
Jensen, Sune Qvotrup, and Ann-Dorte Christensen. "Territorial Stigmatization and Local Belonging: A Study of the Danish Neighbourhood Aalborg East." *City* 16, no. 1–2 (2012): 74–92.
Jimenez, Tomas. *Replenished Ethnicity: Mexican Americans, Immigration, and Identity*. Berkeley: University of California Press, 2010.
Johnson, Allan G. *Privilege, Power, and Difference*. Boston: McGraw-Hill, 2001.
Jones, Nikki, and Christina Jackson. "'You Just Don't Go Down There': Learning to Avoid the Ghetto in San Francisco." In *The Ghetto: Contemporary Global Issues and Controversies*, edited by Bruce Haynes and Ray Hutchinson, 83–109. Boulder: Westview Press, 2012.
Jones, Richard C. "Cultural Retrenchment and Economic Marginality: Mexican Immigrants in San Antonio." In *Immigrants Outside Megalopolis: Ethnic Transformation in the Heartland*, edited by Richard C. Jones, 132–62. Lanham: Lexington Books, 2008.
Jung, Carl. *The Collected Works of C. G. Jung*. Vol. 11, *Psychology and Religion*, translated by R. F. C. Hull. New York: Pantheon Books, 1958.
Kallin, Hamish, and Tom Slater. "Activating Territorial Stigma: Gentrifying Marginality on Edinburgh's Periphery." *Environment and Planning A* 46, no. 6 (2014): 1351–68.
Kasinitz, Phillip, John H. Mollenkopf, Mary C. Waters, and Jennifer Holdaway. *Inheriting the City: The Children of Immigrants Come of Age*. New York: Russell Sage Foundation, 2009.
Katz, Jack. "Time for New Urban Ethnographies." *Ethnography* 11, no. 1 (2010): 25–44.
Kaufman, Jason, and Matthew E. Kaliner. "The Re-accomplishment of Place in Twentieth Century Vermont and New Hampshire: History Repeats Itself, Until It Doesn't." *Theory and Society* 40, no. 2 (2011): 119–54.
Kearns, Ade, Oliver Kearns, and Louise Lawson. "Notorious Places: Image, Reputation, Stigma: The Role of Newspapers in Area Reputations for Social Housing Estates." *Housing Studies* 28, no. 4 (2013): 579–98.
Kelley, Patrick. "Legal and Protective Measures: Field Reports: Utah (Box 111, Folder 01)." *American Social Health Association Records, 1905–1990*, 1949.
Kennedy, David M., Anthony A. Braga, Anne M. Piehl, and Elin J. Waring. *Reducing Gun Violence: The Boston Gun Project's Operation Ceasefire*. Washington, D.C.: U.S. Department of Justice, 2001.

Kirkness, Paul. "The Cités Strike Back: Restive Responses to Territorial Taint in the French Banlieues." *Environment and Planning A* 46, no. 6 (2014): 1281–96.

Kirkness, Paul, and Andreas Tijé-Dra, eds. *Negative Neighbourhood Reputation and Place Attachment: The Production and Contestation of Territorial Stigma*. London: Routledge, 2017.

Kitsuse, John I. "Societal Reaction to Deviant Behavior: Problems of Theory and Method." *Social Problems* 9, no. 3 (1962): 247–56.

Kitsuse, John I., and Aaron V. Cicourel. "A Note on the Uses of Official Statistics." *Social Problems* 11, no. 2 (1963): 131–39.

Klay, Andrew. "Mormons Love Peculiar Baby Names, Blog Says." Fox 13, January 19, 2015. https://fox13now.com/2015/01/19/mormons-love-oddball-baby-names-utah-blog-says/.

Knight, Wendy. "Outdoors Is the Way Up in Ogden." *New York Times*, June 22, 2007. https://www.nytimes.com/2007/06/22/travel/escapes/22ogden.html.

Koch, Makenzie. "Ogden's Rough and Tumble Identity Can Be Traced to Rollicking 25th Street." *Standard-Examiner*, April 6, 2017. https://www.standard.net/news/local/ogden-s-rough-and-tumble-identity-can-be-traced-to/article_58d1b8ac-ec04-572d-ac05-d6bb99f7f0f0.html.

Kotler, Philip, Donald H. Haider, and Irving Rein. *Marketing Places*. New York: Free Press, 2002.

Krakauer, Jon. *Under the Banner of Heaven: A Story of Violent Faith*. New York: Anchor Books, 2004.

Kraus, Michael W., Paul K. Piff, Rodolfo Mendoza-Denton, Michelle L. Rheinschmidt, and Dacher Keltner. "Social Class, Solipsism, and Contextualism: How the Rich Are Different from the Poor." *Psychological Review* 119, no. 3 (2012): 546–72.

Krysan, Maria. "Community Undesirability in Black and White: Examining Racial Residential Preferences through Community Perceptions." *Social Problems* 49, no. 4 (2002): 521–43.

Krysan, Maria, and Michael Bader. "Perceiving the Metropolis: Seeing the City through a Prism of Race." *Social Forces* 86, no. 2 (2007): 699–733.

Krysan, Maria, Mick P. Couper, Reynolds Farley, and Tyrone Forman. "Does Race Matter in Neighborhood Preferences? Results from a Video Experiment." *American Journal of Sociology* 115, no. 2 (2009): 527–59.

Kullberg, Agneta, Toomas Timpka, Tommy Svensson, Nadine Karlsson, and Kent Lindqvist. "Does the Perceived Neighborhood Reputation Contribute to Neighborhood Differences in Social Trust and Residential Wellbeing?" *Journal of Community Psychology* 38, no. 5 (2010): 591–606.

Kusenbach, Margarethe. "Street Phenomenology: The Go-Along as Ethnographic Research Tool." *Ethnography* 4, no. 3 (2003): 455–85.

Lacy, Elaine. "Cultural Enclaves and Transnational Ties: Mexican Immigration and Settlement in South Carolina." In *Latino Immigrants and the Transformation of the U.S. South*, edited by Mary E. Odem and Elaine Lacy, 1–17. Athens: University of Georgia Press, 2009.

Lamont, Michèle, and Virág Molnár. "The Study of Boundaries in the Social Sciences." *Annual Review of Sociology* 28 (2002): 167–95.
Langsdon, Sarah, and Melissa Johnson. *Legendary Locals of Ogden*. Charleston: Arcadia, 2012.
Larsen, Leia. "Nearly 900 ID'd by Ogden Police as Gang Members, Associates." *Standard-Examiner*, November 28, 2015.
Larsen, Shalae, and Sue Wilkerson. *Ogden's Trolley District*. Charleston: Arcadia, 2012.
Layton, Stanford J., ed. *Being Different: Stories of Utah's Minorities*. Salt Lake City: Signature Books, 2001.
Lee, Don. "In Quiet Ogden, Utah, a Surprising Glimpse of Income Equality." *Los Angeles Times*, January 28, 2015. http://www.latimes.com/nation/la-na-utah-town-income-gap-20150719-story.html.
Lee, Jennifer, and Frank D. Bean. "Reinventing the Color Line: Immigration and America's New Racial/Ethnic Divide." *Social Forces* 86, no. 2 (2007): 1–26.
Lees, Loretta. "Gentrification and Social Mixing: Towards an Inclusive Urban Renaissance?" *Urban Studies* 45, no. 12 (2008): 2449–70.
Lees, Loretta, Tom Slater, and Elvin Wyly. *Gentrification*. London: Routledge, 2013.
Lemert, Edwin M. "Beyond Mead: The Societal Reaction to Deviance." *Social Problems* 21, no. 4 (1974): 457–468.
Lewicka, Maria. "Place Attachment: How Far Have We Come in the Last 40 Years?" *Journal of Environmental Psychology* 31, no. 3 (2011): 207–30.
Lewis, Oscar. *Five Families: Mexican Case Studies in the Culture of Poverty*. New York: Basic Books, 1959.
Liazos, Alexander. "The Poverty of the Sociology of Deviance: Nuts, Sluts, and Preverts." *Social Problems* 20, no. 1 (1972): 103–20.
Lichter, Daniel T., and Kenneth M. Johnson. "Immigrant Gateways and Hispanic Migration to New Destinations." *International Migration Review* 43, no. 3 (2009): 496–518.
Lipsitz, George. *The Possessive Investment in Whiteness: How White People Profit from Identity Politics*. Philadelphia: Temple University Press, 2006.
———. "The Racialization of Space and the Spatialization of Race: Theorizing the Hidden Architecture of Landscape." *Landscape Journal* 26, no. 1 (2007): 10–23.
Lloyd, Richard. *Neo-Bohemia: Art and Commerce in the Postindustrial City*. London: Routledge, 2006.
———. "Neo-Bohemia: Art and Neighborhood Redevelopment in Chicago." *Journal of Urban Affairs* 24, no. 5 (2002): 517–32.
Loerzel, Robert. "How the World Media Covers Chicago." *Chicago Magazine*, September 24, 2013. https://www.chicagomag.com/Chicago-Magazine/The-312/September-2013/Chicago-World-Media/.
Lofland, John, David A. Snow, Leon Anderson, and Lyn Lofland. *Analyzing Social Settings: A Guide to Qualitative Observation and Analysis*. 4th ed. Belmont: Wadsworth, 2006.
Lofland, Lyn. *The Public Realm: Quintessential City Life*. Hawthorne: Aldine de Gruyter, 1998.

Lott, Eric. *Love and Theft: Blackface Minstrelsy and the American Working Class.* Oxford: Oxford University Press, 1993.

Lui, Debora A. *Neon Signs, Underground Tunnels and Chinese American Identity: The Many Dimension of Visual Chinatown.* Cambridge: Massachusetts Institute of Technology, 2008.

Lyons, Christopher J, María B. Vélez, and Wayne A. Santoro. "Neighborhood Immigration, Violence, and City-Level Immigrant Political Opportunities." *American Sociological Review* 78, no. 4 (2013): 604–32.

Lythgoe, Dennis L. "Negro Slavery in Utah." *Utah Historical Quarterly* 39, no. 1 (1971): 40–54.

Mahoney, James, and Kathleen Thelen. "A Theory of Gradual Institutional Change." In *Explaining Institutional Change: Ambiguity, Agency, and Power*, edited by James Mahoney and Kathleen Thelen, 1–37. Cambridge: Cambridge University Press, 2010.

Maldonado, Marta Maria. "Latino Incorporation and Racialized Border Politics in the Heartland: Interior Enforcement and Policeability in an English-Only State." *American Behavioral Scientist* 58, no. 14 (2014): 1927–45.

Manzo, Lynne C. "For Better or Worse: Exploring Multiple Dimensions of Place Meaning." *Journal of Environmental Psychology* 25, no. 1 (2005): 67–86.

Manzo, Lynne C., and Douglas D. Perkins. "Finding Common Ground: The Importance of Place Attachment to Community Participation and Planning." *Journal of Planning Literature* 20, no. 4 (2006): 335–50.

Marklew, Tim. "A Brief History of Detroit's Eight Mile Wall." *Culture Trip*, January 4, 2018. https://theculturetrip.com/north-america/usa/michigan/articles/a-brief-history-of-detroits-eight-mile-wall/.

Marrow, Helen. *New Destination Dreaming: Immigration, Race, and Legal Status in the Rural American South.* Stanford: Stanford University Press, 2011.

———. "New Immigrant Destinations and the American Colour Line." *Ethnic and Racial Studies* 32, no. 6 (2009): 1037–57.

Massey, Douglas S., ed. *New Faces in New Places: The Changing Geography of American Immigration.* New York: Russell Sage Foundation, 2008.

———. "Residential Segregation and Neighborhood Conditions in U.S. Metropolitan Areas." In *American Becoming: Racial Trends and Their Consequences*, edited by Neil Smelser, William J. Wilson, and Faith Mitchell, 391–434. Washington, D.C.: National Academy Press, 2001.

Massey, Douglas S., and Nancy A. Denton. *American Apartheid: Segregation and the Making of the Underclass.* Cambridge: Harvard University Press, 1993.

Matsueda, Ross L. "Reflected Appraisals, Parental Labeling, and Delinquency: Specifying a Symbolic Interactionist Theory." *American Journal of Sociology* 97, no. 6 (1992): 1577–611.

Mayer, Edward H. "The Evolution of Culture and Tradition in Utah's Mexican-American Community." In *Being Different: Stories of Utah's Minorities*, edited by Stanford J. Layton, 182–94. Salt Lake City: Signature Books, 2001. Original edition, 1981.

Mazanti, Birgitte, and John Pløger. "Community Planning—from Politicised Places to Lived Spaces." *Journal of Housing and the Built Environment* 18, no. 4 (2003): 309–27.

McGlinchy, Audrey. "Residents of East Austin, Once a Bustling Black Enclave, Make a Suburban Exodus." KUT 90.5, July 12, 2017. http://kut.org/post/residents-east-austin-once-bustling-black-enclave-make-suburban-exodus.

McGrath Goodman, Leah. "As Wealth Inequality Soars, One City Shows the Way." *Newsweek*, September 24, 2015.

McKitrick, Cathy. "Ogden's Warm And Gritty Identity Unveiled: 'Still Untamed.'" *Standard-Examiner*, April 1, 2016. https://www.standard.net/news/government/ogden-s-warm-and-gritty-identity-unveiled-still-untamed.

———. "Union Station Director Pleads for Financial Support." *Standard-Examiner*, June 10, 2015. http://www.standard.net/Government/2015/06/10/Union-Station-Foundation-director-puts-out-plea-for-financial-support.

McKittrick, Katherine. *Demonic Grounds: Black Women and the Cartographies of Struggle*. Minneapolis: University of Minnesota Press, 2006.

———. "On Plantations, Prisons, and a Black Sense of Place." *Social and Cultural Geography* 12, no. 8 (2011): 947–63.

Means, Sean P. "Utah Magazine Owner on 'Women of Color' Headline: 'Lesson Learned.'" *Salt Lake Tribune*, July 11, 2012. http://archive.sltrib.com/article.php?id=54469267&itype=CMSID.

Meares, Tracey L. "The Law and Social Science of Stop and Frisk." *Annual Review of Law and Social Science* 10 (2014): 335–52.

Meinig, Donald W. "The Mormon Culture Region: Strategies and Patterns in the Geography of the American West, 1847–1964." *Annals of the Association of American Geographers* 55, no. 2 (1965): 191–219.

Mesa-Bains, Amalia. "Domesticana: The Sensibility of Chicana Rasquachismo." In *Chicana Feminisms: A Critical Reader*, edited by Gabriela F. Arredondo, Patricia Zavella, Aida Hurtado, Norma Klahn, and Olga Najera-Ramirez, 298–315. Durham: Duke University Press, 2003.

Meyer, Rachel, and Howard Kimeldorf. "Eventful Subjectivity: The Experiential Sources of Solidarity." *Journal of Historical Sociology* 28, no. 4 (2015): 429–57.

Meyerhoffer, Cassi. "'I Have More in Common with Americans Than I Do with Illegal Aliens': Culture, Perceived Threat, and Neighborhood Preferences." *Sociology of Race and Ethnicity* 1, no. 3 (2015): 378–93.

Miller, Chris. "Ogden Redevelopment Plans Inspire Hope and Fear from Residents." KUTV, July 6, 2016. http://kutv.com/news/local/ogden-residents-skeptical-of-efforts-to-improve-city.

Mills, Charles Wade. *The Racial Contract*. Ithaca: Cornell University Press, 1997.

Mohamed, A. Rafik, and Erik D. Fritsvold. *Dorm Room Dealers: Drugs and the Privileges of Race and Class*. Boulder: Lynne Rienner, 2010.

Molotch, Harvey, William Freudenberg, and Krista E. Paulsen. "History Repeats Itself, but How? City Character, Urban Tradition, and the Accomplishment of Place." *American Sociological Review* 65, no. 9 (2000): 791–823.

Moore, Adam. "The Eventfulness of Social Reproduction." *Sociological Theory* 29, no. 4 (2011): 294–314.

Mora, G. Cristina. *Making Hispanics: How Activists, Bureaucrats, and Media Constructed a New American.* Chicago: University of Chicago Press, 2014.

Morris, Alan. "Public Housing in Australia: A Case of Advanced Urban Marginality?" *Economic and Labour Relations Review* 24, no. 1 (2013): 80–96.

Morris, Aldon. *The Scholar Denied: W. E. B. Du Bois and the Birth of Modern Sociology.* Oakland: University of California Press, 2015.

Nelson, Lise, and Nancy Hiemstra. "Latino Immigrants and the Renegotiation of Place and Belonging in Small Town America." *Social and Cultural Geography* 9, no. 3 (2008): 319–42.

Nelson, Lise, and Peter B. Nelson. "The Global Rural: Gentrification and Linked Migration in the Rural U.S.A." *Progress in Human Geography* 35, no. 4 (2010): 441–59.

O'Higgins, Briana. "How Troost Became a Major Divide in Kansas City." KCUR 89.3, March 27, 2014. https://www.kcur.org/post/how-troost-became-major-divide-kansas-city#stream/0.

Ochoa, Gilda Laura. "Mexican Americans' Attitudes toward and Interactions with Mexican Immigrants: A Qualitative Analysis of Conflict and Cooperation." *Social Science Quarterly* 81, no. 1 (2000): 84–105.

Ogden City. *Five Year Consolidated Plan for 2011–2015.* Ogden: Ogden City, 2010. https://www.ogdencity.com/DocumentCenter/View/430/Five-Year-Consolidated-Plan-2011-2015-PDF.

Ogden City. *Neighborhood Revitalization Strategy Area (NRSA) Plan—Ogden City.* Ogden: Ogden City, 2015. https://www.ogdencity.com/DocumentCenter/View/438/Neighborhood-Revitalization-Strategy-Area-NRSA-Plan-PDF.

Ogden United Promise Neighborhoods. *Community Needs Assessment.* Ogden: Ogden United Promise Neighborhoods, 2015.

Olick, Jeffrey K. "Collective Memory: The Two Cultures." *Sociological Theory* 17, no. 3 (1999): 333–48.

Olick, Jeffrey K., and Joyce Robbins. "Social Memory Studies: From 'Collective Memory' to the Historical Sociology of Mnemonic Practices." *Annual Review of Sociology* 24 (1998): 105–40.

Oliver, J. Eric. *The Paradoxes of Integration: Race, Neighborhood, and Civic Life in Multiethnic America.* Chicago: University of Chicago Press, 2010.

Oliver, Melvin L., and Thomas M. Shapiro. *Black Wealth, White Wealth: A New Perspective on Racial Inequality.* New York: Taylor and Francis, 2006.

Ono, Hiromi. "Assimilation, Ethnic Competition, and Ethnic Identities of U.S.-Born Persons of Mexican Origin." *International Migration Review* 36, no. 3 (2002): 726–45.

Oppenheimer, Mark. "A Twist on Posthumous Baptisms Leaves Jews Miffed at Mormon Rite." *New York Times*, March 2, 2012. https://www.nytimes.com/2012/03/03/us/jews-take-issue-with-posthumous-mormon-baptisms-beliefs.html.

Osborne, Katy, Anna Ziersch, and Fran Baum. "Perceptions of Neighbourhood Disorder and Reputation: Qualitative Findings from Two Contrasting Areas of an Australian City." *Urban Policy and Research* 29, no. 3 (2011): 239–56.

Padilla, Laura M. "But You're Not a Dirty Mexican: Internalized Oppression, Latinos and Law." *Texas Hispanic Journal of Law and Policy* 7, no. 1 (2001): 59–113.

———. "Social and Legal Repercussions of Latinos' Colonized Mentality." *University of Miami Law Review* 53 (1999): 769–85.

Pager, Devah, and Hana Shepherd. "The Sociology of Discrimination: Racial Discrimination in Employment, Housing, Credit, and Consumer Markets." *Annual Review of Sociology* 34 (2008): 181–209.

Panek, Tracey E. "Life at Iosepa, Utah's Polynesian Colony." In *Being Different: Stories of Utah's Minorities*, edited by Stanford J. Layton, 87–100. Salt Lake City: Signature Books, 2001. Original edition, 1992.

Papanikolas, Helen Z. "Introduction." In *The Peoples of Utah*, edited by Helen Z. Papanikolas, 1–9. Salt Lake City: Utah State Historical Society, 1976.

Papanikolas, Helen Z., ed. *The Peoples of Utah*. Salt Lake City: Utah State Historical Society, 1976.

Parks, Casey. "Urban Renewal Hurt African Americans, Officials Say: Now Portland Leaders Want to Make Amends." *Oregonian*, November 5, 2016. http://www.oregonlive.com/portland/index.ssf/2016/11/urban_renewal_african_american.html.

Paschall, Keith R., II. "Gentrifying Indy: A Close Look at the Numbers." *Indianapolis Recorder*, August 10, 2017. http://www.indianapolisrecorder.com/opinion/article_8e51df2a-7dd2-11e7-80d6-5bdbc2d07ef7.html.

Paternoster, Raymond, and Leeann Iovanni. "The Labeling Perspective and Delinquency: An Elaboration of the Theory and an Assessment of the Evidence." *Justice Quarterly* 6, no. 3 (1989): 359–94.

Patterson, Orlando. "Culture and Continuity: Causal Structures in Socio-Cultural Persistence." In *Matters of Culture: Cultural Sociology in Practice*, edited by Roger Friedland and John Mohr, 71–109. Cambridge: Cambridge University Press, 2004.

Pattillo, Mary. *Black on the Block: The Politics of Race and Class in the City*. Chicago: University of Chicago Press, 2007.

Pattillo-McCoy, Mary. *Black Picket Fences: Privilege and Peril among the Black Middle Class*. Chicago: University of Chicago Press, 1999.

Peña, Vincent. "Utah Baseball Team's Ex Communication Director Says He Raised Concerns with 'Caucasian Heritage Night.'" *Salt Lake Tribune*, June 20, 2015.

Perlich, Pamela S. *Utah Minorities: The Story Told by 150 Years of Census Data*. Bureau of Economic and Business Research, David S. Eccles School of Business, University of Utah, 2002.

Permentier, Matthieu, Gideon Bolt, and Maarten van Ham. "Determinants of Neighbourhood Satisfaction and Perception of Neighbourhood Reputation." *Urban Studies* 48, no. 5 (2011): 977–96.

Permentier, Matthieu, Maarten van Ham, and Gideon Bolt. "Behavioural Responses to Neighbourhood Reputations." *Journal of Housing and the Built Environment* 22, no. 2 (2007): 199–213.

———. "Neighbourhood Reputation and the Intention to Leave the Neighbourhood." *Environment and Planning A* 41, no. 9 (2009): 2162–80.

———. "Same Neighbourhood . . . Different Views? A Confrontation of Internal and External Neighbourhood Reputations." *Housing Studies* 23, no. 6 (2008): 833–55.

Peterson, F. Ross, and Robert E. Parson. *Ogden City: Its Governmental Legacy*. Ogden: Chapelle Limited, 2001.

Phillips, Rick, Ryan T. Cragun, Barry A. Kosmin, and Ariela Keysar. *Mormons in the United States 1990–2008: Socio-Demographic Trends and Regional Differences*. Hartford: Institute for the Study of Secularism in Society and Culture, 2011.

Pierson, David. "An Urban Legend Has Resurfaced." *Los Angeles Times*, November 26, 2007. http://articles.latimes.com/2007/nov/26/local/me-tunnels26.

Piff, Paul K. "Wealth and the Inflated Self: Class, Entitlement, and Narcissism." *Personality and Social Psychology Bulletin* 40, no. 1 (2014): 34–43.

Piff, Paul K., Daniel M. Stancato, Stéphane Côté, Rodolfo Mendoza-Denton, and Dacher Keltner. "Higher Social Class Predicts Increased Unethical Behavior." *Proceedings of the National Academy of Sciences* 109, no. 11 (2012): 4086–91.

Pinyol, Isaac, Jordi Sabater-Mir, and Guifré Cuní. "How to Talk about Reputation Using a Common Ontology: From Definition to Implementation." *Proceedings of the Ninth Workshop on Trust in Agent Societies* (2007): 90–101.

Pond, Allison. *A Portrait of Mormons in the U.S.* Washington, D.C.: Pew Research Center, 2009.

Quillian, Lincoln, and Devah Pager. "Black Neighbors, Higher Crime? The Role of Racial Stereotypes in Evaluations of Neighborhood Crime." *American Journal of Sociology* 107, no. 3 (2001): 717–67.

Reeve, W. Paul. *Religion of a Different Color: Race and the Mormon Struggle for Whiteness*. Oxford: Oxford University Press, 2015.

Reiman, Jeffrey H. *The Rich Get Richer and the Poor Get Prison: Ideology, Class, and Criminal Justice*. Boston: Allyn and Bacon, 2000.

Reinarman, Craig, and Harry Gene Levine. *Crack in America: Demon Drugs and Social Justice*. Berkeley: University of California Press, 1997.

Riley, Naomi Schaefer. *'Til Faith Do Us Part: How Interfaith Marriage Is Transforming America*. Oxford: Oxford University Press, 2013.

Rios, Victor M. "Decolonizing the White Space in Urban Ethnography." *City and Community* 14, no. 3 (2015): 258–61.

———. *Punished: Policing the Lives of Black and Latino Boys*. New York: New York University Press, 2011.

Rivera, Andreas. "Forty Years Later, Ogden Hi-Fi Murders Are Still the Worst." *Standard-Examiner*, April 21, 2014. https://www.standard.net/forty-years-later-ogden-hi-fi-murders-are-still-the-worst.

Roberts, Richard C., and Richard W. Sadler. *Ogden: Junction City*. Northridge: Windsor, 1985.

Roche, Lisa Riley. "Buttars Apologizes for Potentially Racist Comment." *Deseret News*, February 12, 2008. https://www.deseretnews.com/article/695252618/Buttars-apologizes-for-potentially-racist-comment.html.

Rogers, Rob. "Ogden Mall to See Wrecking Ball." *Deseret News*, January 16, 2002. https://www.deseretnews.com/article/889948/Ogden-mall-to-see-wrecking-ball.html.

Rogler, Lloyd H. "Slum Neighborhoods in Latin America." *Journal of Inter-American Studies* 9, no. 4 (1967): 507–28.

Rosenfeld, Richard, and Robert Fornango. "The Impact of Police Stops on Precinct Robbery and Burglary Rates in New York City, 2003–2010." *Justice Quarterly* 31, no. 1 (2014): 96–122.

Rugh, Susan Sessions. "Branding Utah: Industrial Tourism in the Postwar American West." *Western Historical Quarterly* 37, no. 4 (2006): 445–72.

Rumbaut, Rubén G., and Walter A. Ewing. *The Myth of Immigrant Criminality and the Paradox of Assimilation: Incarceration Rates among Native and Foreign-Born Men.* Washington, D.C.: Immigration Policy Center, 2007.

Ryan, William. *Blaming the Victim.* New York: Vintage Books, 1976.

Saal, Mark. "Black Community Members Recall Backlash in Wake of Horrific Hi-Fi Murders." *Standard-Examiner*, February 11, 2018. https://www.standard.net/news/local/black-community-members-recall-backlash-in-wake-of-horrific-hi-fi-murders.

Sadler, Richard W., and Richard C. Roberts. *Weber County's History.* Ogden: Weber County Commission, 2000.

Sampson, Robert J. "Disparity and Diversity in the Contemporary City: Social (Dis)Order Revisited." *British Journal of Sociology* 60, no. 1 (2009): 1–31.

———. *Great American City: Chicago and the Enduring Neighborhood Effect.* Chicago: University of Chicago Press, 2012.

———. "Rethinking Crime and Immigration." *Contexts* 7, no. 1 (2008): 28–33.

Sampson, Robert J., Jeffrey D. Morenoff, and Thomas Gannon-Rowley. "Assessing 'Neighborhood Effects': Social Processes and New Directions in Research." *Annual Review of Sociology* 28, no. 1 (2002):443–78.

Sampson, Robert J., and Stephen W. Raudenbush. "Neighborhood Stigma and the Perception of Disorder." *Focus* 24, no. 1 (2005): 7–11.

———. "Seeing Disorder: Neighborhood Stigma and the Social Construction of 'Broken Windows.'" *Social Psychology Quarterly* 67, no. 4 (2004): 319–42.

———. "Systematic Social Observation of Public Spaces: A New Look at Disorder in Urban Neighborhoods." *American Journal of Sociology* 105, no. 3 (1999): 603–51.

Sandoval, Gerardo Francisco, and Marta Maria Maldonado. "Latino Urbanism Revisited: Placemaking in New Gateways and the Urban-Rural Interface." *Journal of Urbanism: International Research on Placemaking and Urban Sustainability* 5, no. 2–3 (2012): 193–218.

Sarlin, Benjy. "How America's Harshest Immigration Law Failed." MSNBC, December 16, 2013. http://www.msnbc.com/msnbc/undocumented-workers-immigration-alabama.

Sassen, Saskia. *The Mobility of Labor and Capital: A Study in International Investment and Labor Flow.* Cambridge: Cambridge University Press, 1990.

*Salt Lake Herald.* "Salt Lake Blushes." May 30, 1890.

Schmalzbauer, Leah. "Gender on a New Frontier: Mexican Migration in the Rural Mountain West." *Gender and Society* 23, no. 6 (2009): 747–67.

———. *The Last Best Place: Gender, Family, and Migration in the New West.* Stanford: Stanford University Press, 2014.

Scott, James C. *Weapons of the Weak: Everyday Forms of Peasant Resistance.* New Haven: Yale University Press, 1985.

Scott, Patricia Lyn, and Linda Thatcher. *Women in Utah History: Paradigm or Paradox*. Logan: Utah State University Press, 2005.

Seamon, David. "Body-Subject, Time-Space Routines, and Place-Ballets." In *The Human Experience of Space and Place*, edited by Anne Buttimer and David Seamon, 148–65. New York: St. Martin's Press, 1980.

Semerad, Tony. "Utahns, LDS Church Spent More on Prop. 8 Than Previously Known." *Salt Lake Tribune*, February 9, 2009. http://archive.sltrib.com/story.php?ref=/news/ci_11666895.

Serrano, Alfonso. "Why Undocumented Workers Are Good for the Economy." *Time*, June 14, 2012. http://business.time.com/2012/06/14/the-fiscal-fallout-of-state-immigration-laws/.

Shah, Nayan. *Contagious Divides: Epidemics and Race in San Francisco's Chinatown*. Berkeley: University of California Press, 2001.

Sharkey, Patrick, and Jacob W. Faber. "Where, When, Why, and for Whom Do Residential Contexts Matter? Moving Away from the Dichotomous Understanding of Neighborhood Effects." *Annual Review of Sociology* 40 (2014): 559–79.

Shaw, Mitch. "Ogden Council Approves Food Truck Restrictions." *Standard-Examiner*, August 14, 2014. https://www.standard.net/news/business/ogden-council-approves-food-truck-restrictions/article_9794a46d-f1c5-5d40-b50d-bfcd9db0a45d.html.

———. "Real Ogden: What's the City's 'Most Dangerous' Area? It's a Complex Question." *Standard-Examiner*, August 10, 2017. https://www.standard.net/news/local/real-ogden-what-s-the-city-s-most-dangerous-area/article_dd389aa2-6abc-5821-a93a-f9e1a3bf4ade.html.

Shenefelt, Mark. "Ogden Best in the West or among Most Dangerous?" *Standard-Examiner*, January 19, 2016. http://www.standard.net/News/2016/01/18/Ogden-best-in-the-West-or-among-most-dangerous.

Shutika, Debra Lattanzi. "The Ambivalent Welcome: Cinco de Mayo and the Symbolic Expression of Local Identity and Ethnic Relations." In *New Faces in New Places: The Changing Geography of American Immigration*, edited by Douglas S. Massey, 274–307. New York: Russell Sage Foundation, 2005.

———. *Beyond the Borderlands: Migration and Belonging in the United States and Mexico*. Berkeley: University of California Press, 2011.

———. "Bridging the Community: Nativism, Activism and the Politics of Inclusion in a Mexican Settlement Community." In *New Destinations: Mexican Immigration in the United States*, edited by Victor Zuniga and Ruben Hernandez-Leon, 103–32. New York: Russell Sage Foundation, 2005.

Sidanius, Jim, and Felicia Pratto. *Social Dominance: An Intergroup Theory of Social Hierarchy and Oppression*. Cambridge: Cambridge University Press, 2001.

Sidanius, Jim, Felicia Pratto, Colette van Laar, and Shana Levin. "Social Dominance Theory: Its Agenda and Method." *Political Psychology* 25, no. 6 (2004): 845–80.

Sillito, John R., and Sarah Langsdon. *Ogden*. Charleston: Arcadia, 2008.

Singer, Audrey. *The Rise of New Immigrant Gateways*. Washington, D.C.: Brookings Institution, 2004.

Skogan, Wesley G. "The Validity of Official Crime Statistics: An Empirical Investigation." *Social Science Quarterly* 55, no. 1 (1974): 25–38.

Slater, Tom. "Territorial Stigmatisation, Gentrification and Class Struggle: An Interview with Tom Slater." In *Negative Neighbourhood Reputation and Place Attachment: The Production and Contestation of Territorial Stigma*, edited by Paul Kirkness and Andreas Tijé-Dra, 235–51. London: Routledge, 2017.

———. "Your Life Chances Affect Where You Live: A Critique of the 'Cottage Industry' of Neighbourhood Effects Research." *International Journal of Urban and Regional Research* 37, no. 2 (2013): 367–87.

Slater, Tom, and Ntsiki Anderson. "The Reputational Ghetto: Territorial Stigmatisation in St Paul's, Bristol." *Transactions of the Institute of British Geographers* 37, no. 4 (2012): 530–46.

Small, Mario Luis. "De-exoticizing Ghetto Poverty: On the Ethics of Representation in Urban Ethnography." *City and Community* 14, no. 4 (2015): 352–58.

Small, Mario Luis, David J. Harding, and Michèle Lamont. "Reconsidering Culture and Poverty." *ANNALS of the American Academy of Political and Social Science* 629, no. 1 (2010): 6–27.

Smart, Christopher. "It Took 10 Years, but Ogden Man Beats City Hall." *Salt Lake Tribune*, January 31, 2009. https://archive.sltrib.com/story.php?ref=/news/ci_11599467.

Smith, Neil. *The New Urban Frontier: Gentrification And the Revanchist City*. London: Routledge, 2005.

Sohoni, Deenesh, and Jennifer Bickham Mendez. "Defining Immigrant Newcomers in New Destinations: Symbolic Boundaries in Williamsburg, Virginia." *Ethnic and Racial Studies* 37, no. 3 (2014): 496–516.

Sohoni, Deenesh, and Tracy W. P. Sohoni. "Perceptions of Immigrant Criminality: Crime and Social Boundaries." *Sociological Quarterly* 55, no. 1 (2014): 49–71.

Solórzano, Armando. *We Remember, We Celebrate, We Believe/Recuerdo, Celebración, y Esperanza: Latinos in Utah*. Salt Lake City: University of Utah Press, 2014.

Sorensen, A. Don. "Zion." In *Encyclopedia of Mormonism*, edited by Daniel H. Ludlow, 1624–26. New York: Macmillan Publishing Company, 1992.

Spangler, Jerry. "La Vida Utah: Hispanics Are a Vibrant Part of State's Culture." *Deseret News*, July 23, 2000. https://www.deseretnews.com/article/175021427/La-vida-Utah-Hispanics-are-a-vibrant-part-of-states-culture.html.

Speck, Jeff. *Walkable City: How Downtown Can Save America, One Step at a Time*. New York: North Point Press, 2013.

Spitzer, Steven. "Toward a Marxian Theory of Deviance." *Social Problems* 22, no. 5 (1975): 638–51.

Steinberg, Stephen. *Race Relations: A Critique*. Standford: Stanford University Press, 2007.

Stevens, Ashlie. "Change Is Coming to Louisville's Portland Neighborhood, Like It or Not." 89.3 WFPL, June 27, 2014. https://wfpl.org/change-coming-louisvilles-portland-neighborhood-it-or-not/.

Stevens, Michael J. "Passive-Aggression Among the Latter-day Saints." *Sunstone Magazine*, April 12, 2013.

Stewart, John J. *Mormonism and the Negro*. Orem: Bookmark, 1960.
Strauss, Anselm. *Images of the American City*. New Brunswick: Transaction Books, 1976.
Streeck, Wolfgang, and Kathleen Thelen. "Introduction: Institutional Change in Advanced Political Economies." In *Beyond Continuity: Institutional Change in Advanced Political Economies*, edited by Wolfgang Streeck and Kathleen Thelen, 1–39. Oxford: Oxford University Press, 2005.
Stupi, Elizabeth K., Ted Chiricos, and Marc Gertz. "Perceived Criminal Threat from Undocumented Immigrants: Antecedents and Consequences for Policy Preferences." *Justice Quarterly* 33, no. 2 (2016): 1–28.
Taggart, Stephen G. *Mormonism's Negro Policy: Social and Historical Origins*. Salt Lake City: University of Utah Press, 1970.
Taylor, Emily. "Are Indy Neighborhoods Gentrifying?" *Nuvo*, December 14, 2016. https://www.nuvo.net/arts/general_arts/are-indy-neighborhoods-gentrifying/article_f7ef3602-5992-5043-b61a-25a88b59aabd.html.
Teng, Emma J. "Artifacts of a Lost City: Arnold Genthe's Pictures of Old Chinatown and Its Intertexts." In *Re/Collecting Early Asian America: Essays in Cultural History*, edited by Josephine Lee, Imogene L. Lim and Yuko Matsukawa, 54–77. Philadelphia: Temple University Press, 2002.
Toney, Michael B., Chalon Keller, and Lori M. Hunter. "Regional Cultures, Persistence and Change: A Case Study of the Mormon Culture Region." *Social Science Journal* 40, no. 3 (2003): 431–45.
Trentelman, Carla Koons. "Place Attachment and Community Attachment: A Primer Grounded in the Lived Experience of a Community Sociologist." *Society and Natural Resources* 22, no. 3 (2009): 191–210.
Trentelman, Charles F. "The Good Old Days on 25th Street Were Good and Deadly." *Standard-Examiner*, December 16, 2012. https://www.standard.net/opinion/the-good-old-days-on-th-street-were-good-and/article_1585dfee-fc98-531c-a4bc-6349c8684047.html.
———. "New Economy Means Constantly Changing Focus." *Standard-Examiner*, September 17, 2012. http://www.standard.net/stories/2012/09/17/new-economy-means-constantly-changing-focus.
Trotter, Rachel. "North Ogden Residents Protest Monroe Extension." *Standard-Examiner*, January 15, 2015. https://www.standard.net/news/government/north-ogden-residents-protest-monroe-extension/article_8d8de8fd-701a-5eee-a414-2d44dc916907.html.
Tuan, Yi-Fu. *Space and Place: The Perspective of Experience*. Minneapolis: University of Minnesota Press, 1977.
Tucker, Robert C., ed. *The Marx-Engels Reader*. New York: W. W. Norton, 1972.
Ulibarri, Richard O. "Utah's Ethnic Minorities: A Survey." In *Being Different: Stories of Utah's Minorities*, edited by Stanford J. Layton, 1–18. Salt Lake City: Signature Books, 2001. Original edition, 1972.
Van Riper, Tom. "Best Cities for Raising A Family." *Forbes*, April 16, 2014. https://www.forbes.com/pictures/eddf45gihi/best-cities-for-raising-a-family.

Vandenack, Tim. "Ogden Has Its Charms, but Some Worry the City's Older Core Is on the Decline." *Standard-Examiner*, August 11, 2017. https://www.standard.net/news/local/ogden-has-its-charms-but-some-worry-the-city-s/article_93009af7-18fc-5b63-b289-622381c0cdf6.html.

———. "Ogden's Household Income Level Is Lower, Poverty Is Higher: But Is It a Ghetto?" *Standard-Examiner*, August 11, 2017. https://www.standard.net/news/local/ogden-s-household-income-level-is-lower-poverty-is-higher/article_bec453a5-7c81-5ae8-9cfb-54d9dbca41e7.html.

Vick, Karl. "A Different State of Race Relations: With Few Blacks Living There, Utah Is Feeling Its Way." *Washington Post*, June 1, 2008. http://www.washingtonpost.com/wp-dyn/content/article/2008/05/31/AR2008053100972.html.

Wacquant, Loïc. "Revisiting Territories of Relegation: Class, Ethnicity and State in the Making of Advanced Marginality." *Urban Studies* 53, no. 6 (2016): 1077–88.

———. "Territorial Stigmatization in the Age of Advanced Marginality." *Thesis Eleven* 91, no. 1 (2007): 66–77.

———. "Three Pernicious Premises in the Study of the American Ghetto." *International Journal of Urban and Regional Research* 21, no. 2 (1997): 341–53.

———. *Urban Outcasts: A Comparative Sociology of Advanced Marginality*. Cambridge: Polity, 2008.

———. "Urban Outcasts: Stigma and Division in the Black American Ghetto and the French Urban Periphery." *International Journal of Urban and Regional Research* 17, no. 3 (1993): 366–83.

Wacquant, Loïc, Tom Slater, and Virgílio Borges Pereira. "Territorial Stigmatization in Action." *Environment and Planning A* 46, no. 6 (2014): 1270–80.

Walsh, Tad. "The Church of Jesus Christ of Latter-day Saints Issues New Name Guidelines, Dropping Terms Mormon, LDS in Most Uses." *Deseret News*, August 16, 2018. https://www.deseretnews.com/article/900028401/the-church-of-jesus-christ-of-latter-day-saints-issues-new-name-guidelines-dropping-term-mormon-in-most-uses.html.

———. "Recent Mormon Baptisms for Holocaust Victims Questioned." *Deseret News*, December 21, 2017. https://www.deseretnews.com/article/900006133/mormon-baptisms-on-holocaust-victims-celebrities-violated-church-policy.html.

———. "Utah, LDS Church Join 'Friend of Court' Briefs in Transgender Bathroom Case." *Deseret News*, February 27, 2017. https://www.deseretnews.com/article/865673693/Utah-LDS-Church-join-friend-of-court-briefs-in-transgender-bathroom-case.html.

Wang, Xia. "Undocumented Immigrants as Perceived Criminal Threat: A Test of the Minority Threat Perspective." *Criminology* 50, no. 3 (2012): 743–76.

Weiler, Kathleen. *Utah's African American Voices*. Salt Lake City: KUED, 1999.

Whyte, William H. *City: Rediscovering the Center*. Philadelphia: University of Pennsylvania Press, 2008. Original edition, 1988.

Wickes, Rebecca, John R. Hipp, Renee Zahnow, and Lorraine Mazerolle. "'Seeing' Minorities and Perceptions of Disorder: Explicating the Mediating and Moderating Mechanisms of Social Cohesion." *Criminology* 51, no. 3 (2013): 519–60.

Wilson, James Q., and George E. Kelling. "Broken Windows: The Police and Neighborhood Safety." *Atlantic Monthly*, 29–38, March 1982. https://www.theatlantic.com/magazine/archive/1982/03/broken-windows/304465/.

Wilson, William J. *The Truly Disadvantaged: The Inner City, the Underclass, and Public Policy*. Chicago: University of Chicago Press, 1987.

Winders, Jamie. "Bringing Back the (B)Order: Post-9/11 Politics of Immigration, Borders, and Belonging in the Contemporary U.S. South." *Antipode* 39, no. 5 (2007): 920–42.

———. "New Immigrant Destinations in Global Context." *International Migration Review* 48, no. 1 (2014): S149–S179.

Winslow, Ben. "'Safe and Sound' Seeks to Get LGBT Teens off the Streets." Fox 13, January 22, 2013. https://fox13now.com/2013/01/22/safe-and-sound-seeks-to-get-lgbt-teens-off-the-streets.

Yago, Glenn. "The Sociology of Transportation." *Annual Review of Sociology* 9 (1983): 171–90.

Ybarra-Frausto, Tomás. "Rasquachismo: A Chicano Sensibility." In *Chicano Art: Resistance and Affirmation, 1965–1985*, edited by Richard Griswold del Castillo, Teresa McKenna, and Yvonne Yarbro-Bejarano, 155–62. Los Angeles: Wight Art Gallery, University of California, 1989.

Yinger, John. *Closed Doors, Opportunities Lost: The Continuing Costs of Housing Discrimination*. New York: Russell Sage Foundation, 1995.

Yoo, Sharon. "Neighbors Express Mixed Feelings about Changing Neighborhoods." WAVE 3 News, August 4, 2017. http://www.wave3.com/story/36068052/neighbors-express-mixed-feelings-about-changing-neighborhoods.

Yorgason, Ethan R. *Transformation of the Mormon Culture Region*. Urbana: University of Illinois Press, 2003.

Young, Neil J. "Equal Rights, Gay Rights and the Mormon Church." *New York Times*, June 13, 2012. https://campaignstops.blogs.nytimes.com/2012/06/13/equal-rights-gay-rights-and-the-mormon-church.

Zahnow, Renee, Rebecca Wickes, Michele Haynes, and Lorraine Mazerolle. "Change and Stability in Ethnic Diversity Across Urban Communities: Explicating the Influence of Social Cohesion on Perceptions of Disorder." *Australian and New Zealand Journal of Criminology* 46, no. 3 (2013): 335–56.

Zerubavel, Eviatar. *Time Maps: Collective Memory and the Social Shape of the Past*. Chicago: University of Chicago Press, 2012.

Zuberi, Tukufu. *Thicker Than Blood: How Racial Statistics Lie*. Minneapolis: University of Minnesota Press, 2001.

Zukin, Sharon. "Gentrification: Culture and Capital in the Urban Core." *Annual Review of Sociology* 13, no. 1 (1987): 129–47.

———. *Naked City: The Death and Life of Authentic Urban Places*. Oxford: Oxford University Press, 2010.

Zuniga, Victor, and Ruben Hernandez-Leon, eds. *New Destinations: Mexican Immigration in the United States*. New York: Russell Sage Foundation, 2005.

# INDEX

Note: entries printed in *italics* refer to figures, illustrations, or tables.

Abel, Elijah, 128
African-Americans. *See* blacks; race
American Community Survey (2016), 35
American Social Health Association, 100
Anderson, Elijah, 7–8, 29–30, 31, 190n6
Anholt, Simon, 142
Asian-Americans: immigration and neighborhood racial composition preferences of, 164; and opium trade in nineteenth-century Ogden, 100; as percentage of population in Ogden, Utah, and U.S., *40*; as percentage of Weber County residents in 1870–1920, *98–99*; reputation of Ogden's downtown and stereotypes of, 105; and view of Mormons as racial outsiders in nineteenth century, 131. *See also* Chinese-Americans; Japanese-Americans; race
Association of Statisticians of American Religious Bodies, 179n11
Austin (Texas), 144, 146

Bankston, Carl, 80
Barnes, Lyle, 98, 104, 184n51
Becker, Howard, 14, 177n58
Birmingham (Alabama), 188n57
blacks: and challengers of urban reputations, 32; and early history of Utah, 133; and law enforcement policies in Ogden, 122; as percentage of residents of Weber County, *98–99*; and racial diversity of Ogden, *40*, 181–82n6; and racial policies of Mormon Church, 126, 127, 128, 131, 132, 187n29; segregation and inequality in history of Ogden, 99, 101–2, 103–104, 151; and shifts in demographic makeup of Ogden, 78, 79; and stigmatizing label of "ghetto," 28; and "white spaces" in urban areas, 27. *See also* race
Blumer, Herbert, 110
Bolt, Gideon, 31
Bonilla-Silva, Eduardo, 110
boundary blurring: examples of from history of Utah, 126–34; and suggestions for transformation of urban reputation of Ogden, 138–41
boundary work: and challenges by insiders to outsiders' negative views of Ogden, 46–51; and concept of moral frontiers, 16, 17; and divisions of community in Ogden, 64–75; and perceptions of place by immigrants, 77–91; as theme of study, 19–20. *See also* transformation; urban reputations
Brigham Young University, 114
"broken windows theory," and law enforcement policy, 121, 123, 136
Brooks, Roger, 73
Buttars, Chris, 111

Campbell, Elizabeth, 165
Carr, James, 102
Charles, Camille, 164
Chicago (Illinois), 55–56, 173n2
Chinese-Americans: as immigrants to Ogden, 101, 105; as percentage of

213

population of Weber County, 98–99. *See also* Asian-Americans
Christakis, Nicholas, 153
Christensen, Ann-Dorte, 178n19
Christmas Village (Ogden), 139–40
city brands, and transformation of negative reputations, 146–47. *See also* marketing
City RepTrak, 189n13
civil rights movement: attitudes toward in Utah, 129, 132; and image of Birmingham, Alabama, 188n57
class. *See* social class
"collective forgetfulness," and negative reputation of Ogden, 17, 20–21, 64, 72–75, 143, 155
comparisons, and defense of urban reputation of Ogden, 52–60
conservatism, of politics in Utah, 41–42, 114, 129
contexts: and history of Ogden, 96–106; lack of focus on local in urban research, 8–9; race, class, and cultural status in Ogden, 109–16; as theme of study, 19, 21. *See also* urban reputations
continuity, and social change in history of Ogden, 102–6
"creative class," and disreputable urban areas, 32, 144
crime: in Ogden compared to Salt Lake City, 9, 58, 87; and racial difference in Ogden, 104–5; rates of and statistics on for Ogden, 4, 53, 125, 167–68, 169–72; and urban reputation of Chicago, 173n2. *See also* gangs and gang members; law enforcement
culture: as category of difference in Ogden, 41–42; "culture of poverty" and "culture of abundance" and focus of urban research on inequality, 27, 137, 154; disreputable urban areas as centers of, 27; history of Ogden and transformations of, 101–2; and moral dimension of urban reputations, 153; and urban reputations as cultural symbols, 7–8. *See also* Mormon culture region
Cuní, Guifré, 46

Davie, Rose, 101, 145
Deener, Andrew, 181–82n6
defenses, of Ogden's urban reputation by residents, 49–52
Denver (Colorado), 56
Department of Housing and Urban Development (HUD), 39
Detroit (Michigan), 180n9
deviance: and boundaries of status and morality, 108; social constructionism and theories of, 13–14, 15, 185n8; and urban reputations as moral frontiers, 150
DiAngelo, Robin, 63
difference: and culture of Ogden, 41–42; insider and outsider views of Ogden's urban reputation, 34–42; Ogden's history of, 11, 103; and Park City compared to Ogden, 106; race and immigration as categories of in Ogden, 39–41
disorder, crime rates as measure of, 9. *See also* "internal disorder"
division: of community and urban reputation of Ogden, 64–75; and perceptions of place by Ogden's immigrant population, 86–89; and practices of unity in defense of Ogden's urban reputation, 60–61. *See also* East Branch; Harrison Divide; "micro-differentiations"; Monroe Boulevard; segregation; 25th Street
Donato, Katharine, 80
Douglas, Mary, 177n65
downtown. *See* 25th Street
DuBois, W. E. B., 136
Durán, Robert, 123, 124
Durkheim, Emile, 13–14, 168, 177n64–65

East Bench (Ogden), 36–37, 65, 88
East Saint Louis (Illinois), vii–viii
"ecological fallacies," and assessments of disreputable places, 32–33

education, and working-class character of Ogden, 35–36
Elliott, Delbert, 165
employment, by industry in Ogden, 36. See also Labor
entertainment district, and history of Ogden, 99–102, 105. See also 25th Street
Equal Rights Amendment, 129
Erikson, Kai, 14, 108
ethnography, and research methods, 160, 162, 166
eurocentrism, and history of Utah, 133–34

FBI Uniform Crime Reports, 167
Fine, Gary Alan, 62, 108, 112
Flake, Green, 128
folklore, and urban reputation of Ogden, 10
*Forbes* (newspaper), 4
Foster, Jonathan, 146, 188n57
Fowler, James, 153
Franzini, Luisa, 179n24
freeway systems, as "boundary maintaining devices" in urban areas, 26–27
fur trapping, and history of Ogden, 3

gangs and gang members: and law enforcement policy in Ogden, 123–25, 168; and spatial divisions in Ogden, 69–71
Geertz, Clifford, 159
gentrification, of disreputable urban areas, 32, 123, 146
ghetto: and challengers of bad urban reputations, 30; idea of "iconic," 8; labeling of disreputable places as, 26; and moral boundaries, 13; perception of divisions of Ogden as, 5, 151; race and stigmatizing label of, 28; Wacquant on use of term, 6
Gillespie, James, 101–2, 104
global capitalism, and internal disorder view of urban reputations, 16
go-alongs, and interviews with residents of Ogden, 160, 161, 162, 163–66
Golden Spike Ceremony, 96
Grant, Ulysses S., 57

group position, and racial boundaries in Ogden, 109–12

Harrison Divide (Ogden), 65, 66, 67–68, 90
Hart Celler Act (1965), 79
Henly, Julia, 165
Hester, Raymond, 147
Hispanics. *See* Latinos
"historical echo," and negative reputation of Ogden, 11
Holley, Val, 57, 112
housing: and homelessness of LGBTQ teenagers in Utah, 115; and working-class character of Ogden, 35, 36–37, 39
Hyde, Orson, 132

identity: and boundaries between respectable and deviant, 108; and Mormon culture in Utah, 114, 115; of residents of disreputable places and territorial stigmatization, 63, 175n25
"imagined communities," and urban reputations as cultural symbols, 8
immigration and immigrants: and categories of difference in Ogden, 39–41; and history of Ogden, 97, 103; influence of recent wave on Ogden, 4; and interviews with residents of Ogden, 161; and perceptions of place, 77–91. *See also* Chinese; Latinos; Pacific Islanders; undocumented immigration
Immigration Reform and Control Act (IRCA), 79
income, average household of Ogden, 35, 37, 174n11
industrial center, Ogden as, 4
industry, and employment by sector in Ogden, 36
inequality: of income in Ogden, 174n11; law enforcement policies and reinforcement of, 122. *See also* poverty; social class
insiders/outsiders: as challengers of negative urban reputations, 30–32, 46–51; and cultural explanations for urban reputations, 154; and differing

views of Ogden, 11, *18*, 34–42, 149; "internal" versus "external" views of places, 46; and negative impact of bad urban reputations, 6; as promoters of bad urban reputations, 26–30; as theme of study, 19–20; use of terms, 177n58

"internal disorder": as approach to study of urban reputations, 6, 8, 9, 25; and concepts of boundary blurring and boundary maintenance, 120, 121, 122–23, 125; and moral frontier approach to urban reputations, 16, 154, 156–58; and perceptions of Ogden by Latino residents, 149, 151, 155. *See also* disorder

interviews, with residents of Ogden, 10, 160–66

Irwin, Katherine, 165

Jacobs, Jane, 45

Japanese-Americans, as percentage of population of Weber County, *98–99*. *See also* Asian-Americans

Jensen, Sune Qvotrup, 178n19

Jews, and Mormon Church, 127

Jim Crow era, and history of racial repression in Utah, 110, 132

Kearns, Ade, 7
Kearns, Oliver, 7
Kelling, George, 121
Kusenbach, Margarethe, 160

labeling: of disreputable areas as ghettos, 26; and power dynamics, 108; race and stigmatizing labels, 28; and social constructionist explanations of deviance, 13

labor: and economics of undocumented immigration, 80; race and immigration in history of Ogden, 103. *See also* employment

Las Vegas (Nevada), 73, 176n38, 184n54

Latin America: census and, 181n5; and "Latinization" of Mormonism, 129; organization of cities compared to U.S., 91

Latinos: boundary work and perceptions of place by, 77–91; and gangs in Ogden, 124–25; interviews with and views of Ogden, 11–12, 130, 151, 152–53; as percentage of population in Ogden, 5, 40–41, 181–82n6; reclamation of historical legacy in Utah, 133–34; use of term, 173–74n9. *See also* immigration and immigrants

law enforcement: crime data based on self-reports from, 167–68; policies of and boundary maintenance in Ogden, 120–25. *See also* crime

Lawson, Louise, 7

LGBTQ identity: and rate of homelessness among teenagers in Utah, 115; and transformation of word "queer," 144

Liazos, Alexander, 15

"Little Mexico" (Ogden), 82, 91, 104

London, Belle, 102

*Los Angeles Times*, 4

"magical solutions," and image of Ogden, 64, 181n16

maintenance and transformation. *See* Transformation

marketing, and representations of Ogden, 72–73, 142–43. *See also* city brands

Marx, Karl, 185n8

Mazanti, Birgitte, 7, 137–38

media: depictions of disreputable places in, 28, 29; news stories about Ogden in national, 4, 176n47

Meyerhoffer, Cassi, 77, 176n50, 179n7

"micro-differentiations": urban reputation and subdivisions within Ogden, 11, 20, 61, 74–75; and preservation of status by insiders, 31. *See also* division

Monroe Boulevard (Ogden), 66, 71, 86, 90

moral frontiers: as approach to study of urban reputation, 12–17, 21, 22, 149–58; and Ogden's urban reputation, 17–22; and perceptions of Ogden by immigrants, 90; role of outsiders in

maintenance of, 33, 34. *See also* urban reputations
moral inversions: and research on urban reputations, 155; and transformation of urban reputation of Ogden, 18, 22, 141–46
moral panics, and gangs in Ogden, 123, 124, 125
Mormon culture region: and boundary between Ogden and surrounding region, 112–15; unique characteristics of in Utah, 41–42. *See also* Mormons and Mormonism
Mormons and Mormonism: boundary blurring and racial policies of, 126–34, 187n29, 188n58; and history of Ogden, 3; and history of Utah, 18–19; as percentage of population of Weber County, 42, 179n11; race, class, and cultural status of as dominant group in Utah, 109, 112–15; references to by respondents, 52; use of term, 173n7. *See also* Mormon culture region
Morris, Alan, 178n19

Native Americans, and racial policies of Mormon Church, 127–28, 131
Neighborhood Revitalization Strategy Area, 39
"neo-bohemians," and disreputable urban areas, 32, 144
*Newsweek* (magazine), 4
New York City, 45, 121, 144, 184n54
*New York Times*, 4
North Ogden (Utah), 166

Ogden (Utah): categories of difference and urban reputation of, 34–42; challenges by insiders to outsiders' negative views of, 46–51; and crime rates, 4, 53, 125, 167–68, 169–72; and defense of urban reputation through comparisons, 52–61; discovery of multiple reputations of, 9–12; divisions of community in, 64–75; exploration of urban representations through example of, 148–58; history of, 3, 57, 96–106, 107, 151, 189n24; image of compared to East Saint Louis (Illinois), vii–viii; introduction to, 3–5; income inequality in, 174n11; law enforcement policy and maintenance of boundaries in, 120–25; moral frontiers and urban reputation of, 17–22; and perceptions of place by immigrants, 77–91; race, class, and cultural status in context of, 109–16; research methods for study of, 159–66; suggestions for transformation of urban reputation of, 138–47
Ogden, Peter Skene, 3
Ogden United Promise Neighborhoods, 39
Oliver, Eric, 141
open spaces, geography and built environment of Ogden, 38, 39

Pacific Islanders: Mormon Church and immigration of to Utah, 128, 129; as percentage of population of Ogden, Utah, and U.S., 40
Paiute, and Native Americans in Utah, 133
Park City (Utah), 21, 106
Parson, Robert, 97
Patterson, Orlando, 95–96
Pattillo, Mary, 190n6
Peery, Harman, 100
Permentier, Matthieu, 31
Peterson, F. Ross, 97
Pinyol, Isaac, 46
place: collective groups and differing perceptions of, 26; "internal" and "external" views of, 46; marketing of, 142–43; mechanisms underlying perceptions of, 2; moral quality to designations of, 12; perceptions of by immigrants, 77–91; and problem of image, 5–6. *See also* reputations
Pløger, John, 7, 137–38
politics, Mormons and conservatism in Utah, 41–42, 114, 129
Porters and Waiters Club, 101
poverty, and class stratification in Ogden, 37, 39. *See also* "culture of poverty"

power: and critical race theory, 14–15, 185n8; and labeling of reputations, 108; race and social divisions in Ogden, 109–10; and transformations of negative representations, 144
Prohibition era, and history of Ogden, 100
Promise Neighborhood project (United Way), 85
Promontory Summit, 3, 96
prostitution, and history of Ogden, 100, 101, 102
public places, and boundary blurring in Ogden, 140–41

race: as category of difference in Ogden, 39–41; civil rights movement and image of Birmingham, Alabama, 188n57; concept of internalized, 181n10; and crime in Ogden, 104–5; group position and power relations in Ogden, 109–12; and history of Ogden, 97–99, 103; immigrants and evaluation of place, 91; and Latinos in Ogden, 181–82n6; and negative impact of urban reputations, 6; of Ogden residents from 1960 to 2010, 79; and policies of Mormon Church, 126–34, 187n29, 188n58; power dynamics and theories of, 14–15; and streets as divisions in urban areas, 180–81n9; and "white spaces" in urban areas, 27. *See also* Asian-Americans; blacks; Latinos; Pacific Islanders; segregation
"Race and the Priesthood" (Mormon Church, 2013), 127
railroad, and history of Ogden, 3, 57, 96, 151
Raudenbush, Stephen, 7
Reeve, W. Paul, 131, 132
regional influences, and research on urban reputations, 154–55
religion. *See* Mormons and Mormonism
Republican Party, and Mormon culture in Utah, 114
Reputation Institute (consulting firm), 189n13
reputations: as "beliefs about beliefs," 45–46, 47; and difficulty of change, 62; and power of labeling, 108; uses of, 1–2. *See also* place; urban reputations
restaurants, and Ogden's immigrant community, 81, 140
Richards, Maurice, 101
Rios, Victor, 29, 136, 190n6
Ritchie, Joe, 184n43
Rivera, Andreas, 105
Romney, Mitt, 114
Rust Belt, and description of Ogden, 3

Sabater-Mir, Jordi, 46
St. Louis (Missouri), 181n9
Salt Lake City: comparisons of reputation of Ogden to, 9, 57–60, 87, 167, 168; crime statistics compared to Ogden, 9, 58, 87; and "Mormon culture region," 41; railroads and history of, 96
*Salt Lake Tribune*, 57, 104
sample bias, and research methods, 164–65
Sampson, Robert, 7
secondary sources, and research methods, 162
segregation: racial-spatial divisions and history of Ogden, 99, 103–4, 151; and study of urban reputations, 16
Sessions, Gene, 103
"shady," use of term for spatial divisions in Ogden, 68–69
Singer, Audrey, 78–79
slavery, and history of Utah, 110, 128, 132
Small, Mario Luis, 157
Smith, Joseph, 132
social change, and history of Ogden, 102–6
social class: difference and urban reputation of Ogden, 35–39; and divisions of community in Ogden, 64–65; "magical solutions" for reversing divisions of, 181n16; and negative impact of urban reputations, 6; and Park City compared to Ogden, 106; and streets as divisions in urban areas, 180–81n9. *See also* working class
social constructionism: and explanations of deviance, 13; and perceptions of place, 2

socialization, and racialized mechanisms for evaluating place, 90–91
social networks, and Mormon culture, 114
South (U.S.), as example of negative "nation brand," 8
South Ogden (Utah), 166
Stainback, Melissa, 80
*Standard-Examiner* (newspaper), 4–5
status. *See* immigration; race; social class
"stop and frisk" policies, of law enforcement, 121
*Sunset* magazine, 4

territorial stigmatization: and identity of residents of disreputable areas, 64, 155, 175n25; studies on neighborhood effects compared to, 174–75n23; Wacquant's concept of, 178n19
Tolstoy, Leo, 3, 173n8
tourism, potential for and marketing of Ogden, 72, 73
transcripts, of interviews, 162
transformation: law enforcement and maintenance of boundaries in Ogden, 120–25; suggestions for urban reputation of Ogden, 138–47; as theme of study, 19, 21–22. *See also* urban reputations
25th Street (Ogden), 99–102, 105, 106, 112, 143, 145, 184n43, 184n51

"ultracitizen," Mormon image of, 131–32
undocumented immigration: economics of, 80–81; Mormonism and immigration policy in Utah, 130; national immigration policy and increase in, 79
Union Station (Ogden), 73
U.S. Census, 35, 78, 181n5, 182n7
United Way, 39, 85
unity, and defenses of Ogden's urban reputation, 60–61
urban renewal, and social inequality, 147
urban reputations: exploration of through example of Ogden, 148–58; influence on people's lives and construction of, 2–3; and internal disorder, 6, 9, 16, 25; rankings of, 189n13; and reimagining of urban space, 152–56; rethinking of in urban research, 5–9; varying views of Ogden's, 9–12. *See also* boundary work; contexts; insiders/outsiders; moral frontiers; transformation
Utah: average household income of, 35; examples of boundary blurring in history of, 126–34; and Halloween, 145; "moral inversions" in history of, 18–19; and "Mormon culture region," 41; Mormonism and unique religious culture of, 21, 112–16; population of Latinos in Ogden and, 40; regional racial insensitivity in, 111; social class and race in, 109, 186n21; urban reputation of Ogden among residents of northern, 10. *See also* Ogden; Park City; Salt Lake City
"Utah Compact," and immigration to Utah, 130
*Utah Valley Magazine*, 111
Utes, and Native Americans in Utah, 133

van Ham, Maarten, 31
vice. *See* entertainment district

Wacquant, Loïc, 6, 28, 31, 178n19
Weakley, Anna Belle, 101
Weber County (Utah), percentage of Mormons in population of, 42, 179n11
Weber State University, 35, 36
Wickes, Rebecca, 179n24
Wilson, James, 121
working class, and urban reputation of Ogden, 4, 35–39. *See also* social class

Young, Brigham, 57, 126, 128, 132

Zahnow, Renee, 179n24
"zero tolerance" policing, 121